FLORIDA

HOW TO USE THIS ATLAS

These excerpts from the CONSOLIDATED CHRONOLOGY and the INDIVIDUAL COUNTY CHRONOLOGIES demonstrate the depiction, both textual and cartographic, of county boundary changes and the relationship between these two sections of the atlas.

In addition to the Consolidated Chronology of State and County Boundaries and Individual County Chronologies, Maps, and Areas, the atlas includes the following:

Table of County Creations / Table of Censuses / Census Outline Maps / Bibliography

CONSOLIDATED CHRONOLOGY includes, in chronological order, all boundary changes reported for the state and its counties. Changes for more than one county may appear under one date. Historical sources of information are given in parentheses for every event; more detailed information about sources can be found in the bibliography at the back of the atlas.

Events from the CONSOLIDATED CHRONOLOGY correspond to the events listed in the INDIVIDUAL COUNTY CHRONOLOGY table. These events for Covington are illustrated by maps 4, 5, and 6.

21 January 1824

COVINGTON gained all of BAINBRIDGE; BAINBRIDGE eliminated. (Miss. Laws 1823–1824, 7th sess., ch. 26/p. 35)

JACKSON gained from HANCOCK. (Miss. Laws 1823–1824, 7th sess., ch. 36/pp. 44–45)

23 January 1824

SIMPSON created from COPIAH. (Miss. Laws 1823–1824, 7th sess., ch. 72, sec. 1/p. 87)

1 February 1825

COVINGTON gained from LAWRENCE and WAYNE. Part of COVINGTON's gain from LAWRENCE was unintended; MARION had been authorized to gain from LAWRENCE, but local officials and residents treated the area as part of the territory transferred to COVINGTON. (Miss. Laws 1825, 8th sess., ch. 22/p. 48)

2 February 1825

PIKE gained from LAWRENCE. (Miss. Laws 1825, 8th sess., ch. 33/p. 78)

3 February 1825

PERRY gained from HANCOCK. (Miss. Laws 1825, 8th sess., ch. 43/p. 99)

24 January 1826

JONES created from COVINGTON and WAYNE. (Miss. Laws 1826, 9th sess., p. 59)

4 February 1829

Non-county area (unceded Indian territory) divided into six regions which were attached to: MADISON, MONROE, RANKIN and SIMPSON jointly, WASHINGTON, WAYNE, and YAZOO. (Miss. Laws 1829, 12th sess., ch. 77, secs. 1–2/pp. 81–82)

5 February 1829

MADISON gained from HINDS. (Miss. Laws 1829, 12th sess., ch. 19/p. 17)

30 January 1830

LOWNDES created from MONROE and non-county area attached to MONROE. (Miss. Laws 1830, 13th sess., ch. 14, sec. 1/p. 18)

Part of non-county area detached from RANKIN and SIMPSON, attached to COVINGTON; parts of non-county areas detached from WAYNE and from RANKIN and SIMPSON, attached to JONES. (Miss. Laws 1830, 13th sess., ch. 43/p. 46)

INDIVIDUAL COUNTY CHRONOLOGIES, MAPS, AND AREAS presents boundary changes of a particular county complete with dates of recorded change, a summary of changes, and the resulting area in square miles. When changes cannot be mapped, explanations are provided.

Locator maps identify the county within its state, showing current county configuration. For counties now in other states, the locator map will include appropriate areas.

Numbers in black circles link the maps to the entries in the table.

Map headings show the range of dates for which changes are valid; where more than one range of dates appears, the county was later restored to this configuration.

Heavy lines depict the county boundary during the indicated range of dates.

Underlying map is standard base map drawn by the U.S. Geological Survey.

A standard scale is used throughout unless specifically noted.

When smaller scales are necessary, the alternate scale appears directly beneath small-scale maps.

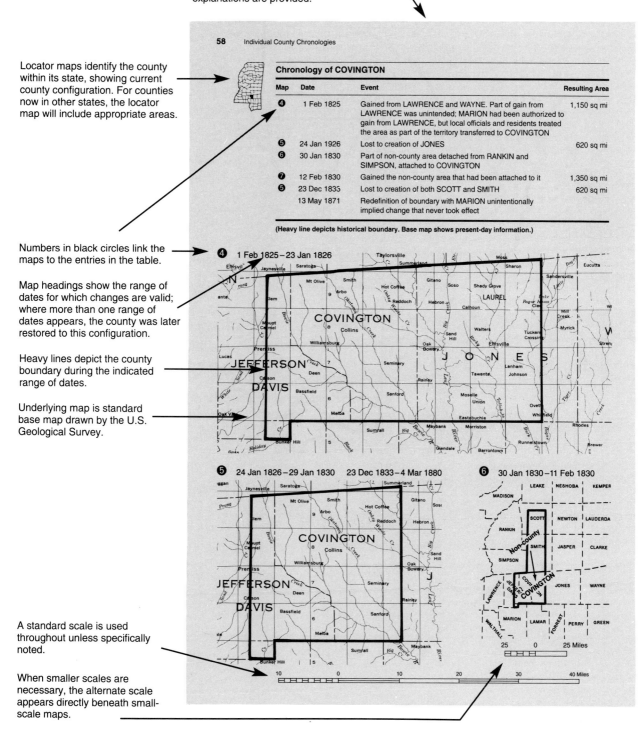

58   Individual County Chronologies

Chronology of COVINGTON

Map	Date	Event	Resulting Area
④	1 Feb 1825	Gained from LAWRENCE and WAYNE. Part of gain from LAWRENCE was unintended; MARION had been authorized to gain from LAWRENCE, but local officials and residents treated the area as part of the territory transferred to COVINGTON	1,150 sq mi
⑤	24 Jan 1926	Lost to creation of JONES	620 sq mi
⑥	30 Jan 1830	Part of non-county area detached from RANKIN and SIMPSON, attached to COVINGTON	
⑦	12 Feb 1830	Gained the non-county area that had been attached to it	1,350 sq mi
⑤	23 Dec 1835	Lost to creation of both SCOTT and SMITH	620 sq mi
	13 May 1871	Redefinition of boundary with MARION unintentionally implied change that never took effect	

(Heavy line depicts historical boundary. Base map shows present-day information.)

④ 1 Feb 1825 – 23 Jan 1826

⑤ 24 Jan 1826 – 29 Jan 1830   23 Dec 1833 – 4 Mar 1880

⑥ 30 Jan 1830 – 11 Feb 1830

This atlas has been supported by a grant from the
National Endowment for the Humanities, an independent federal agency.

FLORIDA

Atlas of Historical County Boundaries

John H. Long, Editor

*Compiled by Peggy Tuck Sinko
and Kathryn Ford Thorne*

A Project of the
Dr. William M. Scholl Center for Family and Community History
The Newberry Library

Charles Scribner's Sons
Simon & Schuster Macmillan
New York

Simon & Schuster Prentice Hall International
London Mexico City New Delhi Singapore Sydney Toronto

Copyright © 1997 by
The Newberry Library

Charles Scribner's Sons
An Imprint of Simon & Schuster Macmillan
1633 Broadway
New York, New York 10019

1 3 5 7 9 11 13 15 17 19   20 18 16 14 12 10 8 6 4 2

Library of Congress Cataloging-in-Publication Data

Atlas of historical county boundaries. Florida / John H. Long, editor;
compiled by Peggy Tuck Sinko and Kathryn Ford Thorne.
    p. cm.
    Includes bibliographical references and index.
    ISBN 0-13-366329-9 (hardcover)
    1. Florida—Administrative and political divisions—Maps.
2. Florida—Historical geography—Maps.   3. Florida—History
I. Long, John Hamilton.   II. Sinko, Peggy Tuck.   III. Thorne,
Kathryn Ford.
G1201.F7 A8 1997 Fla. <G&M>
911'.759—DC20   96-32133
                                              CIP
                                             MAPS

Contents

Preface and Acknowledgments

In 1933 the distinguished historian Frederick Merk lamented the lack of "a set of maps tracing the county divisions of the United States," because such maps "would have been of inestimable service to scholars in various fields" (*New England Quarterly*, 6:622). Merk was concerned primarily with outline maps for the plotting of statistics and, knowing that the federal government had published such maps for the census years 1840 to 1900, he was particularly interested in the earlier censuses, 1790 to 1830. This atlas is an attempt not only to satisfy that longstanding need, but also to provide complete and comprehensive information on all changes in all counties, individually and in aggregate.

A single question has focused the preparation of this atlas: at any time in history, what was the legal, effective arrangement of American county jurisdiction? A great number of people seek answers to that question, and, as Merk knew, their fields vary—demography, economics, genealogy, geography, history, law, political science, and other disciplines—and their interests cover a wide spectrum of place and time, from the national level to the local and from the colonial era to the present. The needs of this diverse audience shaped the primary goal of this atlas and determined its scope, its content, and its forms.

The geographic scope of the atlas encompasses the historical territory of the forty-eight contiguous states and Hawaii, and the chronological coverage extends from the 1630s, when the earliest colonial counties were created, to 1990. The content is not limited strictly to boundary changes, but includes also such other jurisdictional issues as unsuccessful authorizations for change and attachments of unorganized counties and non-county areas to operational counties. Data on the many changes in American counties are presented in both text (consolidated and individual county chronologies) and maps (detailed maps of individual counties and outline maps of the entire state's county network). Unlike the offerings of most reference works, these data come not from a synthesis of previous work but are the fruit of original research in primary sources.

The consolidated chronology should be the starting point for readers concerned with a specific period or date, while those interested in particular counties can use the county-name index built into the table of contents to find their subjects in the section of individual county chronologies and maps. Readers interested in a particular place should consult the index of places that gives the present county of every city, town, and village named on the modern federal map that is the base for the individual county maps. The table of censuses and the set of census outline maps, which cover colonial or territorial and state enumerations or equivalents, in addition to federal censuses, are designed to serve readers interested in statistical analysis and mapping.

The Newberry Library, Chicago, has been both headquarters and institutional sponsor for this atlas; its rich holdings in old maps and in state and local history, its commitment to scholarship, and its knowledgeable and dedicated staff make it the ideal place to conduct this sort of project. Special thanks are due David Buisseret, former director of the library's Hermon Dunlap Smith Center for the History of Cartography, for his contribution to the continuation of the project, and Richard H. Brown, former academic vice president, for his stalwart support of the project and his role in bringing the work to fruition. Thomas Roberts from Denison University, a student fellow of the Newberry Library–Associated Colleges of the Midwest/Great Lakes Colleges Association Humanities Seminar in the fall of 1994, assisted with proofreading, map labeling, typing, checking citations, and other tasks. Research associate Peggy Tuck Sinko compiled all the data on the censuses. The census maps were drafted by John Long with the finished versions executed on the computer by Megan Mack.

Editorial assistants David Strass and Megan Mack merit special recognition. Not only did they format and type (and retype) the chronologies and text for numerous states, they also maintained the master bibliography of over two thousand items, and their editing, proof-reading, and checking of the bibliography and citations contributed greatly to the accuracy and readability of the information presented here.

Because the Newberry Library lacks the resources of a full-fledged law library, the atlas staff made frequent use of the Northwestern University Law Library and the Cook County Law Library, which generously facilitated use of their collections. Marsha Selmer, curator of maps at the University of Illinois at Chicago, rendered valuable assistance with large-scale topographic maps, both new and old.

Librarians, archivists, and local historians throughout Florida contributed to the completeness and accuracy of the data and maps in this atlas by answering queries regarding dates and the details of local geography. Special thanks are due Nadine Doty-Tessel, Florida State Archives; Marylinn Cleveland, State Library of Florida, for providing unpublished WPA material on county boundaries; Alyce F. Tincher, Marion County Historical Society, for information on the attempt to create Bloxham County; Edward Herrmann, Dade City, for material on the boundary between Pasco and Polk counties; Mona Sullivan, Alachua County Environmental Protection Agency, for information on Orange Lake; and Charles A. Tingley and Jacqueline Fretwell, St. Augustine Historical Society, for maps and information on Flagler and St. Johns Counties.

These acknowledgments would be woefully incomplete without special recognition of the important part played by the Reference Materials Program of the National Endowment for the Humanities, an independent federal agency, whose grants have substantially supported the compilation of this atlas. We are especially grateful for the financial support contributed by The Frank Stanley Beveridge Foundation, Jean and Jay Kislak, and J. Thomas Touchton, all of which was matched by the National Endowment for the Humanities.

Introduction

Counties in the United States are, with few exceptions, administrative subdivisions of their states, not self-governing municipalities, as are cities, towns, and boroughs. Their historical significance lies in their important functions, their nearly universal distribution, and their protean nature. United States counties and their equivalents (i.e., parishes in Louisiana and independent cities in Maryland, Missouri, Nevada, and Virginia) today number more than three thousand and embrace within their bounds every part of the forty-eight conterminous states and Hawaii. (Connecticut abolished its counties as operational institutions in 1960 but retained them as geographical units; Alaska is the only state never to have had counties.) County functions vary from state to state, and there is no standard system of operation. Nonetheless, counties everywhere provide judicial administration, and in most states they are responsible for a number of other important functions and services as well. The county's role is smallest in New England, larger in the Middle Atlantic and North Central states, and greatest in the South and West.

The county system was transplanted to North America by early colonists from England. Following the practice in the home country, colonial laws and policies were administered through a network of county courts by sheriffs, judges, and justices of the peace. The county's judicial functions grew from law enforcement and simple legal proceedings to probating wills and handling a variety of legal instruments, such as deeds and certificates of marriage. The recording of births and deaths was a natural addition, and eventually much of the work of census taking was organized around the county. The courthouse, therefore, became both the local seat of justice and the repository of official information concerning every individual within the county's jurisdiction.

Counties also acquired many of the attributes of local government. Welfare administration, road and bridge maintenance, property evaluation and tax collection, and numerous other tasks all became county responsibilities. Although not a product of voluntary action by local inhabitants, the county eventually came under the control of elected officials answerable only to a local constituency. Outside the limits of densely settled urban areas, counties were the obvious geographical units for organizing representation in the provincial, territorial, and state legislatures and for building congressional districts. One result of these developments was that, in the nineteenth century, counties became the grassroots centers for political parties.

Following close on the heels of independence from Great Britain, American settlers began pushing westward onto land formerly occupied only by Indians, and state and territorial governments laid out counties ahead of them. Such acts were more than posturing claims of jurisdiction or fortuitous arrangements; those states and territories were trying to attract settlers with a promise of the orderly provision of governmental services. Unfortunately, a frontier county created in advance of settlement was usually little more than a name and a boundary description in the laws; frequently it was not technically organized and, nearly as often, was attached to a fully operational county for services and record keeping. Some of these counties remained attached and dependent for years, while others experienced such rapid population growth that they were soon organized and separated from their hosts. This atlas not only shows the territory within each county's prescribed boundaries but also maps the arrangement of any temporary attachments. Attachments are not included in calculations of the host county's area.

The functional importance of counties is not matched by a comparable geographic stability. Few, indeed, are the counties that today have their original shapes and areas. Some boundaries change when existing counties are divided to make new ones; other changes may be intended by legislators to serve the convenience of constituents or to raise the efficiency of government, or sometimes for less admirable purposes. The original counties of any state are few in number and may not even cover all of the state's territory. As population increases and spreads, as industry, agriculture, and transportation grow, so do the counties. Before long no place is outside the jurisdiction of one county or another. County lines form a network that divides the land in numerous ways, sometimes along prominent physical features and sometimes into areas whose sizes and shapes have been designed to optimize travel to the county seat or to facilitate control of the electorate. Most important, regardless of design, is the simple fact of change.

These changes in county shapes and sizes make it difficult to interpret county-level historical data. Did the size of the county's population really change or did the county merely gain or lose territory between census enumerations—or both? Could politicians have gerrymandered the state legislature or congressional delegation without explicitly changing the electoral laws, possibly by unobtrusively rearranging the county lines that underlay the system of electoral districts? There are many issues besides statistical shifts that draw researchers to counties. Genealogists, family historians, and attorneys, among others, often need evidence of specific events at particular locations and times—perhaps the initial gathering of a church, a land sale, a death, or a marriage. Knowing a locality's current county may not be adequate, and discovering which county had jurisdiction in the past may be the key to finding old records. State and local agencies may need to examine past attempts at judicial or administrative reorganization and reform. Nearly everyone concerned with local, state, or national politics of the past needs to know what happened to the county configurations in order to judge the significance, and perhaps the causes, of changes in electoral behavior.

The practice of temporarily attaching some sparsely settled counties and non-county areas to fully operational and self-sustaining counties implies some interesting questions concerning the administration of county services, the organization of census data, the conduct of research in county records, and a number of other issues. For example, how extensive a region did a sheriff have to cover when his county became responsible for one or more attached counties? Researchers investigating an event in county A at the time it was attached to county B may find the records still in the archives of county B.

Working with county-based information, especially statistics, has often meant an abundance of topical data and a dearth of information about the configurations of the counties. One can only guess how many researchers have had to interrupt their thematic analyses to piece together the boundary changes of pertinent counties, or how many have revised or abandoned particular projects because compiling the boundary changes loomed as too formidable an obstacle.

History of This Atlas

The impetus for this endeavor came early in the 1970s during the creation of the *Atlas of Early American History: The Revolutionary Era, 1760–1790* (1976) by a team of historians and cartographers, led by editor-in-chief Lester J. Cappon, in Chicago at the Newberry Library. When the staff compiled reference maps of the British North American colonies in 1775, they discovered that, contrary to expectations, there was no authoritative reference source for the historical county lines. There are, instead, a number of separate compilations covering some but not all of the original thirteen states. The quality of those works ranges from superb to unreliable, and they lack anything approaching a common standard or format.

The *Atlas of Early American History* was succeeded by a project to compile the much needed reference work on county development. That original project was conceived as an experiment that would bypass conventional publication by creating a computerized, historical, cartographic data file, thereby making the boundary information available exclusively in a new and flexible format at supposedly reduced costs. The project succeeded in compiling and encoding the data for fourteen eastern and central states, and the data file is distributed by the Inter-university Consortium for Political and Social Research, Ann Arbor, Michigan, under the title, "County Boundaries of Selected United States Territories/States, 1790–1980 (ICPSR 9025)." The original dissemination plan was broadened to include printing the data in maps and text (e.g., chronology, county code lists), thus providing, in addition to the data file, both a printed guide for those who had access to computer facilities and a conventional atlas for those without such equipment. The resulting work, the *Historical Atlas and Chronology of County Boundaries, 1788–1980*, edited by John H. Long, was published in five volumes by G. K. Hall in 1984. In the current project, that five-volume work has been treated as any other secondary compilation of county creations and changes (see Sources, below). This *Atlas of Historical County Boundaries,* a projected forty-volume reference, is a thoroughly new atlas with a broader range of subject matter than the 1984 work, as well as a different format and completely new maps and text.

Also in 1984, Thomas D. Rabenhorst and Carville V. Earle of the Geography Department at the University of Maryland, Baltimore County, produced the *Historical U.S. County Outline Map Collection, 1840–1980*, an expanded set of fifteen unbound maps derived from county outline maps for the federal census years 1840 to 1900 published in the early twentieth century by the U.S. Department of Agriculture. By the 1980s, those federal maps had been so long out of print that they had become virtually unknown. In 1987 William Thorndale and William Dollarhide published their *Map Guide to the U.S. Federal Censuses, 1790–1920,* which provides well-designed state outline maps of both modern and historical counties and gives sources and a description of the authors' methodology. Both of these publications provide only small-scale outline maps for a limited number of dates, leaving the need for a comprehensive and detailed reference unfilled.

This atlas has been designed to leave no gaps. The chronological range for each state extends back to its earliest county, at least, and runs up to 1990. Geographically, the range includes all territory within each state's bounds in 1990, plus (for the relevant historical period) any other territory over which its jurisdiction extended at an earlier time. The table of contents lists all counties included in the volume, identifying those created by another state or now located beyond the state's boundaries; cross-references are provided for counties that have been renamed.

A secondary goal of this atlas is to provide a frame of reference for understanding boundary changes. The maps and chronologies in the volumes of this atlas answer questions of what, when, and where. Venturing to explain why and how changes occurred requires more information and a different focus for the research. It is hoped some readers will undertake this line of inquiry and will find value in the information and references provided here.

While the strictly defined purpose and scope of this project preclude additional research and writing for analytical monographs or narrative histories, compilers uncover more information than is needed to draw the maps and describe the boundary changes. None of this information has been ignored. The bibliographies list a wide range of materials that were useful in compiling the changes and drawing the maps. The chronologies cover more than boundary changes alone, including county name changes, unsuccessful authorizations for new counties, and redefinitions and clarifications of existing lines. Line shifts too small to map at the scales employed here are also regularly identified.

The structural heart of this atlas for each state, the component on which all others depend, is the *consolidated chronology* in which all boundary changes and related events for the state are brought together in a single chronological list. The entries not only tell what happened but refer readers to the sources for each event. Following the consolidated chronology is a section that presents the counties one by one. Here the reader will find *individual county chronologies* and complementary sets of *individual county maps* that depict the various configurations of every county. As an aid to readers concerned with statistical densities and other areal data, figures for *county areas* (not including temporary attachments) accompany the individual county chronologies. A special section covers all censuses in the state's history, including state and colonial or territorial censuses or equivalents (e.g., tax or poll lists), in addition to the more familiar federal enumerations. In this section the reader will find a *table of censuses* describing the available data and a matching series of *census outline maps*. The volume concludes with an annotated *bibliography* and an *index of places,* which lists the present county of every settled place named on the modern federal map that serves as the base for the full-scale individual county maps.

The maps are arranged in two series that serve different purposes. The first series of maps is designed to show the historical jurisdictions of individual counties. With few exceptions there is a separate map for each different configuration of the county lines, so readers can easily see the exact jurisdictional area of the county and the places it encompassed at any time. Most of these maps are derived from the U.S. Geological Survey's State Base series at the scale of 1:500,000 or about eight miles per inch (this atlas's standard base for individual counties), and those maps display considerable detail: water features, cities and towns, state and county boundaries, and, when available, the lines of the federal land survey. Drawing the historical boundary lines on these modern base maps permits a clear comparison of old and new and affords the reader a familiar context and a dependable reference system with which he or she can study the historical boundaries. In most cases, for counties too large to fit on a single page at the standard scale, a small-scale map (1:2,500,000, about one-fifth the scale of the standard maps) is used instead. Small-scale maps are also used to show how unorganized counties and non-county areas were temporarily attached to fully functioning host counties.

A second series of maps presents small-scale outline maps that match available census data. Some maps cover more than one census because during the intervening period either there were no territorial changes or changes were too small to show on these maps. Readers should consult the individual county maps for small changes.

Sources

The principal sources for historical county boundary lines in the United States are colonial, territorial, and state laws. Occasionally, in the earliest days of a proprietary colony or a territory, counties were created or changed by executive proclamation; in the nineteenth century a few counties were created by new state constitutions. Courts or special arbitrators sometimes settled jurisdictional disputes at the international, state, and county levels. The number of changes produced outside the legislative process does not, however, represent a large proportion of the total changes for any state.

The compilers have relied upon the provincial, territorial, and state laws because counties are the creatures of their states, created and for the most part controlled by the state legislatures. State laws are authoritative and convenient, relatively compact and coherent as a corpus, and available throughout the country. Session laws are the immediate, official products of each session of the legislature. Sets of statutes at large are authoritative and convenient, though not available for all states or for all periods. Rationalized sets of state laws, usually termed revised codes, pass through the same legislative process as individual session laws and are equally authoritative. Apparent alterations wrought by codifying a state's laws are infrequent and usually accidental. In Florida the revised and annotated codes include county boundary descriptions, and a few errors have been found. Those errors that were later corrected by legislation are noted in the chronologies.

Before codification became a regular feature of the legislative process, a few individuals compiled and published collections of state laws. The most famous is William W. Hening, whose thirteen-volume *Statutes at Large: Being a Collection of All the Laws of Virginia, from the First Session of the Legislature in the Year 1619 [to 1792],* published in Richmond, 1819–1823, has become a classic and a standard. Some of these collections were commissioned or at least sanctioned by the legislatures, but in all cases they are recognized and accepted as reliable and authoritative. In Florida, John P. Duval's *Compilation of the Public Acts of the Legislative Council of the Territory of Florida Passed prior to 1840* (1839), found listed in this bibliography under Florida Territory, and Leslie A. Thompson's *Manual or Digest of the Statute Law of the State of Florida, Including Law of the United States Relative to the Government of Florida* (1847) proved helpful in reconstructing early county boundaries.

Collections of pertinent sections of county boundary laws, such as the Historical Records Survey of Mississippi's *State and County Boundaries of Mississippi* (Jackson, Miss., 1942), are convenient but demand caution. There is a potential for error in transcription, as well as the possibility that valuable information (e.g., an effective date) may be lost in the editorial process of excerpting the selected passages. Such a compilation can be a marvelous convenience for the researcher, once it has been checked against the session laws and has been found reliable. There are compilations of county creations and changes for a number of states, but they vary greatly in content and in accuracy. It is virtually impossible to judge their reliability until much of the work has been replicated. These secondary sources, therefore, are useful chiefly as guides to the primary laws, proclamations, and decisions. Such a secondary source is available for Florida, although it is largely unknown. The Florida Historical Records Survey researched and prepared a compilation of county boundary laws, but the 1937 typescript was never published. This work, "Record of Acts of the Legislative Council of the Territory of Florida and General Assembly of the State of Florida Relating to County Boundaries, 1821–1937," was used to insure that the compilers' search of session laws was complete.

Although all works used to determine the courses of county boundary lines appear in the bibliography, several deserve special mention. Five volumes of the *Territorial Papers of the United States,* covering Florida from 1821 to 1845, were very important for identifying locations, people, and survey lines; Charles C. Royce's "Indian Land Cessions in the United States" (1899) helped determine the early boundaries of Alachua and Orange Counties, and explained the resurveys of the Indian boundary line. Local histories were helpful for identifying places and confirming referendum dates. Several place-name compilations were also important: *Places in the Sun: The History and Romance of Florida Place-Names,* by Bertha E. Bloodworth and Alton C. Morris (1978); Howard F. Cline's *Provisional Historical Gazeteer* [sic]*, with Locational Notes on Florida Colonial Communities, 1700–1823, and 16 Maps, 3 Figures* (1964. Reprint, 1974); and Allen Morris's *Florida Place Names* (1974).

The histories of United States international and state boundaries, unlike those of county lines, have been thoroughly described and documented in a number of publications. Without the need for further original research at these levels, staff historians have relied heavily upon secondary sources for changes in national, colonial, territorial, and state lines.

Among the most useful modern sources are the large-scale, up-to-date county maps usually published by state departments of transportation or by individual counties. Used for a number of different purposes, both official and unofficial, such maps usually are extremely reliable compilations of the details of boundaries, roads, natural features, and other landmarks.

Historical maps do not frequently play a large role in this sort of work, as they are seldom useful for interpreting boundary descriptions. Throughout the seventeenth and eighteenth centuries, mapmakers knew little about the lay of the land and had to work with relatively inaccurate instruments and data. The accuracy of maps improved during the nineteenth century with the surveying of the land and advancements in cartography, but often those maps are not as valuable for research as one might expect because the boundary landmarks they depict also appear on current maps. On the other hand, historical maps occasionally are indispensable for locating lost landmarks and names. In any case, it is important to remember that a map is, by its nature, more like a secondary work than a primary source.

Sometimes errors on old maps can benefit research. When a boundary description cannot be plotted on a modern base map or does not seem to make sense, the flaw may lie not in the description but in the geographic notions upon which it was based. If the errors on an old map accurately reflect accepted ideas and knowledge, however mistaken they may have been, that map may be the key to the true meaning of contemporaneous boundary descriptions. Florida provides an excellent example of this. In the 1820s and 1830s, the southern interior of Florida was still largely unknown and unexplored. When Monroe County was created in 1823, the northern boundary was described as a line running east from Charlotte

Harbor up the Charlotte River to Lake Macaco (now Lake Okeechobee). The problem is that no river runs from Lake Okeechobee to Charlotte Harbor. Given the swampy conditions and difficult terrain, it is not surprising that such a mistake was made. In 1837, John Williams wrote of the area: "Macaco, or Charlotte River, is supposed to have its source in Myacco Lake [Lake Okeechobee], in the heart of the Peninsula. We have not been so fortunate as to find white man or Indian that had ever visited the lake or the river more than fifty or sixty miles above Charlotte Bay" (*Territory of Florida . . .* , 49). In fact, on a map Williams drew to accompany his book, he included the Macaco River, but left out Lake Okeechobee. I. G. Searcy's 1829 map of Florida shows the Charlotte River running from Lake Okeechobee to Charlotte Harbor, although the lake is placed southwest of its actual location. In this case, the early maps are essential to understanding the information available to legislators, and a line can be drawn to approximate the intended boundary.

The historical maps most frequently consulted for roads, rivers, lakes, and other locations were I. G. Searcy's *Map of Florida Constructed Principally from Authentic Documents in the Land Office at Tallahassee* (1829); the maps accompanying John Williams's two books, *Territory of Florida . . .* (1837) and *View of West Florida . . .* (1827); U.S. Engineer Department's *Map of the Seat of War in Florida . . .* (1839); J. Goldsborough Bruff's *State of Florida, Compiled in the Bureau of Topographical Engineers from the Best Authorities* (1846); and *Atlas of Florida . . .* (1926. Reprint, 1980).

The table of censuses in this atlas does not document the well-known federal enumerations, but it does help readers find extant provincial, territorial, and state statistics or records containing the names of individuals, whether in a publication or in an institution. Whenever possible, the citation directs the reader to Henry J. Dubester's widely available *State Censuses: An Annotated Bibliography of Censuses of Population Taken after the Year 1790 by States and Territories of the United States* (1948), rather than to the document (usually a state government publication) in which the data actually appear. For example, for the 1895 Florida state census the reader is referred simply to page 8 of Dubester, which provides a detailed reference to the Florida Department of Agriculture's *Census Report of the State of Florida, for the Year 1895, under Chapter 4330, Laws of Florida* (Tallahassee, 1897), where the statistics were published. This approach, it is hoped, keeps the citations brief and clear.

The manner in which sources are described in the bibliography, the consolidated chronology, and the table of abbreviations is a composite style fashioned from the guidelines set out in the fourteenth edition of the University of Chicago Press's *Chicago Manual of Style* (Chicago, 1993) and, for legal sources, from the fifteenth edition of *Bluebook: A Uniform System of Citation* (Cambridge, Mass., 1991), compiled jointly by the editors of *Columbia Law Review, Harvard Law Review, University of Pennsylvania Law Review*, and *Yale Law Journal*.

Procedures

There appears to be more than one way to compile the changes in county lines. One attractive approach is to start in the present and work back to the beginning. The most appealing aspect of working from present to past is the apparent logic of the approach—something like following the branches of a family tree back down to its roots or taking down a building brick by brick. But these analogies are misleading. The current array of counties was not constructed by the process of accretion that is at the heart of house building, nor is it like a genealogical diagram in which changes occur only through the addition of new family members. Trying to dismantle the present to reach the past usually yields little more than frustration or error.

In this project, the compiler maps county boundary changes in chronological order, a procedure that provides a built-in checking mechanism. By using a modern map as a base and plotting boundary changes from the past to the present, it is easy to compare the compiler's version of each county's final set of lines with its current configuration. If the two are not the same, there must be an error on the modern map or the compiler has made a mistake, either missing a change or plotting a line incorrectly. Whatever the cause, therefore, a mismatch at the end of research and sketching automatically reveals a problem that must be resolved.

Working directly from originals or photocopies of the verbal boundary descriptions in the laws, the researcher plots the lines on a compilation sheet of tracing paper laid over a base map of the state. These are the graphic equivalents of notes, and the line work is always accompanied by some text, if only the county name, the nature of the change, and the effective date. As each change is plotted, the compiler writes a descriptive entry for the state's boundary chronology and a brief citation to the source of information. Reading straight through the session laws of a state is normally unnecessary, because the titles of acts and the indexes to the laws usually indicate all boundary changes. Occasionally, however, changes in county boundaries are hidden in laws on other topics, as in laws changing the official status of a place from town to borough, establishing a county seat, or providing for the maintenance of roads and bridges. When it becomes clear that a change has been missed, the compiler broadens the search to include enactments on related subjects.

With few exceptions, all boundary changes have been mapped. In some cases it has been necessary to use an asterisk or similar device to indicate the approximate location, along the existing boundary, of a change too small to represent with lines. Changes of unusual proportions (one dimension small, the other large) cannot be represented at all on the maps used here—a change that straightens slight irregularities in a long boundary, for example, or one that shifts a boundary from the center of a stream to one bank or the other. Another unmappable exception is any small change whose location cannot be determined, such as an individual farm identified only by the owner's name or a small area identified only by a landmark now lost. Each unmapped change is noted in the chronology.

Areas of counties are calculated by tracing the boundaries on the individual county maps with a digitizer connected to a microcomputer; data from the digitizer are processed by a program that calculates areas. In order to avoid having the figures appear more precise than is possible, the numbers are rounded to the nearest ten. The county areas published in current reference works commonly are for land area, excluding all bodies of water larger than a certain minimum size. In this atlas, figures for present areas normally match those land-only areas; when there is a difference, the number here usually is larger. It is not difficult to avoid counting large water areas by tracing the shorelines of very large lakes and the seacoast instead of the boundary lines that delineate offshore jurisdiction. No attempt is made to measure and subtract smaller lakes and ponds, nor to add small islands. Thus, for example, the counties of Minnesota are measured without subtracting any of the state's thousands of lakes, but the state's jurisdiction over the waters of Lake Superior is excluded. Many Florida counties contain large numbers of lakes and broad rivers, and, while Lake Okeechobee and large bays were easily excluded from county measurements, smaller lakes and streams were not. The highly irregular coastline also made accurate measurements more difficult. Nevertheless, square mileages are in line with published figures found in various almanacs and gazetteers, which do not always agree among themselves.

Special Topics for Florida

Florida's present northern limit with Georgia is used for events starting in 1763 because that is when it was defined as a straight line running eastward from the confluence of the Chattahoochee and Flint Rivers to the head of the St. Marys River and thence down the St. Marys to the Atlantic Ocean. The disputes over that boundary that flared on and off between Florida and Georgia until final settlement in 1861 concerned the detailed interpretation and implementation of that earlier definition.

Florida began creating counties quite late relative to many eastern states. The Spanish and British governors found no need for sophisticated administrative divisions due to the sparse settlement of the colony. In 1821, following Spain's cession of East and West Florida to the United States two years before, Andrew Jackson assumed the governorship of the territory. He retained the division of Florida into eastern and western parts for administrative purposes, but he moved the dividing line to the Suwannee River from its earlier location along the Chattahoochee and Apalachicola Rivers. Jackson then decreed that East Florida would be called St. Johns County and West Florida would become Escambia County. After 1821, county creations and boundary changes became the responsibility of the legislature.

Three Florida counties changed names permanently, and Hernando County was renamed Benton County for six years. In addition, there was an attempt to change the name of Mosquito (now Orange) County to Leigh Read County. In 1842 the legislature passed a law changing the name of Mosquito County to Leigh Read, in honor of the former legislator who was murdered in 1841, the victim of a longstanding quarrel with the Alston family (Read had killed Augustus Alston in an 1839 duel after repeated challenges from Alston). Although the bill honoring Read passed the legislature, a clerk kept the bill from reaching the governor's desk, effectively killing it. While the change never offically took place, the name Leigh Read can be found in various documents, including a contemporary map, as well as in other acts passed by the 1842 legislature.

With one exception, Florida counties were fully organized at the time of creation and remained fully organized. Dade County, the lone exception, was created in 1836 with a temporary county seat at Indian Key, about halfway between Miami and Key West. However, the lack of population created problems from the start. In 1838 one correspondent reported that there were not enough men in the entire county to form a grand and petit jury. Dade's fortunes diminished further in 1840 when Indians led by Chekika raided Indian Key, killing several citizens and destroying much of the town, and Monroe County began to take over Dade's duties. In 1851 when the legislature ordered the records and files of Dade County removed to Monroe, Dade ceased to exist as a fully organized county and was for all practical purposes attached to Monroe. No single piece of legislation reestablished Dade to fully organized status. Rather, over a period of time beginning in the late 1860s, the county government again began to function, first with the meeting of county commissioners in September 1869, then with the appointment of a clerk of court and sheriff, and finally in 1872 with the reestablishment of judicial functions.

The boundary between Hernando, Hillsborough, and Polk counties presented some especially difficult problems in the mid-1800s that cannot be definitively resolved. Beginning with Hernando's creation in 1843, part of its southern boundary with Hillsborough ran along the Hillsborough River in township 26 south. This part of the boundary was confirmed on 1 January 1847. On 10 February 1874 Polk was given all that part of Hillsborough County that lay in township 26 south, so that Hernando and Polk now shared the boundary in township 26. At some point between 1874 and 1883 Hernando acquired that part of township 26 belonging to Polk, although there is no legislation to that effect and research in other local sources has not identified the reason or source for this change. By 5 March 1883, legislators apparently believed that all of township 26 south, range 22 east, belonged to Hernando, for they transferred three sections of the township from Hernando to Polk. The compiler has decided to use the date "by 1880" for the transfer of township 26 from Polk to Hernando based upon the rendering of the boundary on contemporary maps, especially the annual Rand, McNally business atlases, which show a boundary change beginning with the 1880 edition.

After 1910, county creations dropped sharply in the eastern United States, yet Florida organized thirteen of its sixty-seven counties in the 1920s. (Georgia, which added five counties in the 1920s, is the only other eastern state to create any in that decade.) In the last quarter of the nineteenth century, Florida's population was largely rural and lay concentrated in the northern part of the state. Private and public efforts to attract new residents and capital resulted in steady population growth up to World War I. However, a land-sale boom, improvements in both automobile and rail transportation, the climate, low taxes, and continued advertising and publicity campaigns to spur development in the 1920s helped fuel an unprecedented 51 percent increase in state population from 968,470 in 1920 to 1,468,211 in 1930. Most of this growth was in southern Florida, where nine of the thirteen new counties created during this time are located.

Base Maps

This project relies on maps published by the U.S. Geological Survey. Most of the individual county maps show the historical boundary drawn on a special version of the U.S.G.S. State Base map of Florida published at the scale of 1:500,000, or eight miles per inch. This base map is dated 1967, and therefore does not reflect boundary changes that occurred between 1967 and 1990. However, all post-1967 changes, large and small, are mapped. This map, a product of the Geological Survey's custom printing service, is designed to be as uncluttered as possible without losing essential features. The special printing for this atlas shows the coastline, rivers, outlines of lakes, and the names of water features, all reduced in blackness by a 50 percent, bi-angle screen; place names, longitude and latitude lines, state and county boundary lines, and land survey lines (when available) are all in solid black. Omitted from the regular version of the map of Florida, therefore, are contour lines, boundaries of federal reservations and large municipalities, railroads and miscellaneous symbols, and the small circles for place locations.

The small-scale maps used to show counties too large to fit on a single page using the 1:500,000-scale bases are essentially the same as those used to depict both the state's county network for the various censuses and the attachments of unorganized counties and non-county areas. All these maps are redrawings of the pertinent sections of the U.S. Geological Survey's map of the United States at the scale of 1:2,500,000, or about forty miles per inch.

Although errors on these federal maps are rare, there are two on the Florida map. The boundary between Duval and St. Johns Counties in township 4 south should run along the range line between ranges 27 and 28, rather than along Durbin Creek in township 4 south, range 28 east, as depicted on the federal map. A second error occurs between Lake and Volusia Counties along the St. Johns River. Huntoon's Island is part of Volusia, but is shown as part of Lake on the U.S.G.S. base map. In both cases the boundary is correctly shown on present county highway maps and in this atlas.

All the maps in this atlas have been reduced from their original size for publication. The graphic bar scales provided for the maps make it possible to determine distances accurately. While each small-scale map is accompanied by its own scale bar, the standard maps of individual counties have their graphic scale printed across the bottom of the page.

Dates

Every effort has been made to give the day, month, and year (e.g., 25 February 1785) for all county creations, boundary changes, and other events in this atlas. Occasionally it is impossible to date an event so precisely, but a reasonable estimate is possible. When the precise date is not known or an approximate date is more appropriate, the date is generalized to the month and year (e.g., February 1785) or to the year alone. A lack of evidence may make it impossible to give any date at all for a county's creation, and its occurrence can only be confirmed by the record of a later, related happening, such as the appointment of a sheriff. In such a situation, the date of the later event is used with the simple addition of "by" (e.g., by 25 February 1785) to indicate that the county creation or other event occurred no later than that date and probably earlier.

Several dates may be associated with the creation of a county or a change in county lines. To many individuals the date that makes the most sense is the one when people began to observe the change, but in most cases that date is impossible to ascertain. An alternative is the date on which the law effecting the change passed the legislature or was approved by the governor. The date of passage is an important reference because it helps identify the law; now as in the past, references to a law often include the date of passage. Most other compilations of county changes have adopted the date of passage as their standard for the date of change, but it is not always the best indicator of when change occurred.

The dating standard in this atlas is the legally effective date of change, whether it be for the creation of a new county or for the alteration of lines between existing counties. Through the colonial period and into the nineteenth century, the date a law passed was generally the date it went into effect. As the nineteenth century progressed, legislators recognized the importance of preparing for the establishment of a new county organization or for the shift in jurisdiction that accompanies boundary changes. Some laws, therefore, began to carry two dates: one marking the passage of the law and the other specifying when the line change or new county creation would go into effect. If the date of passage and effective date are different, the law gives both.

Florida counties created before 1858 all have the same passage and effective date. Beginning with the creation of Bradford and Suwannee Counties, many (but not all) counties had different effective dates—in some cases these dates were established in the creation act, and in other cases they were dependent on the outcome of a referendum. The creation of a Bloxham County was authorized by the state legislature, but voters in the affected areas of Levy and Marion Counties voted 460 to 339 against the new county.

Suwannee and Bradford are the only counties for which a precise effective date is not known. Both counties were authorized in a single act approved 21 December 1858, but the creations were dependent on a referendum which was to be held after thirty days' public notice following passage of the act. Neither Bradford, Suwannee, nor the parent county, Columbia, have county commissioners' records from this period, and no record could be found at the state archives or in local historical sources. The earliest possible date for the referendum would have been 20 January 1859, but because of the time lag in communications, it is more likely that the referendum would not have been held until February, hence the effective date "c. February 1959" used in this atlas.

Using effective dates means that many of the dates in this atlas may disagree with dates in other references. As an aid to appreciating how great the differences between the two dates can be and to help correlate the data in this book with other publications, this atlas offers a *table of county creations* that gives both the date of passage and the effective date for all county creations.

Abbreviations

Abbreviated References in Citations

Many citations identify works by author or by author and short title, but most employ abbreviations. Authors and titles for abbreviated references are given below; see the bibliography at the back of the atlas for full descriptions of these works.

Fla. Laws	Florida. *Acts and Resolutions Adopted by the Legislature.*
Fla. Rpts.	Florida Supreme Court. *Florida Reports.*
Fla. Stat.	Florida. *Florida Statutes.*
Fla. Terr. Acts	Florida Territory. *Acts and Resolutions of the Legislative Council.*
HRS Fla., *Okaloosa*	Historical Records Survey, Florida. *Okaloosa County (Crestview).*
HRS Fla., *Pinellas*	Historical Records Survey, Florida. *Pinellas County (Clearwater).*
Terr. Papers U.S.	*Territorial Papers of the United States.*
U.S. Stat.	United States. *Statutes at Large of the United States of America, 1789–1873.*

Other Abbreviations Used in This Atlas

Except where noted, plurals are formed by adding s.

A.D.	*anno Domini,* in the year of our Lord	D.C.	District of Columbia
adj.	adjourned	Dec.	December
Ala.	Alabama	Del.	Delaware
ann.	annotated, annual	dept.	department
Apr.	April	diss.	dissertation
arch.	archives	doc.	document
Ariz.	Arizona	e.	east
Ark.	Arkansas	ed.	edition, editor
art.	article	e.g.	*exempli gratia,* for example
assy.	assembly	et al.	*et alii,* and others
Aug.	August	etc.	*et cetera,* and so forth
bien.	biennial	exec.	executive
bros.	brothers	ext.	extra, extraordinary
c.	*circa,* about	Feb.	February
Calif.	California	Fla.	Florida
ch.	chapter	ft.	fort
co.	company, county	Ga.	Georgia
col.	colonial	gen.	general
Colo.	Colorado	geneal.	genealogical, genealogy
comp.	compiler	gov.	governor
Conn.	Connecticut	hist.	historical, history
corres.	correspondence	HRS	Historical Records Survey
cr.	creek	i.	island

Id.	Idaho	Ph.D.	*Philosophiae Doctor,* Doctor of Philosophy
i.e.	*id est,* that is	pl.	plate
Ill.	Illinois	Ply.	Plymouth
Ind.	Indiana	priv.	private
Jan.	January	pt.	part
jour.	journal	pub.	public
jr.	junior	quad.	quadrennial
Jul.	July	quart.	quarter, quarterly
Jun.	June	r.	river
Kans.	Kansas	rec.	record
Ky.	Kentucky	reg.	register, regular
La.	Louisiana	res.	resolution
loc.	local	rev.	revised
Mar.	March	R.I.	Rhode Island
Mass.	Massachusetts	rpt.	report
Md.	Maryland	s.	south
Me.	Maine	S.C.	South Carolina
mi.	mile	S.Dak.	South Dakota
Mich.	Michigan	sec.	section
Minn.	Minnesota	sec. state	secretary of state
misc.	miscellaneous	sen.	senate
Miss.	Mississippi	Sep.	September
Mo.	Missouri	ser.	series
Mont.	Montana	sess.	session
MS	manuscript	spec.	special
mt.	mount, mountain	sprs.	springs
n.	north, note	sq.	square
N.C.	North Carolina	sq. mi.	square miles
n.d.	no date	st.	saint, state, street
N.Dak.	North Dakota	sta.	station
Nebr.	Nebraska	stat.	statute, statutes
Nev.	Nevada	ste.	sainte
N.H.	New Hampshire	Tenn.	Tennessee
N.J.	New Jersey	terr.	territorial, territory
N.Mex.	New Mexico	Tex.	Texas
no.	number	Univ.	University
Nov.	November	U.S.	United States
n.p.	no place, no publisher	U.S.G.S.	United States Geological Survey
n.s.	new series	v.	versus
N.W. Terr.	Northwest Territory	Va.	Virginia
N.Y.	New York	vol.	volume
Oct.	October	Vt.	Vermont
Okla.	Oklahoma	w.	west
opp.	opposite	Wash.	Washington
Oreg.	Oregon	Wis.	Wisconsin
p. (plural, pp.)	page	W.Va.	West Virginia
Pa.	Pennsylvania	Wyo.	Wyoming
par.	paragraph		

FLORIDA

Florida County Creations

County	Source	Dates	
		Authorization	**Creation Effective**
ALACHUA	Fla. Terr. Acts 1824, 3d sess., sec. 6/p. 261	29 Dec 1824	same
BAKER	Fla. Laws 1860, 10th sess., ch. 1185/p. 179	8 Feb 1861	same
BAY	Fla. Laws 1913, 14th sess., gen., ch. 6505, secs. 1, 24/pp. 347, 353; ch. 6506/p. 354; and ch. 6508/p. 359	24 Apr 1913	1 Jul 1913
BLOXHAM (proposed)	Fla. Laws 1915, 15th sess., gen., ch. 6936, secs. 1, 20–21/pp. 298–303	1 Jun 1915	*
BRADFORD (created as NEW RIVER)	Fla. Laws 1858, 9th sess., ch. 895, secs. 1, 3–4/p. 37	21 Dec 1858	c. Feb 1859
BREVARD (created as original ST. LUCIE)	Fla. Terr. Acts 1844, 22d sess., sec. 1/p. 31	14 Mar 1844	same
BROWARD	Fla. Laws 1915, 15th sess., gen., ch. 6934, secs. 1, 23/pp. 285, 292	30 Apr 1915	1 Oct 1915
CALHOUN	Fla. Terr. Acts 1838, 16th sess., no. 8, sec. 1/p. 9	26 Jan 1838	same
CHARLOTTE	Fla. Laws 1921, 18th sess., gen., ch. 8513, sec. 1/p. 281	23 Apr 1921	same
CITRUS	Fla. Laws 1887, 1st sess., ch. 3772, sec. 1/p. 157	2 Jun 1887	same
CLAY	Fla. Laws 1858, 9th sess., ch. 866, secs. 1–2/p. 19	31 Dec 1858	same
COLLIER	Fla. Laws 1923, 19th sess., gen., ch. 9362, secs. 1, 26/pp. 468, 476	8 May 1923	7 Jul 1923
COLUMBIA	Fla. Terr. Acts 1832, 10th sess., no. 25, sec. 1/p. 33	4 Feb 1832	same
DADE	Fla. Terr. Acts 1836, 14th sess., ch. 937/p. 19	4 Feb 1836	same
DE SOTO	Fla. Laws 1887, 1st sess., ch. 3770, secs. 1–3/pp. 151–152	19 May 1887	same
DIXIE	Fla. Laws 1921, 18th sess., gen., ch. 8514, sec. 1/p. 289	25 Apr 1921	same
DUVAL	Fla. Terr. Acts 1822, 1st sess., sec. 1/p. 3	12 Aug 1822	same
ESCAMBIA	Fla. Terr. Acts 1822, 1st sess., sec. 1/p. xx	21 Jul 1821	same
FAYETTE (extinct)	Fla. Terr. Acts 1832, 10th sess., no. 53/p. 58	9 Feb 1832	same
FLAGLER	Fla. Laws 1917, 16th sess., gen., ch. 7399, secs. 1, 22–23/pp. 277, 284	28 Apr 1917	12 Jun 1917
FRANKLIN	Fla. Terr. Acts 1832, 10th sess., no. 42/p. 44	8 Feb 1832	same
GADSDEN	Fla. Terr. Acts 1823, 2d sess., sec. 1/p. 8	24 Jun 1823	same

County	Source	Dates	
		Authorization	**Creation Effective**
GILCHRIST	Fla. Laws 1925, ext. sess., ch. 11371, secs. 1, 19–20/pp. 66, 70	4 Dec 1925	1 Jan 1926
GLADES	Fla. Laws 1921, 18th sess., gen., ch. 8513, sec. 1/p. 280	23 Apr 1921	same
GULF	Fla. Laws 1925, 20th sess., gen., ch. 10132, secs. 1, 25–26/pp. 237, 244	6 Jun 1925	7 Jul 1925
HAMILTON	Fla. Terr. Acts 1827, 6th sess./p. 8	26 Dec 1827	same
HARDEE	Fla. Laws 1921, 18th sess., gen., ch. 8513, sec. 1/p. 280	23 Apr 1921	same
HENDRY	Fla. Laws 1923, 19th sess., gen., ch. 9360, secs. 1, 26/pp. 459, 467	11 May 1923	10 Jul 1923
HERNANDO	Fla. Terr. Acts 1843, 21st sess., no. 51/p. 48	24 Feb 1843	same
HIGHLANDS	Fla. Laws 1921, 18th sess., gen., ch. 8513, sec. 1/p. 280	23 Apr 1921	same
HILLSBOROUGH	Fla. Terr. Acts 1834, 12th sess., ch. 764/p. 46	25 Jan 1834	same
HOLMES	Fla. Laws 1847, 3d sess., ch. 176, sec. 1/p. 45	8 Jan 1848	same
INDIAN RIVER	Fla. Laws 1925, 20th sess., gen., ch. 10148, sec. 1/p. 294	30 May 1925	29 Jun 1925
JACKSON	Fla. Terr. Acts 1822, 1st sess., sec. 1/p. 3	12 Aug 1822	same
JEFFERSON	Fla. Terr. Acts 1826, 5th sess./p. 151	20 Jan 1827	same
LAFAYETTE	Fla. Laws 1856, 8th sess., ch. 806, secs. 1–2/p. 48	23 Dec 1856	same
LAKE	Fla. Laws 1887, 1st sess., ch. 3771, secs. 1–2/pp. 154–155	27 May 1887	26 July 1887
LEE	Fla. Laws 1887, 1st sess., ch. 3769/p. 150	13 May 1887	same
LEON	Fla. Terr. Acts 1824, 3d sess., sec. 5/p. 261	29 Dec 1824	same
LEVY	Fla. Terr. Acts 1845, 23d sess., no. 30, sec. 1/p. 54	10 Mar 1845	same
LIBERTY	Fla. Laws 1855, adj. sess., ch. 771/p. 50	15 Dec 1855	same
MADISON	Fla. Terr. Acts 1827, 6th sess./p. 8	26 Dec 1827	same
MANATEE	Fla. Laws 1854, 7th sess., ch. 628/p. 47	9 Jan 1855	same
MARION	Fla. Terr. Acts 1844, 22d sess., sec. 1/p. 43	14 Mar 1844	same
MARTIN	Fla. Laws 1925, 20th sess., gen., ch. 10180, secs. 1, 25–26/pp. 359, 368	30 May 1925	4 Aug 1925
MONROE	Fla. Terr. Acts 1823, 2d sess., sec. 1/p. 122	3 Jul 1823	same
MOSQUITO (see ORANGE)			
NASSAU	Fla. Terr. Acts 1824, 3d sess., sec. 8/p. 262	29 Dec 1824	same
NEW RIVER (see BRADFORD)			

County	Source	Dates	
		Authorization	Creation Effective
OKALOOSA	Fla. Laws 1915, 15th sess., gen., ch. 6937, secs. 1, 24–25/pp. 303, 310	3 Jun 1915	7 Sep 1915
OKEECHOBEE	Fla. Laws 1917, 16th sess., gen., ch. 7401, secs. 1, 20–21/pp. 285, 289–290	8 May 1917	7 Aug 1917
ORANGE (created as MOSQUITO)	Fla. Terr. Acts 1824, 3d sess., sec. 10/p. 262	29 Dec 1824	same
OSCEOLA	Fla. Laws 1887, 1st sess., ch. 3768/p. 148	12 May 1887	11 Jul 1887
PALM BEACH	Fla. Laws 1909, 12th sess., ch. 5970, sec. 1/p. 174	30 Apr 1909	1 Jul 1909
PASCO	Fla. Laws 1887, 1st sess., ch. 3772, sec. 8/p. 158	2 Jun 1887	same
PINELLAS	Fla. Laws 1911, 13th sess., ch. 6247, secs. 1, 20–21/pp. 219, 223	23 May 1911	14 Nov 1911
POLK	Fla. Laws 1860, 10th sess., ch. 1201/p. 192	8 Feb 1861	same
PUTNAM	Fla. Laws 1848, 4th sess., ch. 280, sec. 1/p. 87	13 Jan 1849	same
ST. JOHNS	Fla. Terr. Acts 1822, 1st sess., sec. 1/p. xx	21 Jul 1821	same
ST. LUCIE (original; see BREVARD)			
ST. LUCIE	Fla. Laws 1905, 10th sess., ch. 5567, secs. 1, 22/pp. 404, 408	24 May 1905	1 Jul 1905
SANTA ROSA	Fla. Terr. Acts 1842, 20th sess., no. 1, sec. 1/p. 3	18 Feb 1842	same
SARASOTA	Fla. Laws 1921, 18th sess., gen., ch. 8515, secs. 1, 22–23/pp. 294, 300	14 May 1921	15 Jun 1921
SEMINOLE	Fla. Laws 1913, 14th sess., gen., ch. 6511, sec. 1/p. 365	25 Apr 1913	same
SUMTER	Fla. Laws 1852, 6th sess., ch. 548, sec. 1/p. 124	8 Jan 1853	same
SUWANNEE	Fla. Laws 1858, 9th sess., ch. 895, secs. 1–2, 4/p. 37	21 Dec 1858	c. Feb 1859
TAYLOR	Fla. Laws 1856, 8th sess., ch. 806, secs. 1, 3/p. 48	23 Dec 1856	same
UNION	Fla. Laws 1921, 18th sess., gen., ch. 8516, secs. 1, 27/pp. 301, 307	20 May 1921	1 Oct 1921
VOLUSIA	Fla. Laws 1854, 7th sess., ch. 624/p. 44	29 Dec 1854	same
WAKULLA	Fla. Terr. Acts 1843, 21st sess., no. 25/p. 29 and no. 30/p. 33	11 Mar 1843	same
WALTON	Fla. Terr. Acts 1824, 3d sess., sec. 2/p. 260	29 Dec 1824	same
WASHINGTON	Fla. Terr. Acts 1825, 4th sess./p. 35	9 Dec 1825	same

* The Legislature authorized creation of BLOXHAM on 1 June 1915, but voters rejected the proposed county by a vote of 339 in favor to 460 against in an election held 14 September 1915.

Consolidated Chronology of Florida State and County Boundaries

1719

The French commander at New Orleans and the Spanish commander at Pensacola agreed to recognize the Perdido R. as the boundary between their jurisdictions, French Louisiana and Spanish Florida, and their home governments acquiesced in the arrangement. (Cox, 8)

10 February 1763

The Treaty of Paris, ending the Seven Years' War between Great Britain (the victor) and France and Spain, formally transferred Florida from Spain to Britain. The Spanish had incorporated Florida into their empire in the early sixteenth century, when Europeans first visited its coast, and in 1565 they founded St. Augustine; by the time Britain acquired the area, the northern and western limits of Florida had not been fixed definitively but certainly lay at least as far north as the present state line and possibly as far west as the Mississippi R. (Cappon, Petchenik, and Long, 1)

7 October 1763

By royal proclamation King George III organized former Spanish Florida into the new British colonies of East Florida and West Florida. West Florida was to be bounded on the east by the Chattahoochee and Apalachicola Rivers, on the north by the parallel of 31 degrees north latitude, and on the west by the Mississippi R., the Iberville R., and Lake Pontchartrain, including parts of present Louisiana, Mississippi, Alabama, and Florida. East Florida encompassed the territory east of the Apalachicola R. and south of a straight line from where the Apalachicola is formed by the junction of the Chattahoochee and Flint Rivers to the headspring of the St. Marys R. and thence down the St. Marys to the Atlantic Ocean. Demarcation of this boundary line and agreement on its details by Florida and Georgia was not achieved until the 1860s. (Cappon, Petchenik, and Long, 1, 77; Shortt and Doughty, 119–120; Van Zandt, 103)

July 1764

In the commission to West Florida's first governor, Great Britain redefined West Florida, extending its limits northward to a line running due east from the junction of the Yazoo and Mississippi Rivers to the Chattahoochee R. This implicitly reduced the western extent of Georgia and added Natchez and much of present Alabama and Mississippi to West Florida. (Cappon, Petchenik, and Long, 87)

8 May 1781

Spain captured Pensacola, successfully concluding a campaign (started Aug. 1779) to conquer West Florida from Great Britain during the War of the American Revolution. (Cappon, Petchenik, and Long, 53–54)

3 September 1783

Commissioners from Great Britain and the United States signed the Treaty of Paris (ratifications exchanged 12 May 1784), ending the War of the American Revolution, recognizing American independence, and defining U.S. boundaries. The United States was bounded on the west by the Mississippi R. and on the south by the Floridas. Great Britain ceded East and West Florida to Spain by a separate Treaty of Paris, but the boundaries of the Floridas (e.g., 31st parallel of northern latitude) were not specified. (Parry, 48:481, 487, 491–492; Van Zandt, 12)

29 July 1784

Spain claimed most of the southwestern United States (north of West Florida, east of the Mississippi R., south of the Tennessee and Hiwassee Rivers, and west of the Flint R.) based upon its conquest of West Florida and the lower Mississippi during the War of the American Revolution. The United States insisted upon the parallel of 31 degrees north latitude, specified in its 1783 peace treaty with Great Britain, as its southern boundary. Neither side actually controlled the interior. (Cappon, Petchenik, and Long, 14, 74, 87; Whitaker, facing 68, 69)

27 October 1795

Pinckney's Treaty with Spain (ratified 25 Apr. 1796) settled the U.S.–Florida boundary along the parallel of 31 degrees north latitude from the Mississippi R. eastward to the Chattahoochee R., downstream to the mouth of the Flint R., eastward on a straight line to the head of the St. Marys R., and downstream to the Atlantic Ocean. (Parry, 53:9, 12–13; Van Zandt, 22)

30 April 1803

The United States purchased Louisiana from France, taking formal possession 20 December 1803; boundaries were not clearly defined but unquestionably included the western half of the Mississippi drainage basin. The United States took advantage of the ambiguous description of the territory to claim all of West Florida west of the Perdido R. (southern portions of present Alabama and Mississippi and part of present Louisiana), based on the 1719 de facto definition of Louisiana, even though Spain actually governed the area. (Cox, facing 2, 80–101; Parry, 57:27, 30–31)

26 March 1804

The United States created Orleans Territory from that portion of Louisiana south of the parallel of 33 degrees north latitude, west of the Mississippi R., and south of Mississippi Territory east of the river; this included part of West Florida between the Mississippi and Perdido Rivers (southern portions of present Alabama and Mississippi and part of present Louisiana), claimed by the United States as part of Louisiana but actually governed by Spain. (U.S. Stat., vol. 2, ch. 38 [1804], sec. 1/p. 283; Van Zandt, 107)

7 December 1810

FELICIANA (La.) created by Orleans Territory from non-county area; included part of West Florida west of the Perdido R. (southern portions of present Alabama and Mississippi and part of present Louisiana) claimed by the United States as part of Louisiana but actually controlled by Spain [not mapped]. (Orleans Terr. Acts 1811, 2d sess., p. 210)

14 May 1812

Following admission into the Union of the state of Louisiana from Orleans Territory (30 Apr. 1812), the United States formally added to Mississippi Territory the remnant of Orleans Territory lying south of 31 degrees north latitude and between the Pearl and Perdido Rivers (i.e., the southern portions of present Alabama and Mississippi) that the United States claimed as part of Louisiana but actually was controlled by Spain as part of West Florida. (Fuller, 199; U.S. Stat., vol. 2, ch. 84 [1812]/p. 734; Van Zandt, 105)

15 April 1813

American forces captured city of Mobile from Spain, effectively adding to the United States the territory between the Pearl and Perdido Rivers (southern tips of present Alabama and Mississippi) claimed since 1803 by the United States as part of Louisiana. (Cox, facing 2; Fuller, 202)

22 February 1819

Spain ceded East Florida and West Florida (i.e., all territory east of the Perdido R.) to the United States. Exchange of ratifications was delayed until 21 February 1821; American forces formally took possession of East Florida at St. Augustine on 10 July 1821, while West Florida was transferred on 17 July 1821. (Fuller, 307, 323; Parry, 70:1–7; Swindler, 2:309; Van Zandt, 27)

21 July 1821

ESCAMBIA and ST. JOHNS both created from non-county area by decree of Provisional Governor Andrew Jackson. (Fla. Terr. Acts 1822, 1st sess., sec. 1/p. xx)

30 March 1822

Territory of Florida created from Spanish provinces of East and West Florida with same boundaries as present state of Florida. (*Terr. Papers U.S.*, 22:389–399; U.S. Stat., vol. 3, ch. 13 [1822], sec. 1/p. 654)

12 August 1822

DUVAL created from ST. JOHNS; JACKSON created from ESCAMBIA. (Fla. Terr. Acts 1822, 1st sess., sec. 1/p. 3)

24 June 1823

GADSDEN created from JACKSON. DUVAL gained from JACKSON, exchanged with ST. JOHNS. (Fla. Terr. Acts 1823, 2d sess., sec. 1/p. 8)

3 July 1823

MONROE created from ST. JOHNS. (Fla. Terr. Acts 1823, 2d sess., sec. 1/p. 122)

29 December 1824

Territorial legislature created five new counties. (Fla. Terr. Acts 1824, 3d sess., pp. 260–262; for sections on particular counties, see following citations)

ALACHUA created from DUVAL and ST. JOHNS (sec. 6/p. 261)

LEON created from DUVAL and GADSDEN (sec. 5/p. 261)

MOSQUITO (now ORANGE) created from ST. JOHNS (sec. 10/p. 262)

NASSAU created from DUVAL (sec. 8/p. 262)

WALTON created from ESCAMBIA and JACKSON (sec. 2/p. 260)

DUVAL gained from ST. JOHNS. JACKSON gained from ESCAMBIA. Part of ST. JOHNS reverted to non-county area (Indian land). (Fla. Terr. Acts 1824, 3d sess., secs. 7, 9/pp. 261–262)

9 December 1825

WASHINGTON created from JACKSON and WALTON; JACKSON exchanged with WALTON; WALTON gained from ESCAMBIA. (Fla. Terr. Acts 1825, 4th sess./p. 35)

30 December 1826

NASSAU gained from DUVAL. (Fla. Terr. Acts 1826, 5th sess./p. 158)

12 January 1827

JACKSON exchanged with WASHINGTON. (Fla. Terr. Acts 1826, 5th sess./p. 108)

20 January 1827

JEFFERSON created from LEON. (Fla. Terr. Acts 1826, 5th sess./p. 151)

26 December 1827

HAMILTON and MADISON both created from JEFFERSON. (Fla. Terr. Acts 1827, 6th sess./p. 8)

19 January 1828

LEON gained from JEFFERSON. (Fla. Terr. Acts 1827, 6th sess./p. 170)

ALACHUA lost to Indian lands when treaty line was resurveyed. As a result of the resurvey MOSQUITO (now ORANGE) also apparently lost to Indian lands. (Fla. Terr. Acts 1827, 6th sess./p. 171; Royce, 704–705, pl. 121)

29 October 1828

JACKSON exchanged with WASHINGTON. (Fla. Terr. Acts 1828, 7th sess./p. 6)

23 November 1828

All county boundaries redefined; an overlap resulted when a single area was assigned to both DUVAL and NASSAU [corrected 2 Jan. 1857]. (Fla. Terr. Acts 1828, 7th sess., secs. 5–6/pp. 220–221)

14 November 1829

JEFFERSON gained from LEON. (Fla. Terr. Acts 1829, 8th sess./p. 37)

13 February 1831

LEON gained from JEFFERSON. (Fla. Terr. Acts 1831, 9th sess./p. 31)

30 January 1832

JEFFERSON gained from LEON. (Fla. Terr. Acts 1832, 10th sess., no. 11/p. 10)

4 February 1832

COLUMBIA created from ALACHUA. (Fla. Terr. Acts 1832, 10th sess., no. 25, sec. 1/p. 33)

8 February 1832

FRANKLIN created from GADSDEN and WASHING-TON. (Fla. Terr. Acts 1832, 10th sess., no. 42/p. 44)

9 February 1832

FAYETTE created from JACKSON. (Fla. Terr. Acts 1832, 10th sess., no. 53/p. 58)

11 February 1832

JACKSON exchanged with WASHINGTON. (Fla. Terr. Acts 1832, 10th sess., no. 72/p. 113)

9 February 1833

MADISON gained from JEFFERSON. (Fla. Terr. Acts 1833, 11th sess., ch. 686/p. 52)

16 February 1833

FAYETTE gained from WASHINGTON, lost to JACK-SON. (Fla. Terr. Acts 1833, 11th sess., ch. 688/p. 53)

JACKSON gained from WASHINGTON. (Fla. Terr. Acts 1833, 11th sess., ch. 687/p. 52)

25 January 1834

HILLSBOROUGH created from ALACHUA and from non-county area (former Indian lands). (Fla. Terr. Acts 1834, 12th sess., ch. 764/p. 46)

1 February 1834

JACKSON gained all of FAYETTE; FAYETTE eliminated. (Fla. Terr. Acts 1834, 12th sess., ch. 765/p. 47)

10 February 1835

ALACHUA gained from COLUMBIA. (Fla. Terr. Acts 1835, 13th sess., ch. 869/p. 325)

4 February 1836

DADE created from MONROE. (Fla. Terr. Acts 1836, 14th sess., ch. 937/p. 19)

26 January 1838

CALHOUN created from FRANKLIN, JACKSON, and WASHINGTON. WASHINGTON apparently gained small area from FRANKLIN. (Fla. Terr. Acts 1838, 16th sess., no. 8, sec. 1/p. 9)

25 February 1840

CALHOUN exchanged with WASHINGTON. (Fla. Terr. Acts 1840, 18th sess., no. 21/p. 23)

18 February 1842

SANTA ROSA created from ESCAMBIA. (Fla. Terr. Acts 1842, 20th sess., no. 1, sec. 1/p. 3)

22 February 1843

JEFFERSON gained from MADISON. (Fla. Terr. Acts 1843, 21st sess., no. 48/p. 47)

24 February 1843

HERNANDO created from ALACHUA and HILLSBOR-OUGH. (Fla. Terr. Acts 1843, 21st sess., no. 51/p. 48)

11 March 1843

WAKULLA created from LEON. (Fla. Terr. Acts 1843, 21st sess., no. 25/p. 29 and no. 30/p. 33)

5 February 1844

MADISON gained from JEFFERSON. (Fla. Terr. Acts 1844, 22d sess./p. 1)

6 March 1844

HERNANDO gained from HILLSBOROUGH; HER-NANDO renamed BENTON. (Fla. Terr. Acts 1844, 22d sess./p. 16)

14 March 1844

MARION created from ALACHUA, HILLSBOROUGH, MOSQUITO (now ORANGE), and ST. JOHNS. (Fla. Terr. Acts 1844, 22d sess., sec. 1/p. 43)

Original ST. LUCIE (now BREVARD) created from HILLSBOROUGH and MOSQUITO (now ORANGE). MOSQUITO apparently gained from HILLSBOROUGH. (Fla. Terr. Acts 1844, 22d sess., sec. 1/p. 31)

15 March 1844

COLUMBIA exchanged small areas with ALACHUA; DUVAL gained from COLUMBIA. Boundary between ALACHUA and DUVAL adjusted [not mapped]. (Fla. Terr. Acts 1844, 22d sess./p. 55)

30 January 1845

MOSQUITO renamed ORANGE. (Fla. Terr. Acts 1845, 23d sess., no. 31/p. 56)

27 February 1845

ORANGE gained from original ST. LUCIE (now BREVARD). (Fla. Terr. Acts 1845, 23d sess., no. 35/p. 58)

3 March 1845

Congress created the state of Florida from Florida Territory, with boundaries the same as those set in 1822; Florida Territory eliminated. (Swindler, 2:332; U.S. Stat., vol. 5, ch. 48 [1845], secs. 1, 5/pp. 742–743)

10 March 1845

LEVY created from ALACHUA. (Fla. Terr. Acts 1845, 23d sess., no. 30, sec. 1/p. 54)

CALHOUN gained from JACKSON. (Fla. Terr. Acts 1845, 23d sess., no. 29/p. 53)

25 December 1846

ORANGE and ST. JOHNS both gained from MARION along the St. Johns R. and Lake George. (Fla. Laws 1846, 2d sess., ch. 106/p. 63)

28 December 1846

Original ST. LUCIE (now BREVARD) gained from ORANGE. (Fla. Laws 1846, 2d sess., ch. 105/p. 62)

1 January 1847

HILLSBOROUGH gained from BENTON (now HERNANDO). (Fla. Laws 1846, 2d sess., ch. 107/p. 63)

4 January 1847

WASHINGTON gained from JACKSON. (Fla. Laws 1846, 2d sess., ch. 108/p. 64)

28 December 1847

JACKSON exchanged with WASHINGTON. (Fla. Laws 1847, 3d sess., ch. 180/p. 49)

8 January 1848

HOLMES created from JACKSON and WALTON. (Fla. Laws 1847, 3d sess., ch. 176, sec. 1/p. 45)

30 December 1848

ST. JOHNS gained from MARION. (Fla. Laws 1848, 4th sess., ch. 289/p. 96)

6 January 1849

WAKULLA gained from LEON. (Fla. Laws 1848, 4th sess., ch. 288/p. 96)

10 January 1849

ORANGE exchanged with original ST. LUCIE (now BREVARD). (Fla. Laws 1848, 4th sess., ch. 290/p. 97)

13 January 1849

PUTNAM created from ALACHUA and ST. JOHNS. (Fla. Laws 1848, 4th sess., ch. 280, sec. 1/p. 87)

24 December 1850

BENTON renamed HERNANDO. (Fla. Laws 1850, 5th sess., ch. 415/p. 148)

7 January 1851

DADE no longer fully organized, attached to MONROE for administrative and judicial purposes. (Fla. Laws 1850, 5th sess., ch. 400/p. 140; Hudson, 14–15)

11 January 1851

WALTON gained part of Santa Rosa I. from ESCAMBIA; SANTA ROSA exchanged with WALTON. (Fla. Laws 1850, 5th sess., ch. 411/p. 146)

13 January 1851

FRANKLIN gained from WAKULLA when boundary shifted from west bank to east bank of Ochlockonee R., and exchanged with GADSDEN. (Fla. Laws 1850, 5th sess., chs. 412, 413/p. 147)

22 January 1851

WAKULLA gained from LEON. (Fla. Laws 1850, 5th sess., ch. 414/p. 148)

8 January 1853

SUMTER created from MARION. (Fla. Laws 1852, 6th sess., ch. 548, sec. 1/p. 124)

14 January 1853

SANTA ROSA gained from WALTON. (Fla. Laws 1852, 6th sess., ch. 571/p. 145)

29 December 1854

VOLUSIA created from ORANGE. (Fla. Laws 1854, 7th sess., ch. 624/p. 44)

6 January 1855

Original ST. LUCIE renamed BREVARD. (Fla. Laws 1854, 7th sess., ch. 651/p. 61)

9 January 1855

MANATEE created from HILLSBOROUGH. (Fla. Laws 1854, 7th sess., ch. 628/p. 47)

15 December 1855

LIBERTY created from GADSDEN [mistake in description corrected 5 Jan. 1859]. (Fla. Laws 1855, adj. sess., ch. 771/p. 50)

23 December 1856

LAFAYETTE and TAYLOR both created from MADISON. (Fla. Laws 1856, 8th sess., ch. 806, secs. 1–3/p. 48)

2 January 1857

1828 overlap between DUVAL and NASSAU ended; based upon their most recently defined configurations, NASSAU appeared to exchange with DUVAL, while DUVAL appeared to lose to NASSAU. (Fla. Laws 1856, 8th sess., ch. 811/p. 55)

21 December 1858

LAFAYETTE gained from TAYLOR. (Fla. Laws 1858, 9th sess., ch. 921/p. 55)

31 December 1858

CLAY created from ALACHUA, COLUMBIA, and DUVAL. (Fla. Laws 1858, 9th sess., ch. 866, secs. 1–2/p. 19)

5 January 1859

LIBERTY boundaries clarified, correcting mistake of 15 December 1855 [no change]. (Fla. Laws 1858, 9th sess., ch. 949/p. 120)

13 January 1859

MANATEE gained from MONROE, exchanged with BREVARD. (Fla. Laws 1858, 9th sess., ch. 922/p. 56)

15 January 1859

DUVAL gained from NASSAU. (Fla. Laws 1858, 9th sess., ch. 920/p. 55)

MARION gained small area from SUMTER to accommodate local resident [location unknown, not mapped]. (Fla. Laws 1858, 9th sess., ch. 973/p. 133)

PUTNAM gained from CLAY, exchanged with ST. JOHNS in the St. Johns R. and Crescent Lake. (Fla. Laws 1858, 9th sess., ch. 923/p. 57)

c. February 1859

NEW RIVER (now BRADFORD) and SUWANNEE both created from COLUMBIA. (Fla. Laws 1858, 9th sess., ch. 895, secs. 1–4/p. 37)

12 December 1859

COLUMBIA gained from SUWANNEE. (Fla. Laws 1859, adj. sess., ch. 1048/p. 69)

22 December 1859

CLAY gained from PUTNAM and gained small areas in the St. Johns R. from DUVAL and ST. JOHNS when boundary shifted from west bank to west margin of the channel. (Fla. Laws 1859, adj. sess., ch. 1039/p. 63)

GADSDEN exchanged with LIBERTY. (Fla. Laws 1859, adj. sess., ch. 1046/p. 68)

8 February 1861

BAKER created from NEW RIVER (now BRADFORD). (Fla. Laws 1860, 10th sess., ch. 1185/p. 179)

POLK created from BREVARD and HILLSBOROUGH. (Fla. Laws 1860, 10th sess., ch. 1201/p. 192; "Lonnie Clemons v. W. W. Chase, as Sheriff" in Fla. Rpts., 120:429–431)

6 December 1861

NEW RIVER renamed BRADFORD. (Fla. Laws 1861, 11th sess., ch. 1300/p. 53)

27 November 1863

SUWANNEE gained small area from COLUMBIA so as to include entire town of Wellborn in SUWANNEE. (Fla. Laws 1863, 12th sess., ch. 1391/p. 11)

6 December 1866

ORANGE gained from BREVARD. (Fla. Laws 1866, 14th sess., ch. 1621/p. 82)

8 December 1866

DADE gained from BREVARD, exchanged with MONROE. (Fla. Laws 1866, 14th sess., ch. 1592/p. 62)

10 December 1866

HILLSBOROUGH gained small area from POLK to accommodate local resident. (Fla. Laws 1866, 14th sess., ch. 1622/p. 82)

13 December 1866

SUMTER gained from HILLSBOROUGH. (Fla. Laws 1866, 14th sess., ch. 1589/p. 61)

30 July 1868

PUTNAM gained from ST. JOHNS. (Fla. Laws 1868, 1st sess., ch. 1673/p. 174)

3 February 1870

BRADFORD gained from ALACHUA. (Fla. Laws 1870, 3d sess., ch. 1765/p. 45)

14 February 1870

Boundary between ORANGE and VOLUSIA clarified to run west of Huntoon's Island [no change]. (Fla. Laws 1870, 3d sess., ch. 1764/p. 45)

30 January 1871

POLK gained from SUMTER. (Fla. Laws 1871, 4th sess., ch. 1848/p. 36)

1872

DADE fully organized, detached from MONROE. (Hudson, 18–21)

14 February 1872

ORANGE gained from SUMTER. (Fla. Laws 1872, 5th sess., ch. 1895/p. 52)

14 February 1873

JACKSON gained from CALHOUN. (Fla. Laws 1873, 6th sess., ch. 1954/p. 28)

WASHINGTON gained from CALHOUN [mistake in WASHINGTON description corrected 2 Jun. 1893]. (Fla. Laws 1873, 6th sess., ch. 1950/p. 27)

18 February 1873

BREVARD gained from ORANGE. (Fla. Laws 1873, 6th sess., ch. 1964/p. 36)

19 February 1874

DADE gained from BREVARD, lost to MONROE; MANATEE gained from BREVARD, exchanged with MONROE; ORANGE gained from BREVARD; POLK gained from HILLSBOROUGH. (Fla. Laws 1874, 7th sess., ch. 1998/p. 63)

February 1875

CALHOUN gained from JACKSON. (Fla. Laws 1875, 8th sess., ch. 2061/p. 67)

15 February 1875

ST. JOHNS gained from VOLUSIA, exchanged with DUVAL and PUTNAM. (Fla. Laws 1875, 8th sess., ch. 2068/p. 70)

6 February 1877

LEVY gained from MARION. (Fla. Laws 1877, 9th sess., ch. 3060/p. 120)

13 February 1877

TAYLOR gained from LAFAYETTE. (Fla. Laws 1877, 9th sess., ch. 3061/p. 121)

21 February 1877

MANATEE exchanged with MONROE. (Fla. Laws 1877, 9th sess., ch. 3062/p. 121)

5 March 1879

ORANGE and SUMTER gained from POLK. (Fla. Laws 1879, 10th sess., ch. 3177/p. 141)

11 March 1879

BREVARD gained from VOLUSIA. (Fla. Laws 1879, 10th sess., ch. 3175/p. 140)

LEON gained from JEFFERSON. (Fla. Laws 1879, 10th sess., ch. 3176/p. 140)

by 1880

HERNANDO gained from POLK. (Rand, McNally, 1880, 254–255)

27 January 1881

WALTON and WASHINGTON granted concurrent jurisdiction over the waters of Choctawhatchee Bay [not mapped]. (Fla. Laws 1881, 11th sess., ch. 3258/p. 73)

7 February 1881

JEFFERSON gained from LEON. (Fla. Laws 1881, 11th sess., ch. 3304/p. 101)

31 January 1883

LAFAYETTE gained from TAYLOR [mistake in description corrected 12 Feb. 1885]. (Fla. Laws 1883, 12th sess., ch. 3470/p. 79)

26 February 1883

CLAY gained from PUTNAM. (Fla. Laws 1883, 12th sess., ch. 3469/p. 79)

5 March 1883

POLK gained small area from HERNANDO. (Fla. Laws 1883, 12th sess., ch. 3471/p. 80)

12 February 1885

Boundary between LAFAYETTE and TAYLOR redefined, correcting mistake of 31 January 1883 [no change]. (Fla. Laws 1885, 13th sess., ch. 3625/p. 64)

16 February 1885

FRANKLIN gained narrow strip of territory all along boundary with LIBERTY. (Fla. Laws 1885, 13th sess., ch. 3624/p. 63)

13 May 1887

LEE created from MONROE. (Fla. Laws 1887, 1st sess., ch. 3769/p. 150)

19 May 1887

DE SOTO created from MANATEE. (Fla. Laws 1887, 1st sess., ch. 3770, secs. 1–3/pp. 151–152)

28 May 1887

MARION exchanged with PUTNAM. (Fla. Laws 1887, 1st sess., ch. 3767/p. 147)

TAYLOR gained from LAFAYETTE. (Fla. Laws 1887, 1st sess., ch. 3766/p. 147)

2 June 1887

CITRUS and PASCO both created from HERNANDO. (Fla. Laws 1887, 1st sess., ch. 3772, secs. 1, 8/pp. 157–159)

11 July 1887

OSCEOLA created from BREVARD and ORANGE; BREVARD apparently gained small area from ORANGE. (Fla. Laws 1887, 1st sess., ch. 3768/p. 148)

26 July 1887

LAKE created from ORANGE and SUMTER. (Fla. Laws 1887, 1st sess., ch. 3771, secs. 1–2/pp. 154–155)

30 May 1889

COLUMBIA exchanged with SUWANNEE. (Fla. Laws 1889, ext. sess., ch. 3948/p. 181)

31 May 1889

LAKE gained small area from ORANGE. (Fla. Laws 1889, ext. sess., ch. 3944/p. 176)

POLK gained from SUMTER. (Fla. Laws 1889, ext. sess., ch. 3932/p. 167)

10 June 1891

POLK gained small area from LAKE and gained from PASCO. (Fla. Laws 1891, 3d sess., ch. 4066/p. 108)

2 June 1893

WASHINGTON boundaries redefined, correcting mistake of 14 February 1873 [no change]. (Fla. Laws 1893, 4th sess., ch. 4236/p. 169)

31 May 1897

CALHOUN exchanged with JACKSON. (Fla. Laws 1897, 6th sess., ch. 4576/p. 119)

4 June 1897

CALHOUN exchanged with WASHINGTON. (Fla. Laws 1897, 6th sess., ch. 4577/p. 119)

24 May 1899

VOLUSIA gained small area from ST. JOHNS. (Fla. Laws 1899, 7th sess., ch. 4811, secs. 1–2/pp. 209–210)

1 July 1905

ST. LUCIE created from BREVARD. (Fla. Laws 1905, 10th sess., ch. 5567, secs. 1, 22/pp. 404, 408)

3 June 1907

Boundary between ST. JOHNS and VOLUSIA clarified [no change]. (Fla. Laws 1907, 11th sess., ch. 5730, secs. 1–2/pp. 244–245)

5 May 1909

PUTNAM gained small area from CLAY in the town of Melrose. (Fla. Laws 1909, 12th sess., ch. 5978/p. 184)

29 May 1909

COLUMBIA boundaries clarified [no change]. (Fla. Laws 1909, 12th sess., ch. 5979/p. 184)

1 July 1909

PALM BEACH created from DADE. (Fla. Laws 1909, 12th sess., ch. 5970, sec. 1/p. 174)

1 January 1910

GADSDEN exchanged with LIBERTY. (Fla. Laws 1909, 12th sess., ch. 5966, secs. 1–2, 4/pp. 169–171)

19 May 1911

BAKER gained from DUVAL; NASSAU gained from BAKER. (Fla. Laws 1911, 13th sess., ch. 6244/p. 216)

24 May 1911

LAFAYETTE gained from TAYLOR. (Fla. Laws 1911, 13th sess., ch. 6246/p. 218)

2 June 1911

CITRUS gained non-county area in the Withlacoochee R. along the LEVY line when the boundary shifted from the middle of river to the north bank [not mapped]. (Fla. Laws 1911, 13th sess., ch. 6245/p. 217)

3 June 1911

ALACHUA exchanged with LEVY. (Fla. Laws 1911, 13th sess., ch. 6243/p. 215)

14 November 1911

PINELLAS created from HILLSBOROUGH. (Fla. Laws 1911, 13th sess., ch. 6247, secs. 1, 20–21/pp. 219, 223; Grismer, *St. Petersburg*, 35; HRS Fla., *Pinellas*, 9)

25 April 1913

SEMINOLE created from ORANGE [mistake in description corrected 31 May 1961 and 22 Jun. 1961]. (Fla. Laws 1913, 14th sess., gen., ch. 6511, sec. 1/p. 365)

17 May 1913

WALTON gained from WASHINGTON. (Fla. Laws 1913, 14th sess., gen., ch. 6508, sec. 1/p. 359)

6 June 1913

Legislature authorized creation of BROWARD from DADE, dependent on local referendum that failed [no change]. (Fla. Laws 1913, 14th sess., gen., ch. 6504, secs. 1, 22/pp. 341, 346; McIver, 64)

7 June 1913

LEVY gained small area from ALACHUA. (Fla. Laws 1913, 14th sess., gen., ch. 6509/p. 363)

1 July 1913

BAY created from CALHOUN and WASHINGTON. (Fla. Laws 1913, 14th sess., gen., ch. 6505, secs. 1, 24/pp. 347, 353; ch. 6506/p. 354; and ch. 6508/p. 359)

1 June 1915

Legislature authorized creation of BLOXHAM from LEVY and MARION, dependent on local referendum that failed [no change]. (Fla. Laws 1915, 15th sess., gen., ch. 6936, secs. 1, 20–21/pp. 298–303; Morris, 25; "Battle of Bloxham")

8 August 1915

HOLMES gained from WASHINGTON; WASHINGTON gained from JACKSON. (Fla. Laws 1915, 15th sess., gen., ch. 6935, secs. 1–2, 16/pp. 292–293, 297)

7 September 1915

OKALOOSA created from SANTA ROSA and WALTON. (Fla. Laws 1915, 15th sess., gen., ch. 6937, secs. 1, 24–25/pp. 303, 310; HRS Fla., *Okaloosa*, 6)

1 October 1915

BROWARD created from DADE and PALM BEACH. (Fla. Laws 1915, 15th sess., gen., ch. 6934, secs. 1, 23/pp. 285, 292)

12 June 1917

FLAGLER created from ST. JOHNS and VOLUSIA. (Fla. Laws 1917, 16th sess., gen., ch. 7399, secs. 1, 22–23/pp. 277, 284)

7 August 1917

OKEECHOBEE created from OSCEOLA, PALM BEACH, and ST. LUCIE. (Fla. Laws 1917, 16th sess., gen., ch. 7401, secs. 1, 20–21/pp. 285, 289–290; Van Landingham and Hetherington, 66)

23 April 1921

CHARLOTTE, GLADES, HARDEE, and HIGHLANDS created from DE SOTO. (Fla. Laws 1921, 18th sess., gen., ch. 8513, sec. 1/pp. 279–281)

25 April 1921

DIXIE created from LAFAYETTE. (Fla. Laws 1921, 18th sess., gen., ch. 8514, sec. 1/p. 289)

15 June 1921

SARASOTA created from MANATEE. (Fla. Laws 1921, 18th sess., gen., ch. 8515, secs. 1, 22–23/pp. 294, 300; Grismer, *Sarasota*, 200–201)

1 October 1921

UNION created from BRADFORD. (Fla. Laws 1921, 18th sess., gen., ch. 8516, secs. 1, 27/pp. 301, 307)

c. May 1923

JEFFERSON exchanged with MADISON. (Fla. Laws 1923, 19th sess., gen., ch. 9361/p. 467)

7 July 1923

COLLIER created from LEE. (Fla. Laws 1923, 19th sess., gen., ch. 9362, secs. 1, 26/pp. 468, 476)

10 July 1923

HENDRY created from LEE. (Fla. Laws 1923, 19th sess., gen., ch. 9360, secs. 1, 26/pp. 459, 467)

8 May 1925

GLADES gained part of Lake Okeechobee from PALM BEACH. (Fla. Laws 1925, 20th sess., spec., ch. 10596/p. 1860)

14 May 1925

HENDRY gained small part of Lake Okeechobee from PALM BEACH. (Fla. Laws 1925, 20th sess., gen., ch. 10090/p. 112)

4 June 1925

LEVY gained small area from DIXIE when the boundary shifted from the east bank to the middle of the Suwannee R. [not mapped]. (Fla. Laws 1925, 20th sess., spec., ch. 10778/p. 2518)

29 June 1925

INDIAN RIVER created from ST. LUCIE. (Fla. Laws 1925, 20th sess., gen., ch. 10148, sec. 1/p. 294)

7 July 1925

GULF created from CALHOUN. (Fla. Laws 1925, 20th sess., gen., ch. 10132, secs. 1, 25–26/pp. 237, 244)

4 August 1925

MARTIN created from PALM BEACH and ST. LUCIE. (Fla. Laws 1925, 20th sess., gen., ch. 10180, secs. 1, 25–26/pp. 359, 368; Hutchinson, front endpapers)

1 January 1926

GILCHRIST created from ALACHUA. (Fla. Laws 1925, ext. sess., ch. 11371, secs. 1, 19–20/pp. 66, 70; McCarthy, 73)

6 June 1927

PUTNAM gained small areas from BRADFORD and CLAY. (Fla. Laws 1927, 21st sess., gen., ch. 12489, sec. 1/ p. 1585)

4 May 1933

GADSDEN gained from LEON when boundary shifted from west bank to the middle of the Ochlockonee R. [not mapped]. (Fla. Laws 1933, 24th sess., spec., ch. 16436/ p. 493)

7 September 1937

HENDRY gained small area from GLADES. (Fla. Laws 1937, 26th sess., spec., ch. 18568, secs. 1, 6/pp. 535, 537)

15 May 1939

PINELLAS gained small area from HILLSBOROUGH. (Fla. Laws 1939, 27th sess., gen., ch. 19058/p. 116)

12 June 1941

Part of the boundary between SEMINOLE and VOLUSIA clarified [no discernible change]. (Fla. Laws 1941, 28th sess., gen., ch. 20888/p. 2358)

29 July 1942

All county boundaries redefined. Only change was PASCO gained from POLK. HENDRY boundaries redefined [mistake in description corrected 11 June 1945, no change]. (Fla. Stat., 1941, 1:secs. 7.22, 7.26, 7.51, 7.53)

11 June 1945

HENDRY boundaries clarified, correcting mistake of 29 July 1942 [no change]. (Fla. Laws 1945, 30th sess., gen., ch. 22858, sec. 7/p. 862)

31 May 1947

OKALOOSA gained from ESCAMBIA. (Fla. Laws 1947, 31st sess., gen., ch. 23867/p. 483)

13 June 1949

GLADES gained small area from HIGHLANDS. (Fla. Laws 1949, 32d sess., gen., ch. 25612, sec. 1/p. 1342)

31 December 1949

POLK gained from PASCO. (Fla. Laws 1949, 32d sess., gen., ch. 25440, secs. 1–2/pp. 1055–1056; Fla. Laws 1949, ext. sess., ch. 26347/p. 125)

11 June 1951

SANTA ROSA gained small area from ESCAMBIA. (Fla. Laws 1951, 33d sess., gen., ch. 26860/p. 742)

1 January 1954

ALACHUA gained small area from COLUMBIA, exchanged small areas with BRADFORD. (Fla. Laws 1953, 34th sess., gen., ch. 28312, secs. 1–3, 6/pp. 973–979)

29 June 1957

SANTA ROSA gained small area from ESCAMBIA along the right-of-way of the toll bridge and road on Santa Rosa Sound and Island. (Fla. Laws 1957, 36th sess., gen., ch. 57-834/p. 1181)

20 June 1959

Boundary between FLAGLER and PUTNAM in Crescent Lake clarified [no discernible change]. (Fla. Laws 1959, 37th sess., gen., ch. 59-488, secs. 1–2/pp. 1629–1630)

3 November 1959

INDIAN RIVER gained small area from BREVARD. (Fla. Laws 1959, 37th sess., gen., ch. 59-486/p. 1626)

13 May 1961

DADE gained small area from MONROE. (Fla. Laws 1961, 38th sess., gen., ch. 61-16/p. 44)

31 May 1961

SEMINOLE boundaries redefined, correcting mistake of 25 April 1913 [no change]. (Fla. Laws 1961, 38th sess., gen., ch. 61-167, secs. 1–2/pp. 279–281)

22 June 1961

ORANGE boundaries redefined, correcting mistake of 25 April 1913 [no change]. (Fla. Laws 1961, 38th sess., gen., ch. 61-483/p. 1075)

29 May 1963

GLADES, HENDRY, MARTIN, and OKEECHOBEE gained parts of Lake Okeechobee from PALM BEACH. (Fla. Laws 1963, 39th sess., gen., ch. 63-200, secs. 1–5/ pp. 451–454)

12 June 1963

HENDRY gained small area from GLADES along Route 80. (Fla. Laws 1963, 39th sess., gen., ch. 63-391/p. 1048)

14 June 1967

VOLUSIA boundaries redefined [no change]. (Fla. Laws 1967, 41st sess., gen., ch. 67-190/p. 389)

4 August 1967

PINELLAS boundary in Gulf of Mexico clarified [no change]. (Fla. Laws 1967, 41st sess., gen., ch. 67-601/ p. 1789)

1 January 1968

OSCEOLA exchanged with POLK. (Fla. Laws 1967, 41st sess., gen., ch. 67-592, secs. 1–3/pp. 1728–1730)

30 March 1972

FRANKLIN gained Forbes I. from GULF. (Fla. Laws 1972, reg. sess., gen., ch. 72-119/p. 388)

c. 1973

MARION gained from ALACHUA when part of Lake Orange was drained. (Rand, McNally, 1972, pp. 158–159; Rand, McNally, 1973, pp. 158–159)

1 July 1976

CLAY gained small area from DUVAL along Interstate 295. (Fla. Laws 1976, reg. sess., gen., ch. 76-17/p. 25)

27 June 1978

CLAY boundaries redefined [no change]. (Fla. Laws 1978, 2d reg. sess., gen., ch. 78-421/p. 1394)

1 October 1978

BROWARD gained small area from DADE. (Fla. Laws 1978, 2d reg. sess., gen., ch. 78-119, secs. 1–3/pp. 447–449)

31 December 1980

CLAY gained small area from DUVAL along Interstate 295. (Fla. Laws 1980, reg. sess., gen., ch. 80-9, secs. 1–3/pp. 64–66)

14 June 1983

ESCAMBIA boundaries clarified to extend into the Gulf of Mexico [no change]. (Fla. Laws 1983, reg. and spec. sess., gen., ch. 83-130/p. 434)

24 June 1983

VOLUSIA boundaries redefined [no change]. (Fla. Laws 1983, reg. and spec. sess., gen., ch. 83-217, sec. 1/p. 984)

14 June 1984

CLAY gained small area from PUTNAM. (Fla. Laws 1984, reg. sess., gen., ch. 84-211, secs. 1–3/pp. 664–666)

1 October 1986

WAKULLA gained from FRANKLIN when boundary shifted from east bank to middle of the Ochlockonee R. and Bay. (Fla. Laws 1986, reg. sess., gen., ch. 86-288/p. 2109)

Individual County Chronologies, Maps, and Areas for Florida

ALACHUA / 20
BAKER / 28
BAY / 29
BENTON (see
  HERNANDO)
BLOXHAM (proposed) / 30
BRADFORD (created as
  NEW RIVER) / 31
BREVARD (created as
  original ST. LUCIE) / 34
BROWARD / 40
CALHOUN / 41
CHARLOTTE / 50
CITRUS / 51
CLAY / 52
COLLIER / 56
COLUMBIA / 57
DADE / 61
DE SOTO / 66
DIXIE / 67

DUVAL / 68
ESCAMBIA / 78
FAYETTE (extinct) / 82
FLAGLER / 83
FRANKLIN / 84
GADSDEN / 88
GILCHRIST / 94
GLADES / 95
GULF / 98
HAMILTON / 100
HARDEE / 101
HENDRY / 102
HERNANDO / 104
HIGHLANDS / 109
HILLSBOROUGH / 110
HOLMES / 117
INDIAN RIVER / 118
JACKSON / 119
JEFFERSON / 135
LAFAYETTE / 145

LAKE / 150
LEE / 152
LEON / 153
LEVY / 161
LIBERTY / 164
MADISON / 167
MANATEE / 169
MARION / 172
MARTIN / 178
MONROE / 179
MOSQUITO (see
ORANGE)
NASSAU / 186
NEW RIVER (see
BRADFORD)
OKALOOSA / 191
OKEECHOBEE / 192
ORANGE (created
as MOSQUITO) / 194
OSCEOLA / 203

PALM BEACH / 206
PASCO / 210
PINELLAS / 211
POLK / 212
PUTNAM / 219
ST. JOHNS / 227
ST. LUCIE (original;
see BREVARD)
ST. LUCIE / 238
SANTA ROSA / 241
SARASOTA / 246
SEMINOLE / 247
SUMTER / 248
SUWANNEE / 255
TAYLOR / 258
UNION / 262
VOLUSIA / 263
WAKULLA / 266
WALTON / 268
WASHINGTON / 275

Chronology of ALACHUA

Map	Date	Event	Resulting Area
❶	29 Dec 1824	ALACHUA created from DUVAL and ST. JOHNS	12,650 sq mi
❷	19 Jan 1828	ALACHUA lost to Indian lands when treaty line was resurveyed	11,150 sq mi

(Heavy line depicts historical boundary. Base map shows present-day information.)

❶ ALACHUA Boundaries
29 Dec 1824 – 18 Jan 1828

❷ ALACHUA Boundaries
19 Jan 1828 – 3 Feb 1832

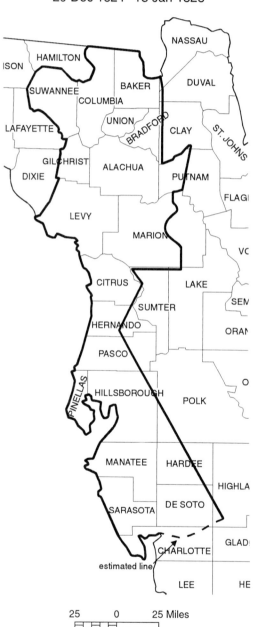

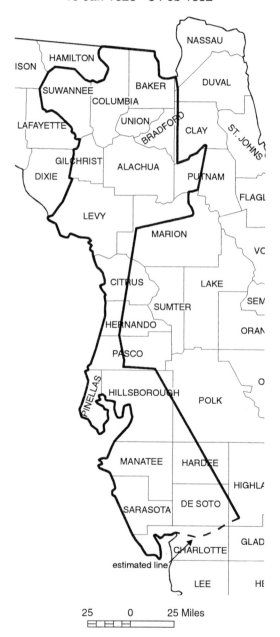

Chronology of ALACHUA

Map	Date	Event	Resulting Area
❸	4 Feb 1832	ALACHUA lost to creation of COLUMBIA	8,000 sq mi
❹	25 Jan 1834	ALACHUA lost to creation of HILLSBOROUGH	3,300 sq mi
❺	10 Feb 1835	ALACHUA gained from COLUMBIA	3,800 sq mi

(Heavy line depicts historical boundary. Base map shows present-day information.)

❹ ALACHUA Boundaries
25 Jan 1834 – 9 Feb 1835

❸ ALACHUA Boundaries
4 Feb 1832 – 24 Jan 1834

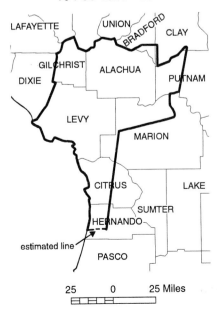

❺ ALACHUA Boundaries
10 Feb 1835 – 23 Feb 1843

Chronology of ALACHUA

Map	Date	Event	Resulting Area
❻	24 Feb 1843	ALACHUA lost to creation of HERNANDO	3,230 sq mi
❼	14 Mar 1844	ALACHUA lost to creation of MARION	2,600 sq mi
❼	15 Mar 1844	ALACHUA exchanged small areas with COLUMBIA. Boundary between ALACHUA and DUVAL adjusted	2,600 sq mi
❽	10 Mar 1845	ALACHUA lost to creation of LEVY	1,680 sq mi

(Heavy line depicts historical boundary. Base map shows present-day information.)

❻ ALACHUA Boundaries
24 Feb 1843–13 Mar 1844

❼ ALACHUA Boundaries
14 Mar 1844–9 Mar 1845

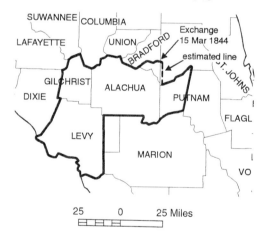

❽ ALACHUA Boundaries
10 Mar 1845–12 Jan 1849

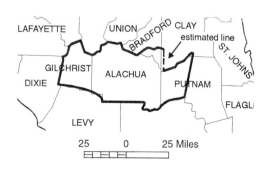

Chronology of ALACHUA

Map	Date	Event	Resulting Area
⑨	13 Jan 1849	ALACHUA lost to creation of PUTNAM	1,380 sq mi

(Heavy line depicts historical boundary. Base map shows present-day information.)

⑨ ALACHUA Boundaries
13 Jan 1849 – 30 Dec 1858

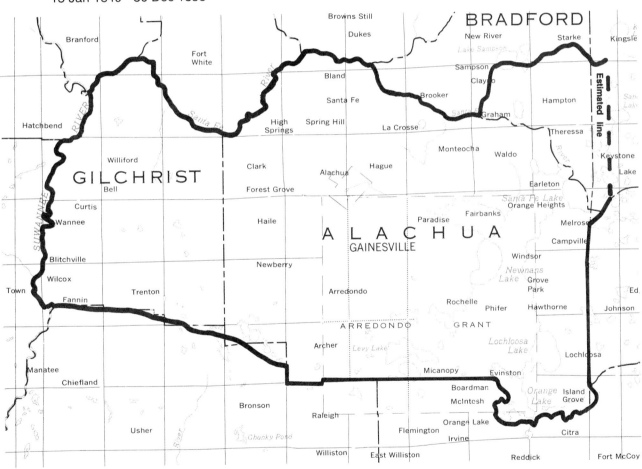

Chronology of ALACHUA

Map	Date	Event	Resulting Area
⑩	31 Dec 1858	ALACHUA lost to creation of CLAY	1,350 sq mi

(Heavy line depicts historical boundary. Base map shows present-day information.)

⑩ ALACHUA Boundaries
31 Dec 1858 – 2 Feb 1870

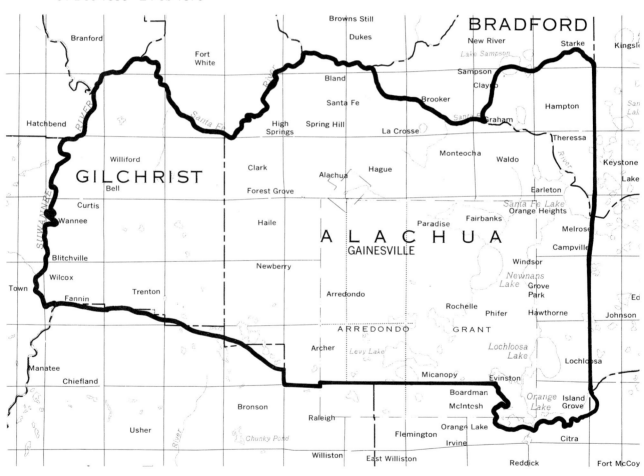

Chronology of ALACHUA

Map	Date	Event	Resulting Area
⑪	3 Feb 1870	ALACHUA lost to BRADFORD	1,260 sq mi

(Heavy line depicts historical boundary. Base map shows present-day information.)

⑪   ALACHUA Boundaries
3 Feb 1870 – 2 Jun 1911

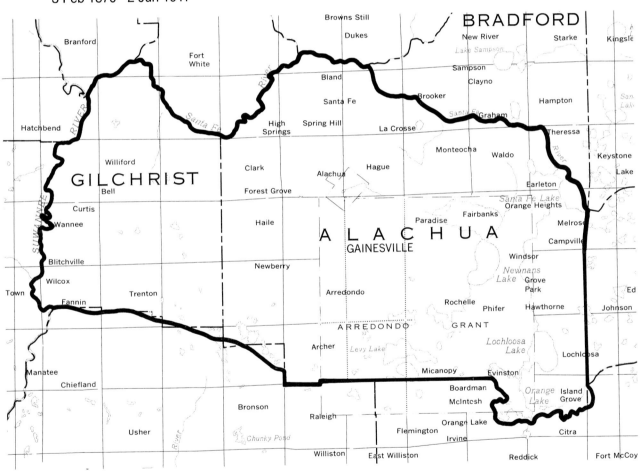

Chronology of ALACHUA

Map	Date	Event	Resulting Area
⑫	3 Jun 1911	ALACHUA exchanged with LEVY	1,250 sq mi
⑫	7 Jun 1913	ALACHUA lost small area to LEVY	1,250 sq mi

(Heavy line depicts historical boundary. Base map shows present-day information.)

⑫ ALACHUA Boundaries
3 Jun 1911–31 Dec 1925

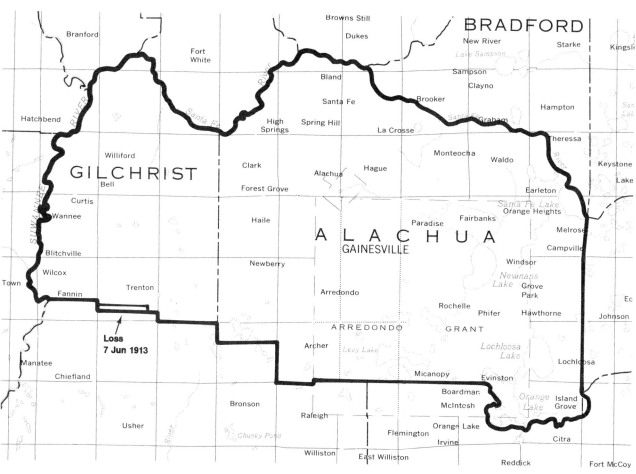

Chronology of ALACHUA

Map	Date	Event	Resulting Area
⑬	1 Jan 1926	ALACHUA lost to creation of GILCHRIST	900 sq mi
⑬	1 Jan 1954	ALACHUA gained small area from COLUMBIA, exchanged small areas with BRADFORD	900 sq mi
⑬	c. 1973	ALACHUA lost to MARION when part of Lake Orange was drained	900 sq mi

(Heavy line depicts historical boundary. Base map shows present-day information.)

⑬ ALACHUA Boundaries
1 Jan 1926–1990

10   0   10   20   30   40 Miles

Chronology of BAKER

Map	Date	Event	Resulting Area
❶	8 Feb 1861	BAKER created from NEW RIVER (now BRADFORD)	600 sq mi
❷	19 May 1911	BAKER gained from DUVAL, lost to NASSAU	600 sq mi

(Heavy line depicts historical boundary. Base map shows present-day information.)

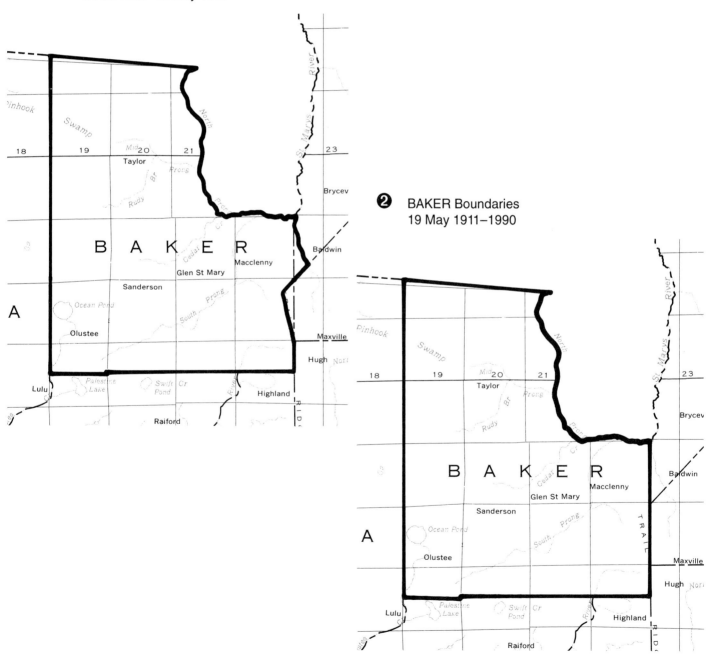

❶ BAKER Boundaries
8 Feb 1861–18 May 1911

❷ BAKER Boundaries
19 May 1911–1990

Chronology of BAY

Map	Date	Event	Resulting Area
❶	1 Jul 1913	BAY created from CALHOUN and WASHINGTON	780 sq mi

(Heavy line depicts historical boundary. Base map shows present-day information.)

❶   BAY Boundaries
1 Jul 1913–1990

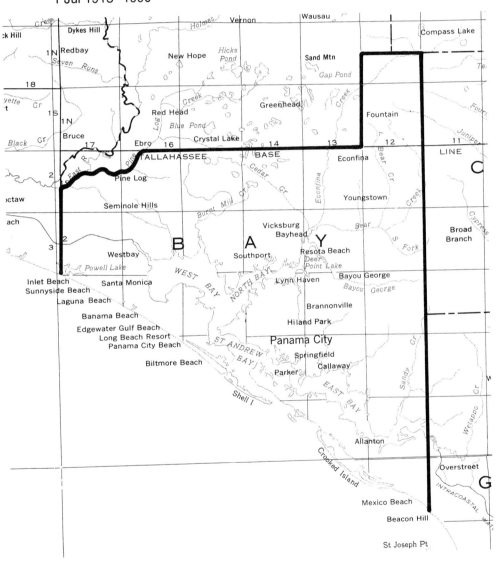

Chronology of BLOXHAM (proposed)

Map	Date	Event	Resulting Area
❶	1 Jun 1915	Legislature authorized creation of BLOXHAM from LEVY and MARION, dependent on local referendum that failed	

(Heavy line depicts historical boundary. Base map shows present-day information.)

❶ BLOXHAM (proposed) Boundaries
1 Jun 1915

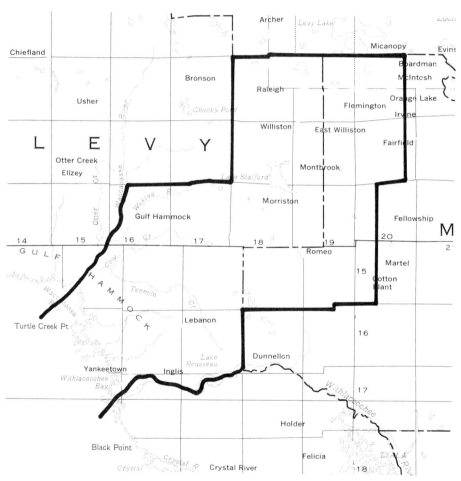

10   0   10   20   30   40 Miles

Chronology of BRADFORD (created as NEW RIVER)

Map	Date	Event	Resulting Area
❶	c. Feb 1859	BRADFORD created as NEW RIVER from COLUMBIA	1,060 sq mi

(Heavy line depicts historical boundary. Base map shows present-day information.)

❶ NEW RIVER Boundaries
c. Feb 1859 – 7 Feb 1861

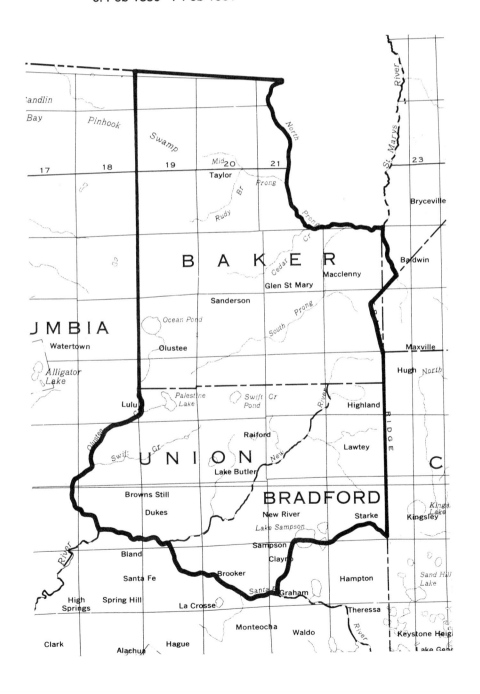

Chronology of BRADFORD (created as NEW RIVER)

Map	Date	Event	Resulting Area
❷	8 Feb 1861	NEW RIVER lost to creation of BAKER	460 sq mi
	6 Dec 1861	NEW RIVER renamed BRADFORD	
❸	3 Feb 1870	BRADFORD gained from ALACHUA	550 sq mi

(Heavy line depicts historical boundary. Base map shows present-day information.)

❷   NEW RIVER Boundaries
   8 Feb 1861–2 Feb 1870

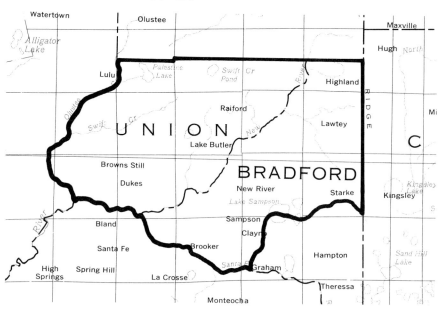

❸   BRADFORD Boundaries
   3 Feb 1870–30 Sep 1921

Chronology of BRADFORD (created as NEW RIVER)

Map	Date	Event	Resulting Area
❹	1 Oct 1921	BRADFORD lost to creation of UNION	300 sq mi
❹	6 Jun 1927	BRADFORD lost small area to PUTNAM	300 sq mi
❹	1 Jan 1954	BRADFORD exchanged small areas with ALACHUA	300 sq mi

(Heavy line depicts historical boundary. Base map shows present-day information.)

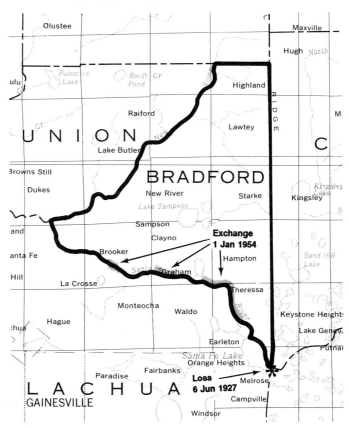

❹ BRADFORD Boundaries
1 Oct 1921–1990

Chronology of BREVARD (created as original ST. LUCIE)

Map	Date	Event	Resulting Area
❶	14 Mar 1844	BREVARD created as original ST. LUCIE from HILLSBOROUGH and MOSQUITO (now ORANGE)	7,800 sq mi
❷	27 Feb 1845	Original ST. LUCIE lost to ORANGE	5,800 sq mi

(Heavy line depicts historical boundary. Base map shows present-day information.)

❶ Original ST. LUCIE Boundaries
14 Mar 1844 – 26 Feb 1845

❷ Original ST. LUCIE Boundaries
27 Feb 1845 – 27 Dec 1846

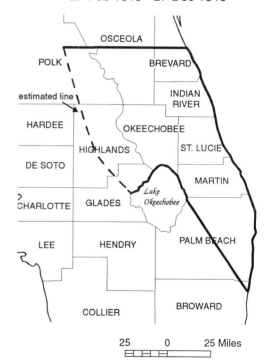

Chronology of BREVARD (created as original ST. LUCIE)

Map	Date	Event	Resulting Area
❸	28 Dec 1846	Original ST. LUCIE gained from ORANGE	6,200 sq mi
❹	10 Jan 1849	Original ST. LUCIE exchanged with ORANGE	7,300 sq mi
	6 Jan 1855	Original ST. LUCIE renamed BREVARD	

(Heavy line depicts historical boundary. Base map shows present-day information.)

❸ Original ST. LUCIE Boundaries
28 Dec 1846 – 9 Jan 1849

25   0   25 Miles

❹ Original ST. LUCIE Boundaries
10 Jan 1849 – 12 Jan 1859

25   0   25 Miles

Chronology of BREVARD (created as original ST. LUCIE)

Map	Date	Event	Resulting Area
❺	13 Jan 1859	BREVARD exchanged with MANATEE	7,320 sq mi
❻	8 Feb 1861	BREVARD lost to creation of POLK	6,450 sq mi

(Heavy line depicts historical boundary. Base map shows present-day information.)

❺ BREVARD Boundaries
13 Jan 1859 – 7 Feb 1861

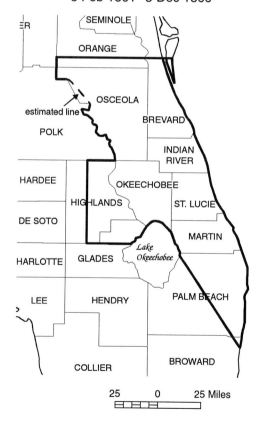

❻ BREVARD Boundaries
8 Feb 1861 – 5 Dec 1866

Chronology of BREVARD (created as original ST. LUCIE)

Map	Date	Event	Resulting Area
❼	6 Dec 1866	BREVARD lost to ORANGE	5,350 sq mi
❽	8 Dec 1866	BREVARD lost to DADE	3,790 sq mi
❾	18 Feb 1873	BREVARD gained from ORANGE	4,560 sq mi

(Heavy line depicts historical boundary. Base map shows present-day information.)

❽ BREVARD Boundaries
8 Dec 1866 – 17 Feb 1873

❼ BREVARD Boundaries
6 Dec 1866 – 7 Dec 1866

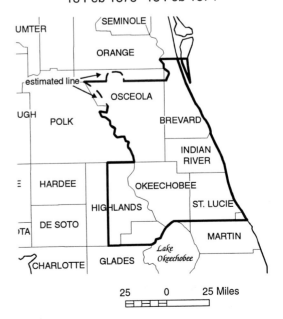

❾ BREVARD Boundaries
18 Feb 1873 – 18 Feb 1874

Chronology of BREVARD (created as original ST. LUCIE)

Map	Date	Event	Resulting Area
⑩	19 Feb 1874	BREVARD lost to DADE, MANATEE, and ORANGE	3,730 sq mi
⑪	11 Mar 1879	BREVARD gained from VOLUSIA	4,030 sq mi
⑫	11 Jul 1887	BREVARD lost to creation of OSCEOLA, apparently gained small area from ORANGE	2,420 sq mi

(Heavy line depicts historical boundary. Base map shows present-day information.)

⑩ BREVARD Boundaries
19 Feb 1874 – 10 Mar 1879

⑪ BREVARD Boundaries
11 Mar 1879 – 10 Jul 1887

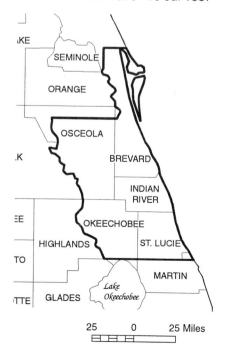

⑫ BREVARD Boundaries
11 Jul 1887 – 30 Jun 1905

Chronology of BREVARD (created as original ST. LUCIE)

Map	Date	Event	Resulting Area
⑬	1 Jul 1905	BREVARD lost to creation of ST. LUCIE	1,000 sq mi
⑬	3 Nov 1959	BREVARD lost small area to INDIAN RIVER	1,000 sq mi

(Heavy line depicts historical boundary. Base map shows present-day information.)

⑬   BREVARD Boundaries
1 Jul 1905 – 1990

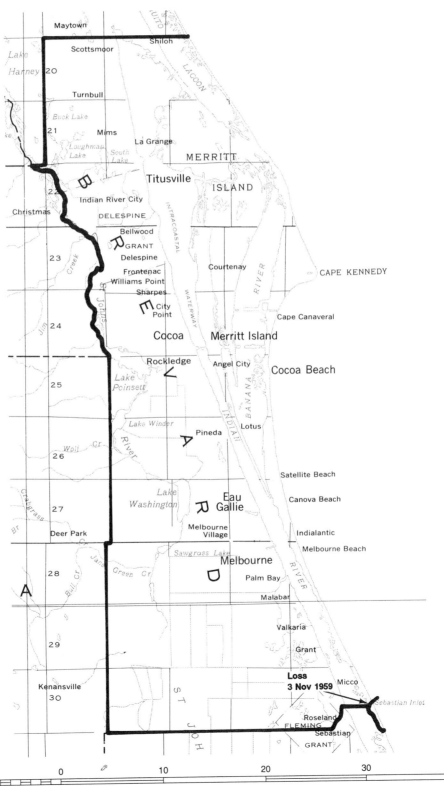

Chronology of BROWARD

Map	Date	Event	Resulting Area
❶	6 Jun 1913	Legislature authorized creation of BROWARD from DADE, dependent on local referendum that failed	
❷	1 Oct 1915	BROWARD created from DADE and PALM BEACH	1,210 sq mi
❷	1 Oct 1978	BROWARD gained small area from DADE	1,210 sq mi

(Heavy line depicts historical boundary. Base map shows present-day information.)

❶ BROWARD (proposed) Boundaries
6 Jun 1913

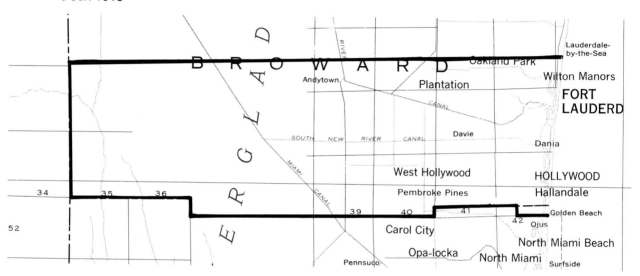

❷ BROWARD Boundaries
1 Oct 1915–1990

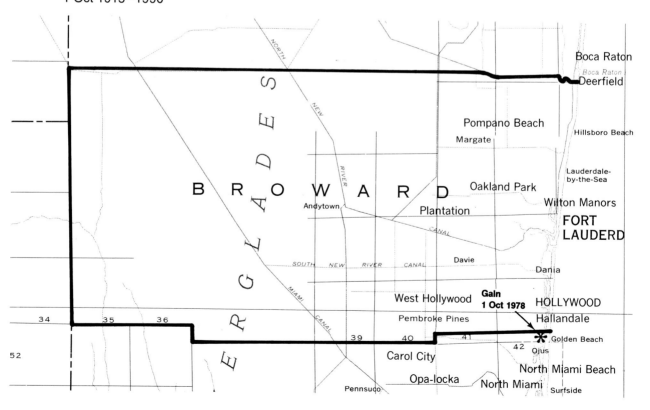

Chronology of CALHOUN

Map	Date	Event	Resulting Area
❶	26 Jan 1838	CALHOUN created from FRANKLIN, JACKSON, and WASHINGTON	600 sq mi

(Heavy line depicts historical boundary. Base map shows present-day information.)

❶   CALHOUN Boundaries
26 Jan 1838 – 24 Feb 1840

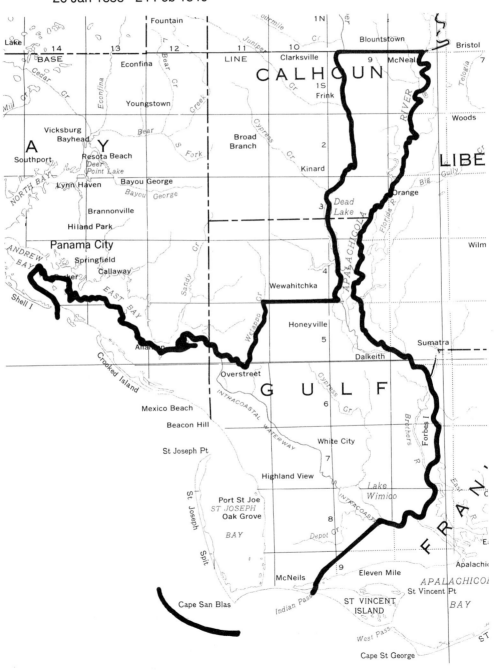

Chronology of CALHOUN

Map	Date	Event	Resulting Area
❷	25 Feb 1840	CALHOUN exchanged with WASHINGTON	770 sq mi

(Heavy line depicts historical boundary. Base map shows present-day information.)

❷ CALHOUN Boundaries
25 Feb 1840 – 9 Mar 1845

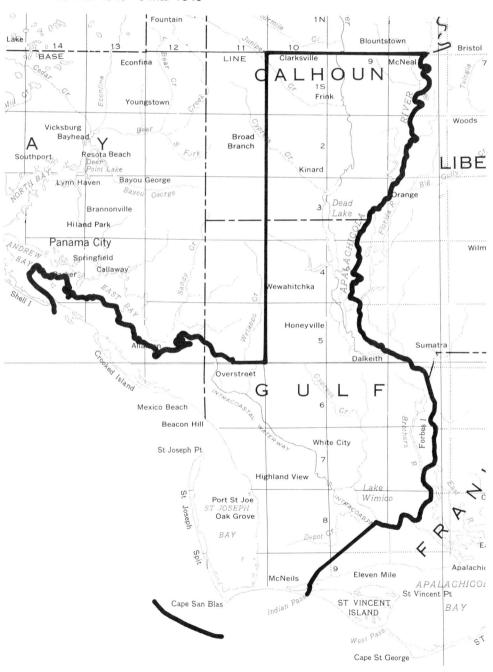

Chronology of CALHOUN

Map	Date	Event	Resulting Area
❸	10 Mar 1845	CALHOUN gained from JACKSON	1,110 sq mi

(Heavy line depicts historical boundary. Base map shows present-day information.)

❸ CALHOUN Boundaries
10 Mar 1845 – 13 Feb 1873

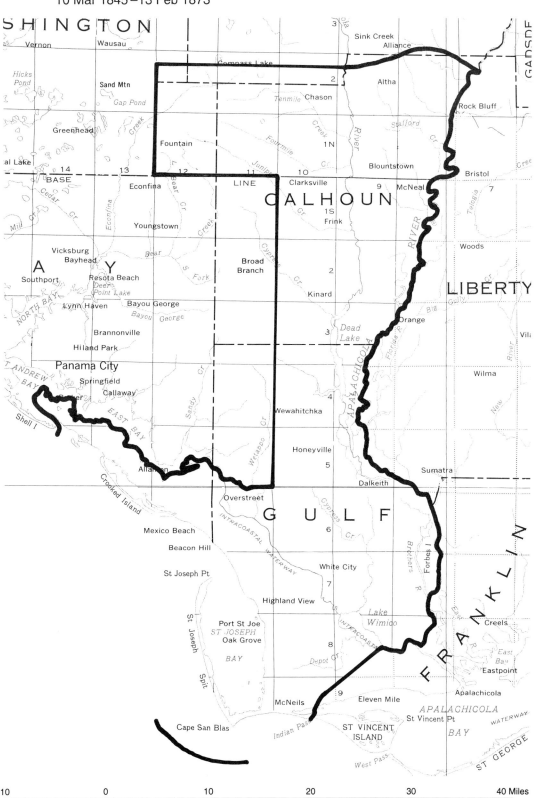

10   0   10   20   30   40 Miles

Chronology of CALHOUN

Map	Date	Event	Resulting Area
❹	14 Feb 1873	CALHOUN lost to both JACKSON and WASHINGTON	1,000 sq mi

(Heavy line depicts historical boundary. Base map shows present-day information.)

❹   CALHOUN Boundaries
14 Feb 1873 – Feb 1875

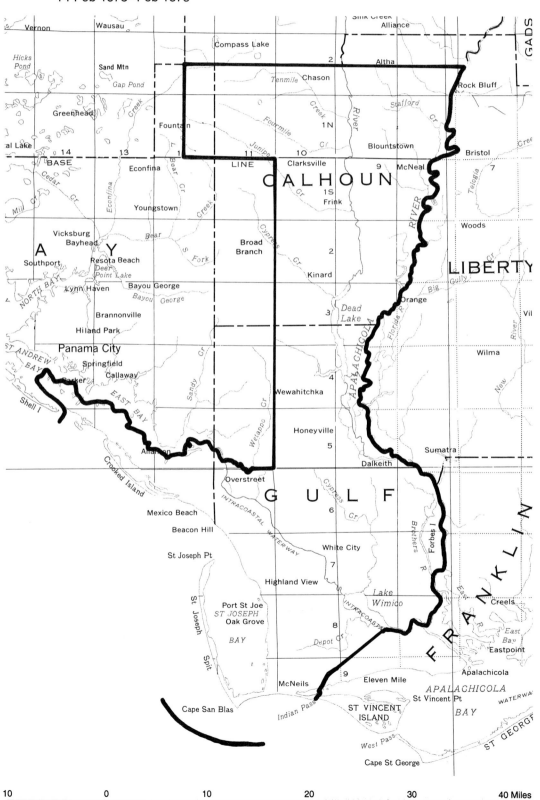

10	0	10	20	30	40 Miles

Chronology of CALHOUN

Map	Date	Event	Resulting Area
❺	Feb 1875	CALHOUN gained from JACKSON	1,070 sq mi

(Heavy line depicts historical boundary. Base map shows present-day information.)

❺ CALHOUN Boundaries
Feb 1875 – 30 May 1897

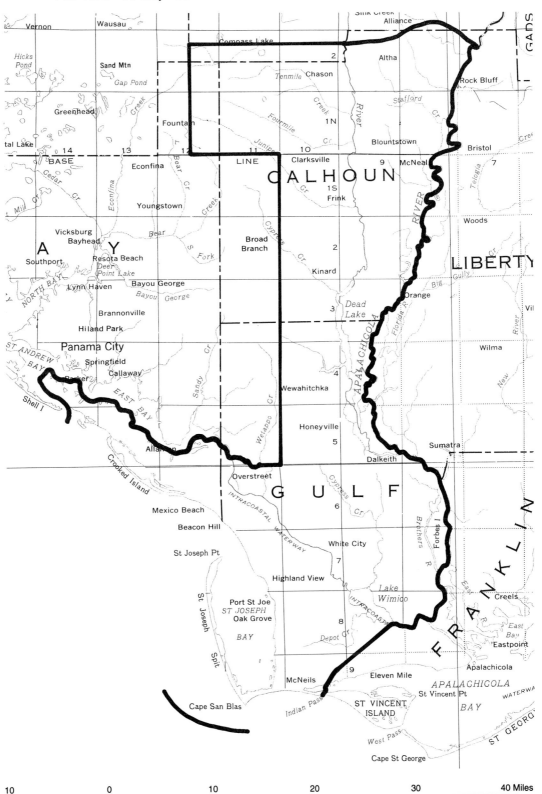

10   0   10   20   30   40 Miles

Chronology of CALHOUN

Map	Date	Event	Resulting Area
❻	31 May 1897	CALHOUN exchanged with JACKSON	1,040 sq mi

(Heavy line depicts historical boundary. Base map shows present-day information.)

❻ CALHOUN Boundaries
31 May 1897– 3 Jun 1897

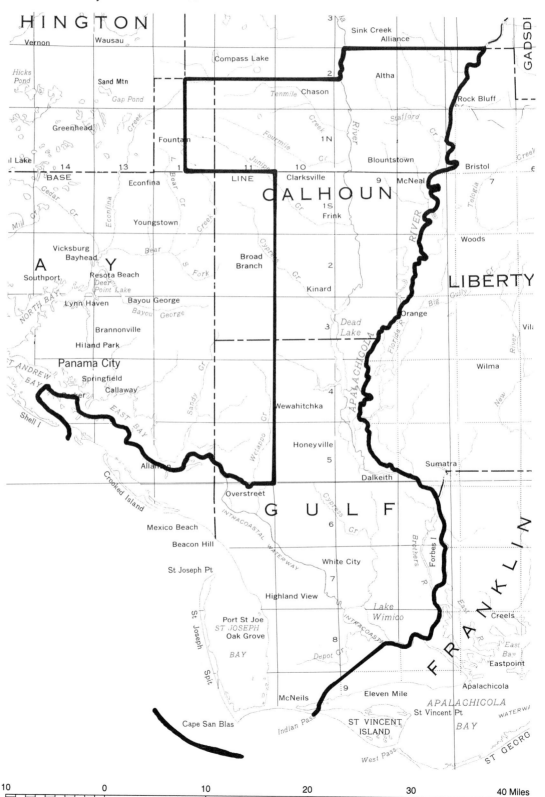

10   0   10   20   30   40 Miles

Chronology of CALHOUN

Map	Date	Event	Resulting Area
❼	4 Jun 1897	CALHOUN exchanged with WASHINGTON	1,190 sq mi

(Heavy line depicts historical boundary. Base map shows present-day information.)

❼   CALHOUN Boundaries
4 Jun 1897– 30 Jun 1913

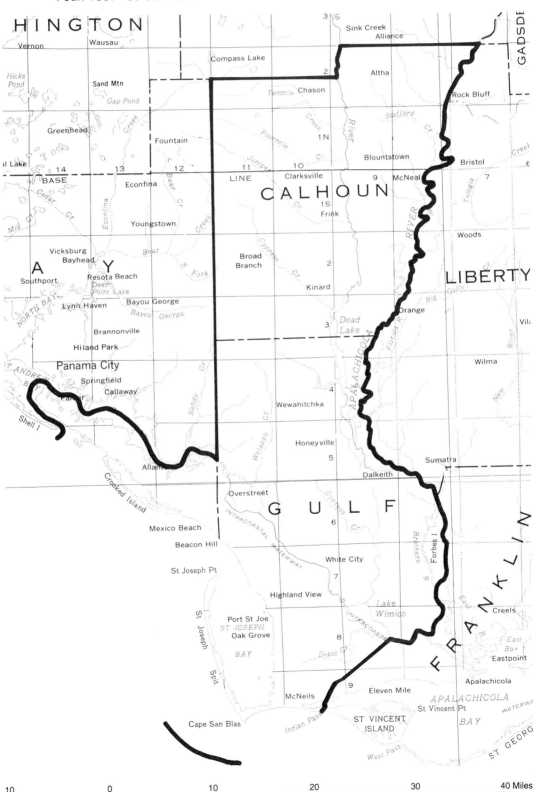

Chronology of CALHOUN

Map	Date	Event	Resulting Area
❽	1 Jul 1913	CALHOUN lost to creation of BAY	1,130 sq mi

(Heavy line depicts historical boundary. Base map shows present-day information.)

❽   CALHOUN Boundaries
1 Jul 1913 – 6 Jul 1925

| 10 | 0 | 10 | 20 | 30 | 40 Miles |

Chronology of CALHOUN

Map	Date	Event	Resulting Area
⑨	7 Jul 1925	CALHOUN lost to creation of GULF	570 sq mi

(Heavy line depicts historical boundary. Base map shows present-day information.)

⑨   CALHOUN Boundaries
7 Jul 1925–1990

10   0   10   20   30   40 Miles

Chronology of CHARLOTTE

Map	Date	Event	Resulting Area
❶	23 Apr 1921	CHARLOTTE created from DE SOTO	700 sq mi

(Heavy line depicts historical boundary. Base map shows present-day information.)

❶ CHARLOTTE Boundaries
23 Apr 1921–1990

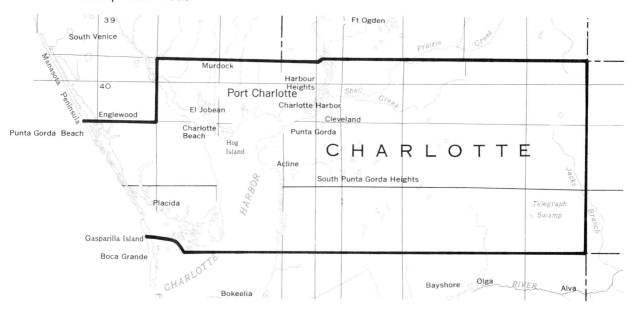

10   0   10   20   30   40 Miles

Chronology of CITRUS

Map	Date	Event	Resulting Area
❶	2 Jun 1887	CITRUS created from HERNANDO	620 sq mi
	2 Jun 1911	CITRUS gained non-county area in Withlacoochee R. along the LEVY line when the boundary shifted from middle of river to the north bank [not mapped]	

(Heavy line depicts historical boundary. Base map shows present-day information.)

❶ CITRUS Boundaries
2 Jun 1887–1990

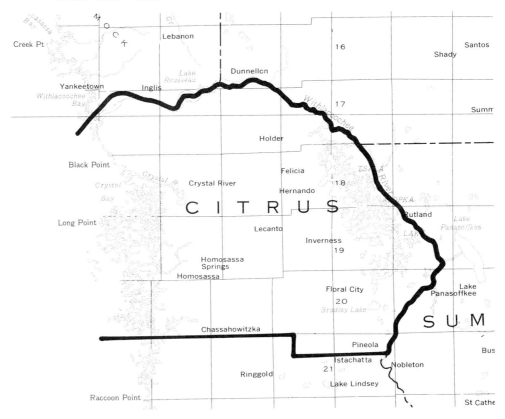

10	0	10	20	30	40 Miles

Chronology of CLAY

Map	Date	Event	Resulting Area
❶	31 Dec 1858	CLAY created from ALACHUA, COLUMBIA, and DUVAL	550 sq mi
❷	15 Jan 1859	CLAY lost to PUTNAM	490 sq mi

(Heavy line depicts historical boundary. Base map shows present-day information.)

❶ CLAY Boundaries
31 Dec 1858 – 14 Jan 1859

❷ CLAY Boundaries
15 Jan 1859 – 21 Dec 1859

10   0   10   20   30   40 Miles

Chronology of CLAY

Map	Date	Event	Resulting Area
❸	22 Dec 1859	CLAY gained from PUTNAM, and gained small areas in the St. Johns R. from DUVAL and ST. JOHNS when boundary shifted from west bank to west margin of the channel	550 sq mi

(Heavy line depicts historical boundary. Base map shows present-day information.)

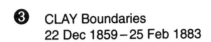

❸ CLAY Boundaries
22 Dec 1859 – 25 Feb 1883

| 10 | 0 | 10 | 20 | 30 | 40 Miles |

Chronology of CLAY

Map	Date	Event	Resulting Area
❹	26 Feb 1883	CLAY gained from PUTNAM	600 sq mi
❹	5 May 1909	CLAY lost small area to PUTNAM in the town of Melrose	600 sq mi

(Heavy line depicts historical boundary. Base map shows present-day information.)

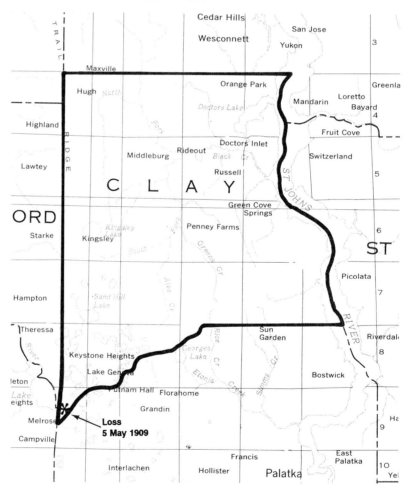

❹ CLAY Boundaries
26 Feb 1883 – 5 Jun 1927

10   0   10   20   30   40 Miles

Chronology of CLAY

Map	Date	Event	Resulting Area
⑤	6 Jun 1927	CLAY lost small area to PUTNAM	600 sq mi
⑤	1 Jul 1976	CLAY gained small area from DUVAL along Interstate 295	600 sq mi
	27 Jun 1978	CLAY boundaries redefined [no change]	
⑤	31 Dec 1980	CLAY gained small area from DUVAL along Interstate 295	600 sq mi
⑤	14 Jun 1984	CLAY gained small area from PUTNAM	600 sq mi

(Heavy line depicts historical boundary. Base map shows present-day information.)

⑤ CLAY Boundaries
6 Jun 1927–1990

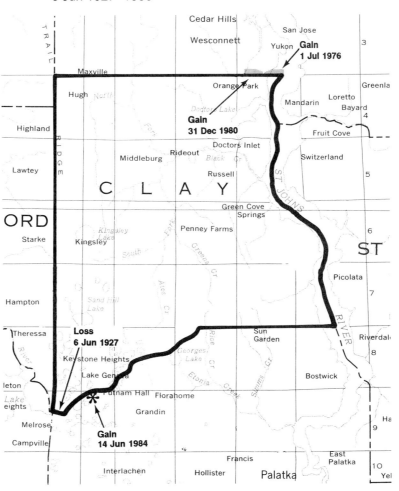

Chronology of COLLIER

Map	Date	Event	Resulting Area
❶	7 Jul 1923	COLLIER created from LEE	2,000 sq mi

(Heavy line depicts historical boundary. Base map shows present-day information.)

❶ COLLIER Boundaries
7 Jul 1923–1990

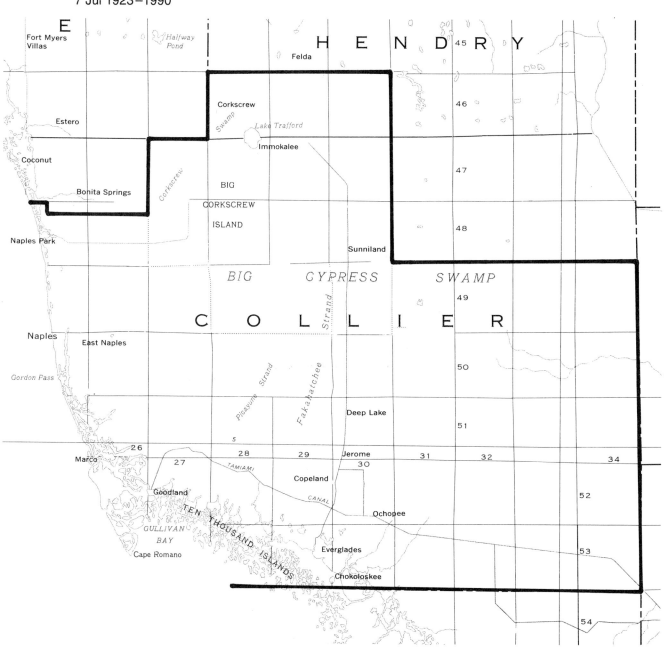

Chronology of COLUMBIA

Map	Date	Event	Resulting Area
❶	4 Feb 1832	COLUMBIA created from ALACHUA	3,140 sq mi
❷	10 Feb 1835	COLUMBIA lost to ALACHUA	2,640 sq mi
❸	15 Mar 1844	COLUMBIA exchanged small areas with ALACHUA, lost to DUVAL	2,590 sq mi
❸	31 Dec 1858	COLUMBIA lost to creation of CLAY	2,580 sq mi

(Heavy line depicts historical boundary. Base map shows present-day information.)

❶ COLUMBIA Boundaries
4 Feb 1832 – 9 Feb 1835

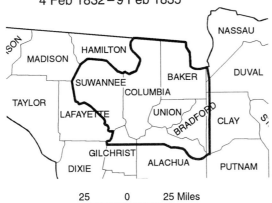

❷ COLUMBIA Boundaries
10 Feb 1835 – 14 Mar 1844

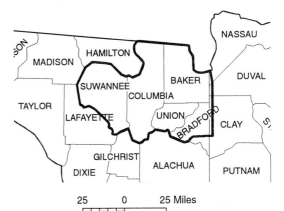

❸ COLUMBIA Boundaries
15 Mar 1844 – c. Feb 1859

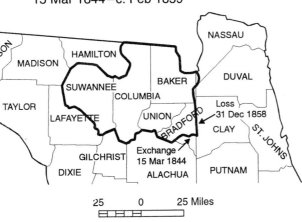

Chronology of COLUMBIA

Map	Date	Event	Resulting Area
❹	c. Feb 1859	COLUMBIA lost to creation of both NEW RIVER (now BRADFORD) and SUWANNEE	760 sq mi

(Heavy line depicts historical boundary. Base map shows present-day information.)

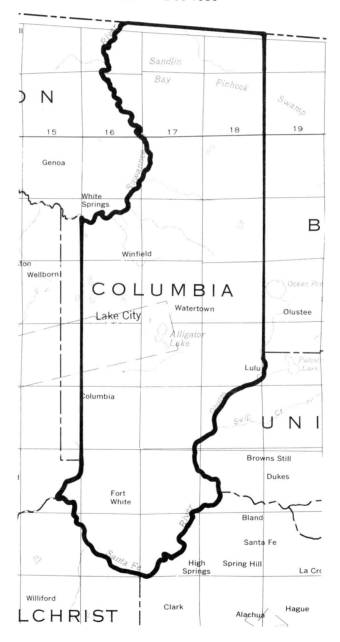

❹   COLUMBIA Boundaries
c. Feb 1859–11 Dec 1859

Chronology of COLUMBIA

Map	Date	Event	Resulting Area
⑤	12 Dec 1859	COLUMBIA gained from SUWANNEE	810 sq mi
⑤	27 Nov 1863	COLUMBIA lost small area to SUWANNEE so as to include entire town of Wellborn in SUWANNEE	810 sq mi

(Heavy line depicts historical boundary. Base map shows present-day information.)

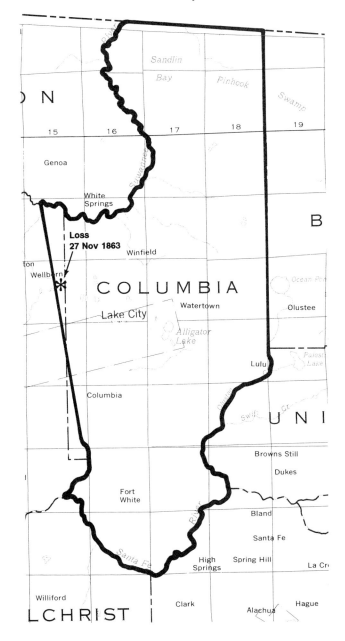

⑤   COLUMBIA Boundaries
12 Dec 1859 – 29 May 1889

Chronology of COLUMBIA

Map	Date	Event	Resulting Area
❻	30 May 1889	COLUMBIA exchanged with SUWANNEE	810 sq mi
	29 May 1909	COLUMBIA boundaries clarified [no change]	
❻	1 Jan 1954	COLUMBIA lost small area to ALACHUA	810 sq mi

(Heavy line depicts historical boundary. Base map shows present-day information.)

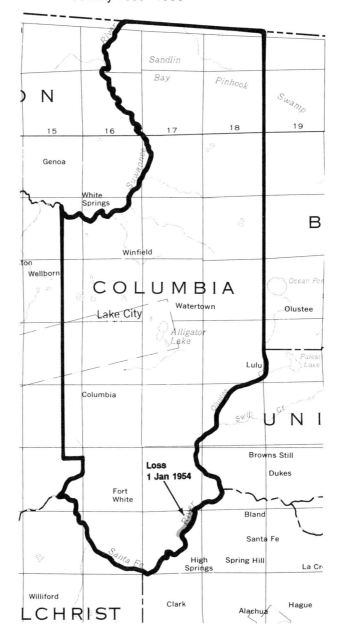

❻ COLUMBIA Boundaries
30 May 1889 – 1990

Chronology of DADE

Map	Date	Event	Resulting Area
❶	4 Feb 1836	DADE created from MONROE	4,600 sq mi
❷	7 Jan 1851	DADE no longer fully organized, attached to MONROE for administrative and judicial purposes	

(Heavy line depicts historical boundary. Base map shows present-day information.)

❶ DADE Boundaries
4 Feb 1836–7 Dec 1866

25   0   25 Miles

❷ DADE Attachment
7 Jan 1851–7 Dec 1866

25   0   25 Miles

Chronology of DADE

Map	Date	Event	Resulting Area
❸/❹	8 Dec 1866	DADE gained from BREVARD, exchanged with MONROE / Area attached to MONROE for administrative and judicial purposes was enlarged	7,600 sq mi
❸	1872	DADE fully organized, detached from MONROE	7,600 sq mi

(Heavy line depicts historical boundary. Base map shows present-day information.)

❸ DADE Boundaries
8 Dec 1866 – 18 Feb 1874

❹ DADE Attachment
8 Dec 1866 – 1872

25   0   25 Miles

25   0   25 Miles

Chronology of DADE

Map	Date	Event	Resulting Area
❺	19 Feb 1874	DADE gained from BREVARD, lost to MONROE	5,700 sq mi

(Heavy line depicts historical boundary. Base map shows present-day information.)

❺ DADE Boundaries
19 Feb 1874 – 30 Jun 1909

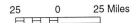

25   0   25 Miles

Chronology of DADE

Map	Date	Event	Resulting Area
⑥	1 Jul 1909	DADE lost to creation of PALM BEACH	2,650 sq mi
	6 Jun 1913	Legislature authorized creation of BROWARD from DADE, dependent on local referendum that failed [no change; see BROWARD, map 1]	

(Heavy line depicts historical boundary. Base map shows present-day information.)

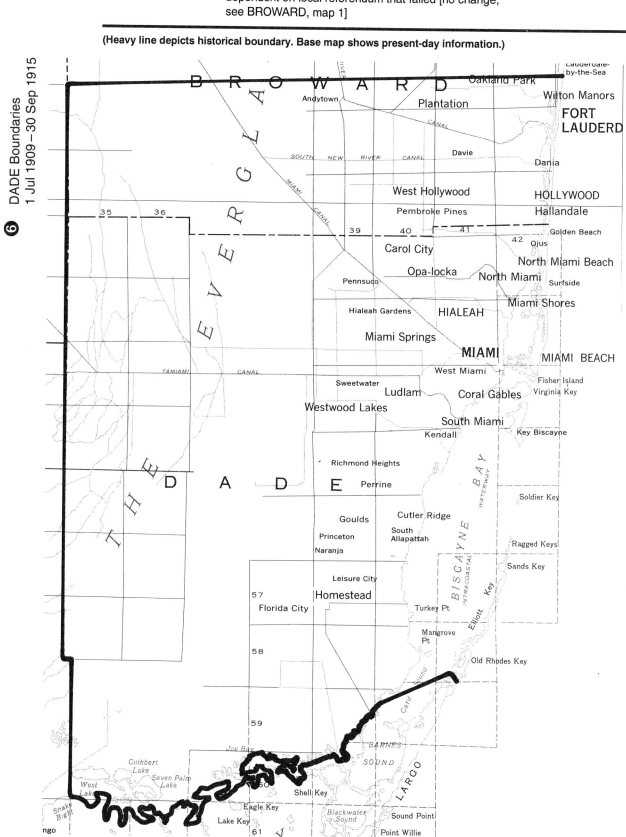

⑥ DADE Boundaries 1 Jul 1909 – 30 Sep 1915

B R O W A R D

Lauderdale-by-the-Sea

Oakland Park

Andytown

Plantation

Wilton Manors

FORT LAUDERD

CANAL

SOUTH NEW RIVER CANAL

Davie

Dania

MIAMI CANAL

West Hollywood

HOLLYWOOD

Pembroke Pines

Hallandale

35   36

39   40   41   42

Golden Beach

Ojus

Carol City

North Miami Beach

Opa-locka

North Miami

Surfside

Pennsuco

Miami Shores

Hialeah Gardens

HIALEAH

Miami Springs

MIAMI   **MIAMI BEACH**

TAMIAMI   CANAL

West Miami

Fisher Island

Sweetwater

Ludlam

Coral Gables

Virginia Key

Westwood Lakes

South Miami

Kendall

Key Biscayne

T H E   E V E R G L A D E S

D   A   D   E

Richmond Heights

Perrine

BISCAYNE   BAY

WATERWAY

Soldier Key

Goulds

Cutler Ridge

Princeton

South Allapattah

Ragged Keys

Naranja

INTRACOASTAL

Sands Key

Leisure City

BISCAYNE

57   Homestead

Florida City

Turkey Pt

Elliott Key

58

Mangrove Pt

Old Rhodes Key

Card Sound

59

BARNES   SOUND

Joe Bay

LARGO

Cuthbert Lake

Seven Palm Lake

West Lake

60

Shell Key

Snake Bight

Eagle Key

Blackwater Sound

Sound Point

ngo

Lake Key   61

Point Willie

10   0   10   20   30   40 Miles

Chronology of DADE

Map	Date	Event	Resulting Area
❼	1 Oct 1915	DADE lost to creation of BROWARD	1,950 sq mi
❼	13 May 1961	DADE gained small area from MONROE	1,950 sq mi
❼	1 Oct 1978	DADE lost small area to BROWARD	1,950 sq mi

(Heavy line depicts historical boundary. Base map shows present-day information.)

❼ DADE Boundaries
   1 Oct 1915–1990

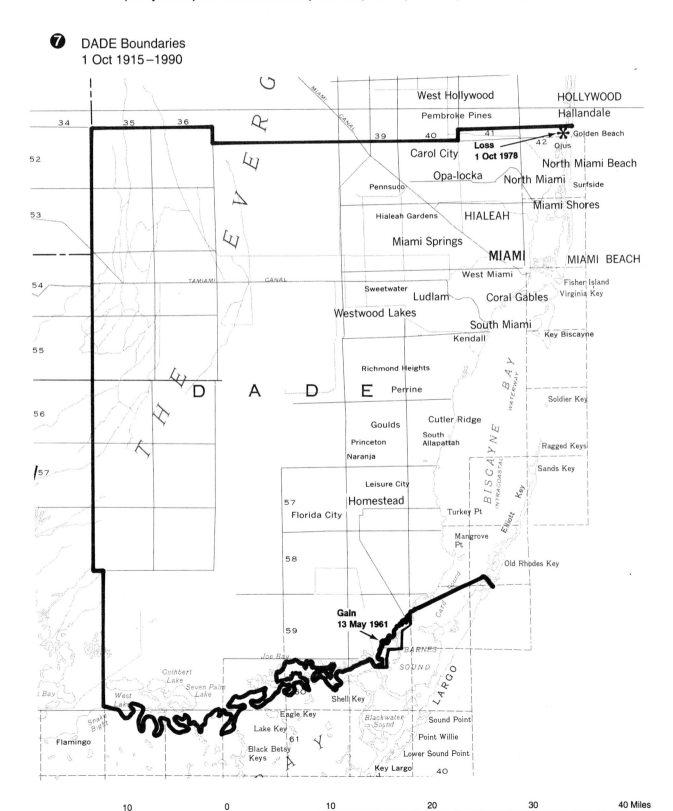

Chronology of DE SOTO

Map	Date	Event	Resulting Area
❶	19 May 1887	DE SOTO created from MANATEE	3,750 sq mi
❷	23 Apr 1921	DE SOTO lost to creation of CHARLOTTE, GLADES, HARDEE, and HIGHLANDS	650 sq mi

(Heavy line depicts historical boundary. Base map shows present-day information.)

❶ DE SOTO Boundaries
19 May 1887–22 Apr 1921

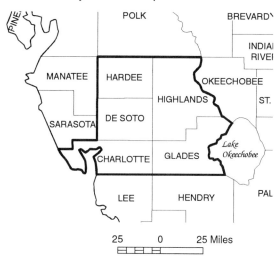

25   0   25 Miles

❷ DE SOTO Boundaries
23 Apr 1921–1990

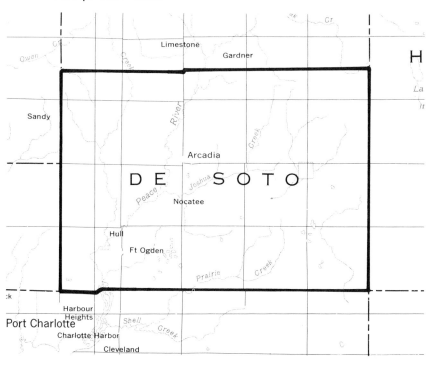

10   0   10   20   30   40 Miles

Chronology of DIXIE

Map	Date	Event	Resulting Area
❶	25 Apr 1921	DIXIE created from LAFAYETTE	700 sq mi
	4 Jun 1925	DIXIE lost small area to LEVY when the boundary shifted from east bank to middle of the Suwannee R. [not mapped]	

(Heavy line depicts historical boundary. Base map shows present-day information.)

❶ DIXIE Boundaries
25 Apr 1921–1990

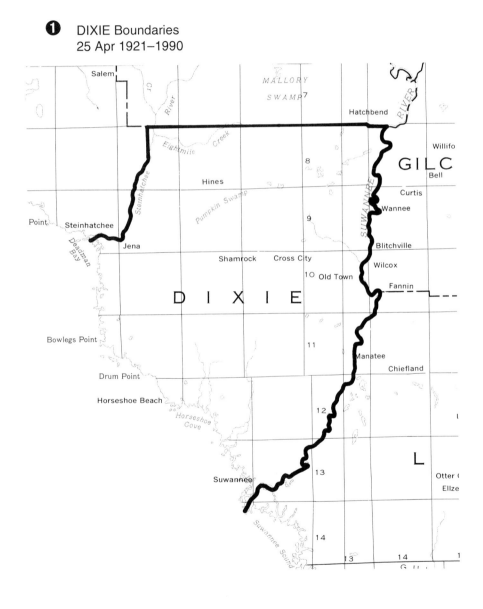

10   0   10   20   30   40 Miles

Chronology of DUVAL

Map	Date	Event	Resulting Area
❶	12 Aug 1822	DUVAL created from ST. JOHNS	4,630 sq mi
❷	24 Jun 1823	DUVAL gained from JACKSON, exchanged with ST. JOHNS	4,450 sq mi

(Heavy line depicts historical boundary. Base map shows present-day information.)

❶ DUVAL Boundaries
12 Aug 1822 – 23 Jun 1823

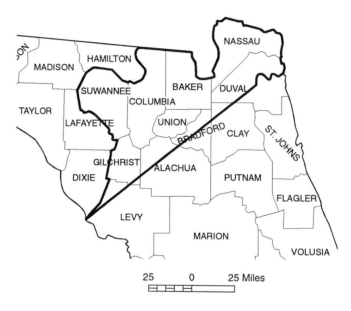

❷ DUVAL Boundaries
24 Jun 1823 – 28 Dec 1824

Chronology of DUVAL

Map	Date	Event	Resulting Area
❸	29 Dec 1824	DUVAL gained from ST. JOHNS, lost to creation of ALACHUA, LEON, and NASSAU	1,580 sq mi

(Heavy line depicts historical boundary. Base map shows present-day information.)

❸ DUVAL Boundaries
29 Dec 1824 – 29 Dec 1826

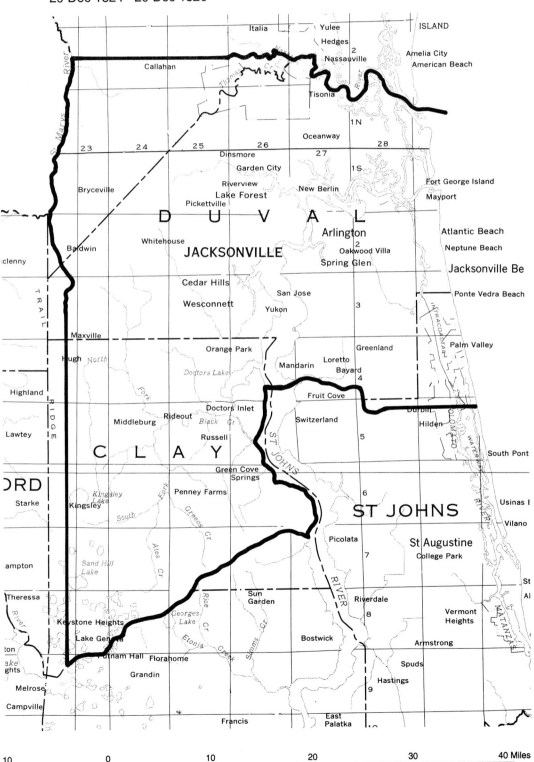

Chronology of DUVAL

Map	Date	Event	Resulting Area
❹	30 Dec 1826	DUVAL lost to NASSAU	1,350 sq mi

(Heavy line depicts historical boundary. Base map shows present-day information.)

❹ DUVAL Boundaries
30 Dec 1826 – 22 Nov 1828

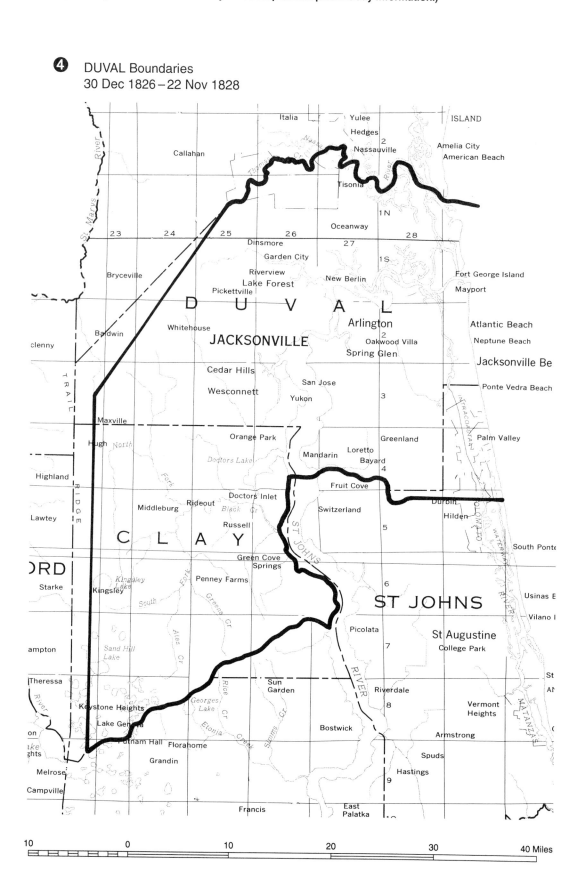

Chronology of DUVAL

Map	Date	Event	Resulting Area
❺	23 Nov 1828	Overlap resulted when a single area was assigned to both DUVAL and NASSAU [corrected 2 Jan 1857]	1,480 sq mi

(Heavy line depicts historical boundary. Base map shows present-day information.)

❺   DUVAL Boundaries
23 Nov 1828 – 14 Mar 1844

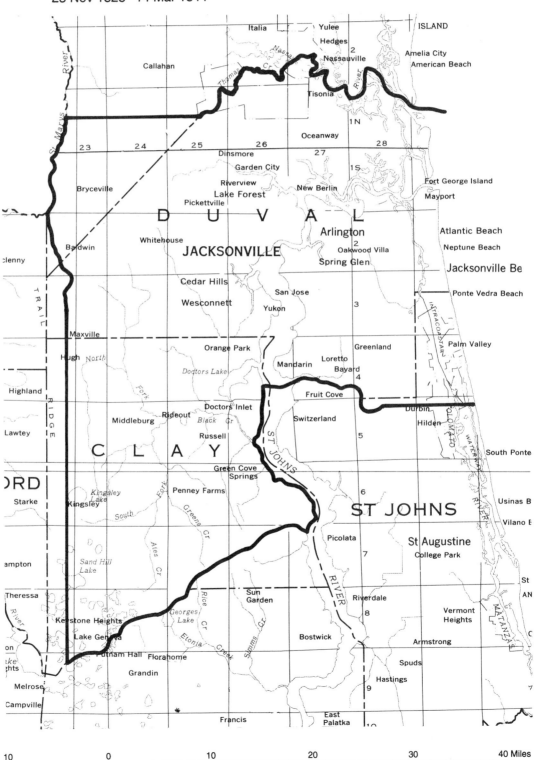

Chronology of DUVAL

Map	Date	Event	Resulting Area
❻	15 Mar 1844	DUVAL gained from COLUMBIA; boundary with ALACHUA adjusted	1,510 sq mi

(Heavy line depicts historical boundary. Base map shows present-day information.)

❻   **DUVAL Boundaries**
   15 Mar 1844–1 Jan 1857

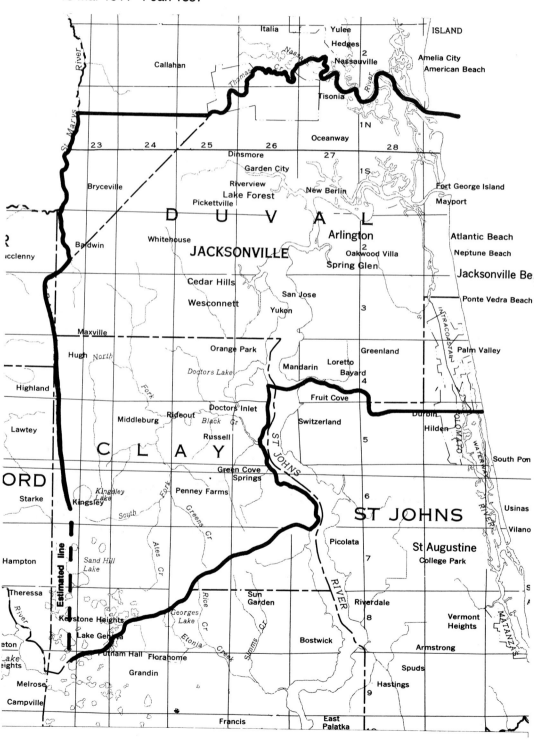

10   0   10   20   30   40 Miles

Chronology of DUVAL

Map	Date	Event	Resulting Area
❼	2 Jan 1857	1828 overlap between DUVAL and NASSAU ended; based upon its most recently defined configuration, DUVAL appeared to lose to NASSAU	1,370 sq mi

(Heavy line depicts historical boundary. Base map shows present-day information.)

❼ DUVAL Boundaries
2 Jan 1857– 30 Dec 1858

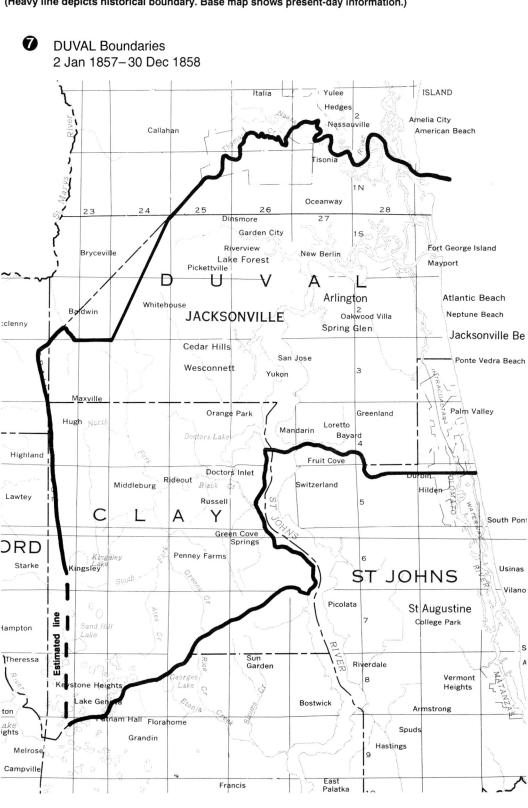

Chronology of DUVAL

Map	Date	Event	Resulting Area
❽	31 Dec 1858	DUVAL lost to creation of CLAY	810 sq mi

(Heavy line depicts historical boundary. Base map shows present-day information.)

❽ DUVAL Boundaries
31 Dec 1858 – 14 Jan 1859

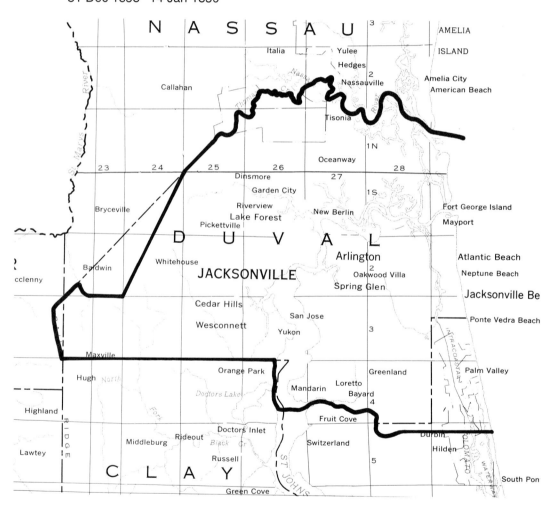

| 10 | 0 | 10 | 20 | 30 | 40 Miles |

Chronology of DUVAL

Map	Date	Event	Resulting Area
⑨	15 Jan 1859	DUVAL gained from NASSAU	840 sq mi
⑨	22 Dec 1859	DUVAL lost small area in the St. Johns R. to CLAY when boundary shifted from west bank to west margin of the channel	840 sq mi

(Heavy line depicts historical boundary. Base map shows present-day information.)

⑨   DUVAL Boundaries
    15 Jan 1859 – 14 Feb 1875

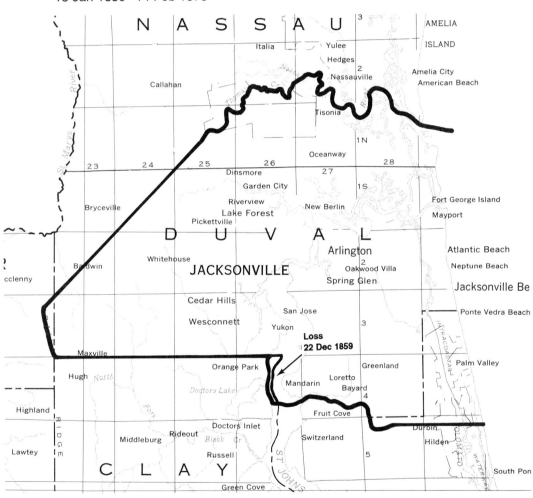

Chronology of DUVAL

Map	Date	Event	Resulting Area
⑩	15 Feb 1875	DUVAL exchanged with ST. JOHNS	780 sq mi

(Heavy line depicts historical boundary. Base map shows present-day information.)

⑩ DUVAL Boundaries
15 Feb 1875 – 18 May 1911

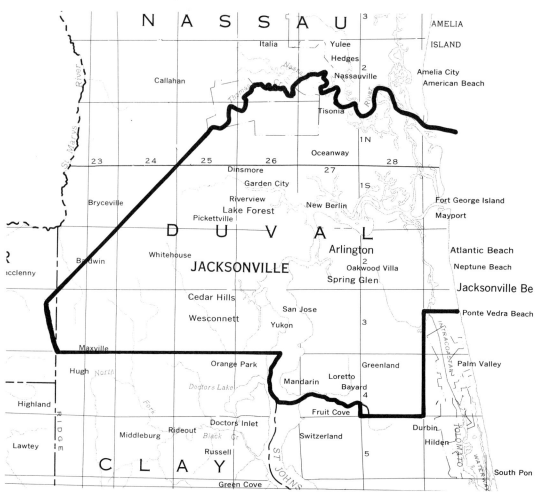

Chronology of DUVAL

Map	Date	Event	Resulting Area
⑪	19 May 1911	DUVAL lost to BAKER	780 sq mi
⑪	1 July 1976	DUVAL lost small area to CLAY along Interstate 295	780 sq mi
⑪	31 Dec 1980	DUVAL lost small area to CLAY along Interstate 295	780 sq mi

(Heavy line depicts historical boundary. Base map shows present-day information.)

⑪   DUVAL Boundaries
19 May 1911–1990

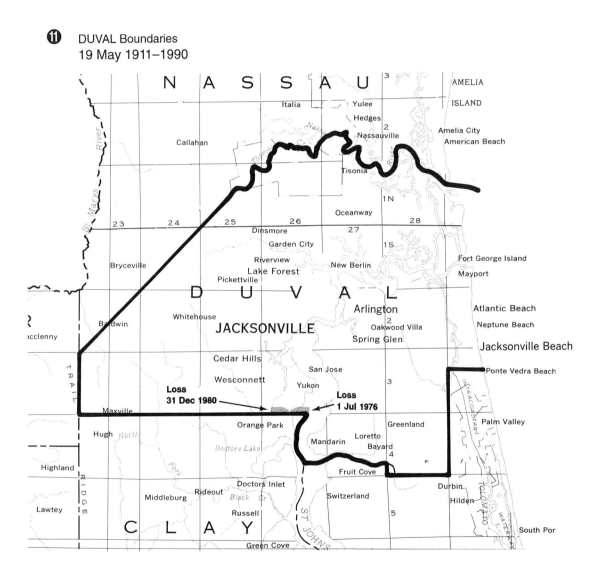

Chronology of ESCAMBIA

Map	Date	Event	Resulting Area
❶	21 Jul 1821	ESCAMBIA created from non-county area by decree of Provisional Governor Andrew Jackson	15,000 sq mi
❷	12 Aug 1822	ESCAMBIA lost to creation of JACKSON	3,750 sq mi
❸	29 Dec 1824	ESCAMBIA lost to JACKSON and to creation of WALTON	2,400 sq mi
❹	9 Dec 1825	ESCAMBIA lost to WALTON	2,150 sq mi

(Heavy line depicts historical boundary. Base map shows present-day information.)

❶ ESCAMBIA Boundaries
21 Jul 1821–11 Aug 1822

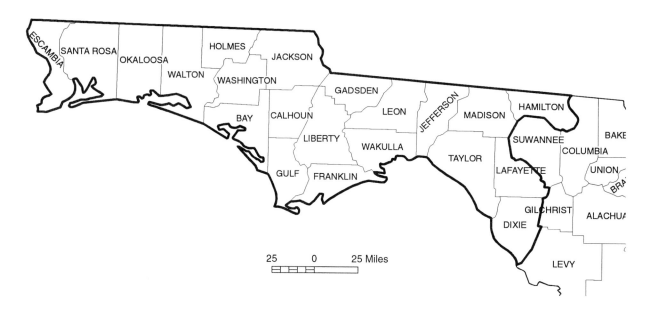

❷ ESCAMBIA Boundaries
12 Aug 1822 – 28 Dec 1824

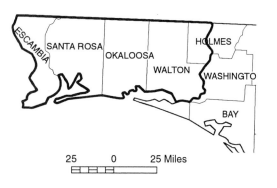

❸ ESCAMBIA Boundaries
29 Dec 1824 – 8 Dec 1825

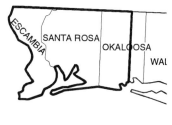

❹ ESCAMBIA Boundaries
9 Dec 1825 – 17 Feb 1842

Chronology of ESCAMBIA

Map	Date	Event	Resulting Area
❺	18 Feb 1842	ESCAMBIA lost to creation of SANTA ROSA	670 sq mi
❺	11 Jan 1851	ESCAMBIA lost part of Santa Rosa I. to WALTON	670 sq mi

(Heavy line depicts historical boundary. Base map shows present-day information.)

❺   ESCAMBIA Boundaries
18 Feb 1842 – 30 May 1947

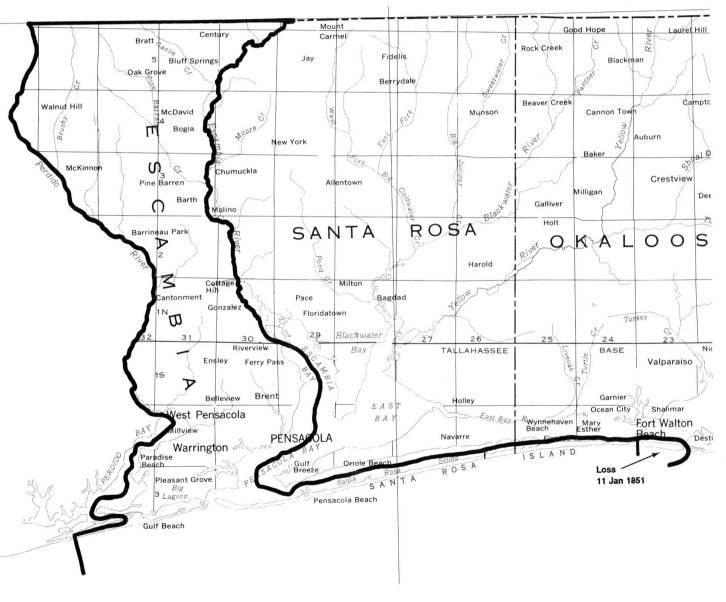

Chronology of ESCAMBIA

Map	Date	Event	Resulting Area
❻	31 May 1947	ESCAMBIA lost to OKALOOSA	660 sq mi

(Heavy line depicts historical boundary. Base map shows present-day information.)

❻ ESCAMBIA Boundaries
31 May 1947–10 Jun 1951

| 10 | 0 | 10 | 20 | 30 | 40 Miles |

Chronology of ESCAMBIA

Map	Date	Event	Resulting Area
❼	11 Jun 1951	ESCAMBIA lost small area to SANTA ROSA	660 sq mi
❼	29 Jun 1957	ESCAMBIA lost small area to SANTA ROSA along the right-of-way of the toll bridge and road on Santa Rosa Sound and Island	660 sq mi
	14 Jun 1983	ESCAMBIA boundaries clarified to extend into the Gulf of Mexico [no change]	

(Heavy line depicts historical boundary. Base map shows present-day information.)

❼   ESCAMBIA Boundaries
11 Jun 1951–1990

Chronology of FAYETTE (extinct)

Map	Date	Event	Resulting Area
❶	9 Feb 1832	FAYETTE created from JACKSON	620 sq mi
❷	16 Feb 1833	FAYETTE gained from WASHINGTON, lost to JACKSON	370 sq mi
	1 Feb 1834	FAYETTE lost all territory to JACKSON; FAYETTE eliminated	

(Heavy line depicts historical boundary. Base map shows present-day information.)

❶ FAYETTE Boundaries
9 Feb 1832–15 Feb 1833

❷ FAYETTE Boundaries
16 Feb 1833–31 Jan 1834

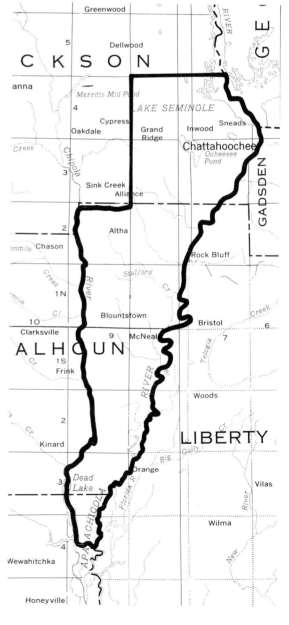

10   0   10   20   30   40 Miles

Chronology of FLAGLER

Map	Date	Event	Resulting Area
❶	12 Jun 1917	FLAGLER created from ST. JOHNS and VOLUSIA	490 sq mi
	20 Jun 1959	Boundary between FLAGLER and PUTNAM in Crescent Lake clarified [no discernible change]	

(Heavy line depicts historical boundary. Base map shows present-day information.)

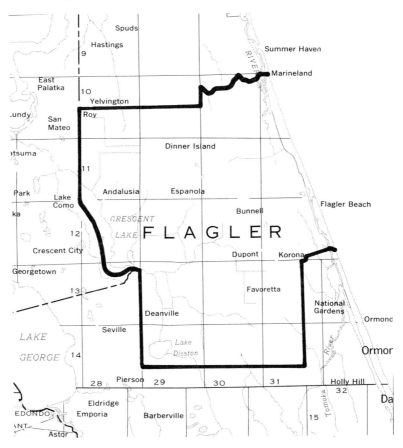

❶   FLAGLER Boundaries
12 Jun 1917–1990

10   0   10   20   30   40 Miles

Chronology of FRANKLIN

Map	Date	Event	Resulting Area
❶	8 Feb 1832	FRANKLIN created from GADSDEN and WASHINGTON	770 sq mi

(Heavy line depicts historical boundary. Base map shows present-day information.)

❶ FRANKLIN Boundaries
8 Feb 1832 – 25 Jan 1838

| 10 | 0 | 10 | 20 | 30 | 40 Miles |

Chronology of FRANKLIN

Map	Date	Event	Resulting Area
❷	26 Jan 1838	FRANKLIN lost to creation of CALHOUN, apparently lost small area to WASHINGTON	360 sq mi

(Heavy line depicts historical boundary. Base map shows present-day information.)

❷ FRANKLIN Boundaries
26 Jan 1838 – 12 Jan 1851

Chronology of FRANKLIN

Map	Date	Event	Resulting Area
❸	13 Jan 1851	FRANKLIN gained from WAKULLA when boundary shifted from west bank to east bank of Ochlockonee R., and exchanged with GADSDEN	540 sq mi
❸	16 Feb 1885	FRANKLIN gained narrow strip of territory all along boundary with LIBERTY	540 sq mi

(Heavy line depicts historical boundary. Base map shows present-day information.)

❸ FRANKLIN Boundaries
13 Jan 1851–29 Mar 1972

Chronology of FRANKLIN

Map	Date	Event	Resulting Area
❹	30 Mar 1972	FRANKLIN gained Forbes I. from GULF	550 sq mi
❹	1 Oct 1986	FRANKLIN lost to WAKULLA when boundary shifted from east bank to middle of Ochlockonee R. and Bay	550 sq mi

(Heavy line depicts historical boundary. Base map shows present-day information.)

❹ FRANKLIN Boundaries
30 Mar 1972–1990

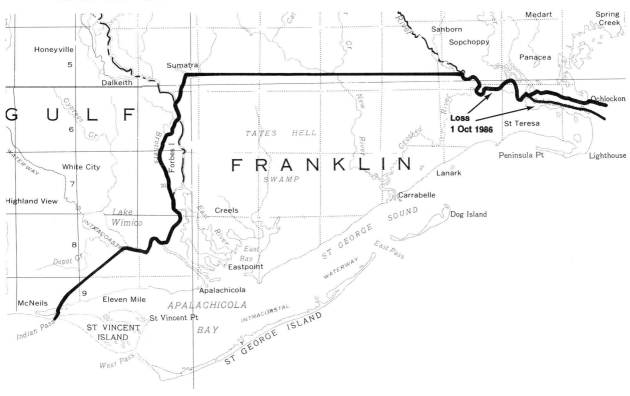

Chronology of GADSDEN

Map	Date	Event	Resulting Area
❶	24 Jun 1823	GADSDEN created from JACKSON	6,950 sq mi

(Heavy line depicts historical boundary. Base map shows present-day information.)

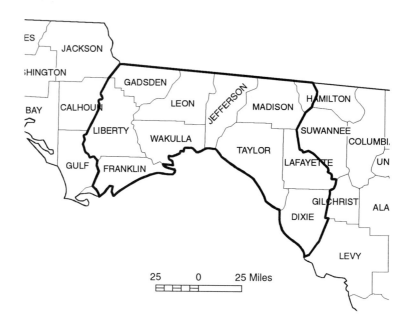

❶ GADSDEN Boundaries
24 Jun 1823 – 28 Dec 1824

Chronology of GADSDEN

Map	Date	Event	Resulting Area
❷	29 Dec 1824	GADSDEN lost to creation of LEON	1,920 sq mi

(Heavy line depicts historical boundary. Base map shows present-day information.)

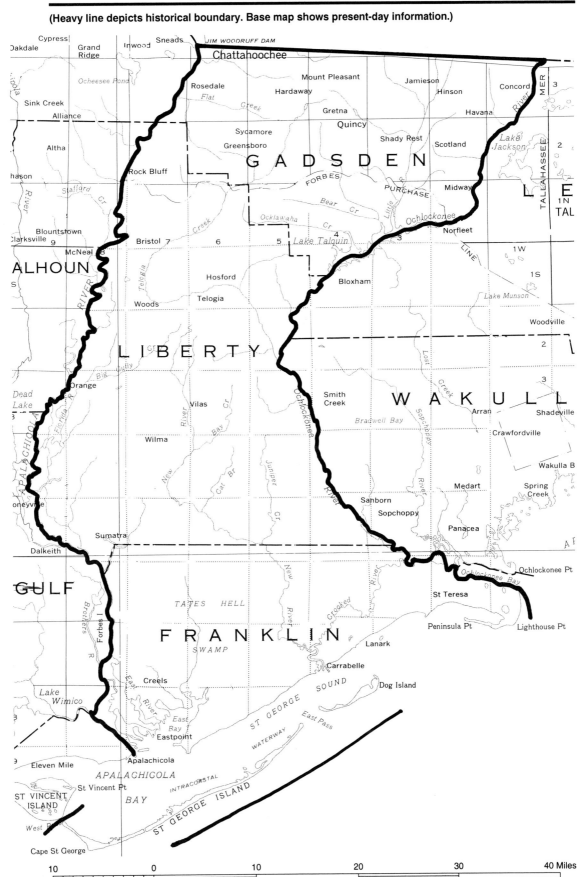

❷ GADSDEN Boundaries
29 Dec 1824 – 7 Feb 1832

10   0   10   20   30   40 Miles

Chronology of GADSDEN

Map	Date	Event	Resulting Area
❸	8 Feb 1832	GADSDEN lost to creation of FRANKLIN	1,590 sq mi

(Heavy line depicts historical boundary. Base map shows present-day information.)

❸ GADSDEN Boundaries
8 Feb 1832 – 12 Jan 1851

Chronology of GADSDEN

Map	Date	Event	Resulting Area
❹	13 Jan 1851	GADSDEN exchanged with FRANKLIN	1,400 sq mi

(Heavy line depicts historical boundary. Base map shows present-day information.)

❹ GADSDEN Boundaries
13 Jan 1851–14 Dec 1855

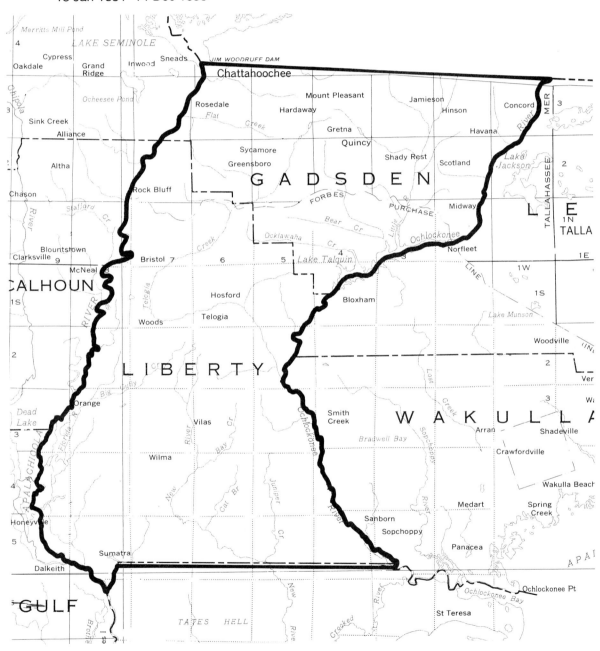

Chronology of GADSDEN

Map	Date	Event	Resulting Area
❺	15 Dec 1855	GADSDEN lost to creation of LIBERTY [mistake in description corrected 5 Jan 1859]	530 sq mi
	5 Jan 1859	Boundary between GADSDEN and LIBERTY clarified, correcting mistake of 15 Dec 1855 [no change]	
❻	22 Dec 1859	GADSDEN exchanged with LIBERTY	550 sq mi

(Heavy line depicts historical boundary. Base map shows present-day information.)

❺ GADSDEN Boundaries
15 Dec 1855 – 21 Dec 1859

❻ GADSDEN Boundaries
22 Dec 1859 – 31 Dec 1909

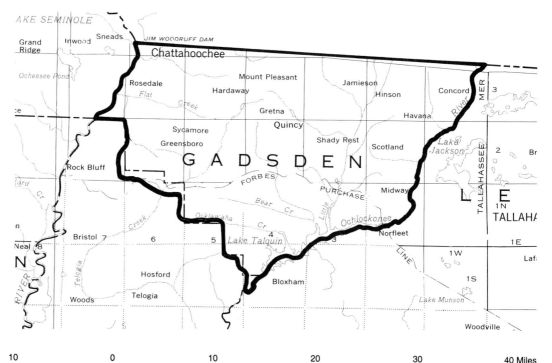

10	0	10	20	30	40 Miles

Chronology of GADSDEN

Map	Date	Event	Resulting Area
❼	1 Jan 1910	GADSDEN exchanged with LIBERTY	540 sq mi
	4 May 1933	GADSDEN gained from LEON when boundary shifted from west bank to middle of the Ochlockonee R. [not mapped]	

(Heavy line depicts historical boundary. Base map shows present-day information.)

❼ GADSDEN Boundaries
1 Jan 1910–1990

Chronology of GILCHRIST

Map	Date	Event	Resulting Area
❶	1 Jan 1926	GILCHRIST created from ALACHUA	350 sq mi

(Heavy line depicts historical boundary. Base map shows present-day information.)

❶   GILCHRIST Boundaries
1 Jan 1926–1990

| 10 | 0 | 10 | 20 | 30 | 40 Miles |

Chronology of GLADES

Map	Date	Event	Resulting Area
❶	23 Apr 1921	GLADES created from DE SOTO	760 sq mi

(Heavy line depicts historical boundary. Base map shows present-day information.)

❶ GLADES Boundaries
23 Apr 1921–7 May 1925

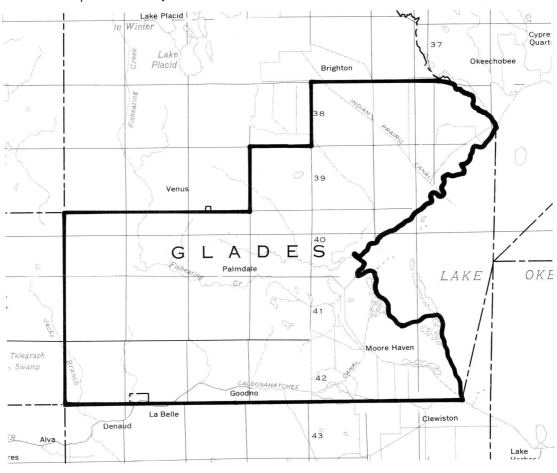

10	0	10	20	30	40 Miles

Chronology of GLADES

Map	Date	Event	Resulting Area
❷	8 May 1925	GLADES gained part of Lake Okeechobee from PALM BEACH	760 sq mi
❷	7 Sep 1937	GLADES lost small area to HENDRY	760 sq mi
❷	13 Jun 1949	GLADES gained small area from HIGHLANDS	760 sq mi

(Heavy line depicts historical boundary. Base map shows present-day information.)

❷ GLADES Boundaries
8 May 1925 – 28 May 1963

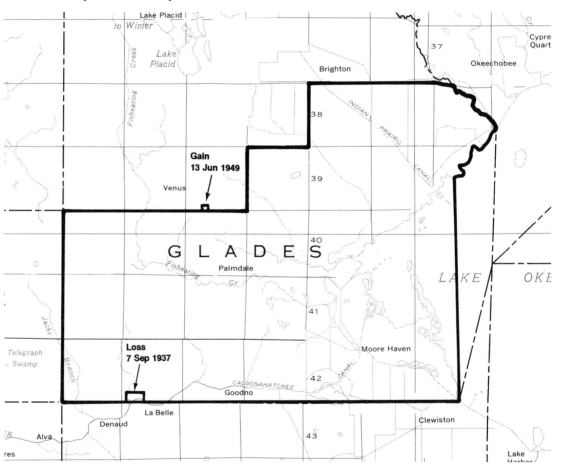

Chronology of GLADES

Map	Date	Event	Resulting Area
❸	29 May 1963	GLADES gained part of Lake Okeechobee from PALM BEACH	760 sq mi
❸	12 Jun 1963	GLADES lost small area to HENDRY along Route 80	760 sq mi

(Heavy line depicts historical boundary. Base map shows present-day information.)

❸ GLADES Boundaries
29 May 1963–1990

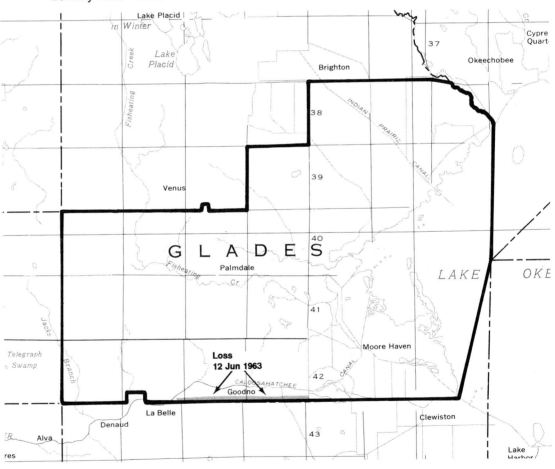

Chronology of GULF

Map	Date	Event	Resulting Area
❶	7 Jul 1925	GULF created from CALHOUN	570 sq mi

(Heavy line depicts historical boundary. Base map shows present-day information.)

❶ GULF Boundaries
7 Jul 1925 – 29 Mar 1972

Chronology of GULF

Map	Date	Event	Resulting Area
❷	30 Mar 1972	GULF lost Forbes I. to FRANKLIN	560 sq mi

(Heavy line depicts historical boundary. Base map shows present-day information.)

❷   GULF Boundaries
30 Mar 1972–1990

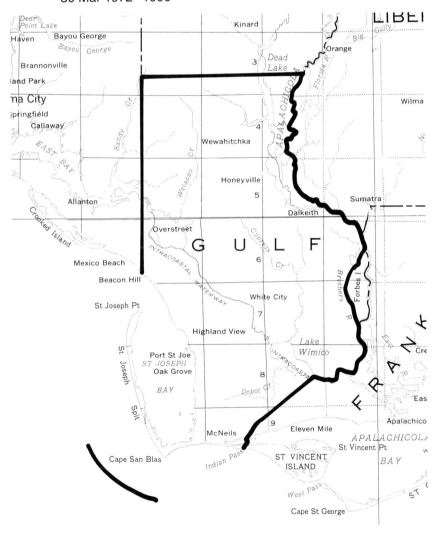

Chronology of HAMILTON

Map	Date	Event	Resulting Area
❶	26 Dec 1827	HAMILTON created from JEFFERSON	520 sq mi

(Heavy line depicts historical boundary. Base map shows present-day information.)

❶ HAMILTON Boundaries
26 Dec 1827–1990

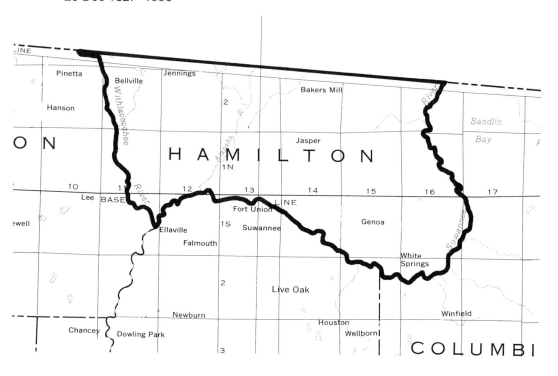

10   0   10   20   30   40 Miles

Chronology of HARDEE

Map	Date	Event	Resulting Area
❶	23 Apr 1921	HARDEE created from DE SOTO	650 sq mi

(Heavy line depicts historical boundary. Base map shows present-day information.)

❶ HARDEE Boundaries
23 Apr 1921–1990

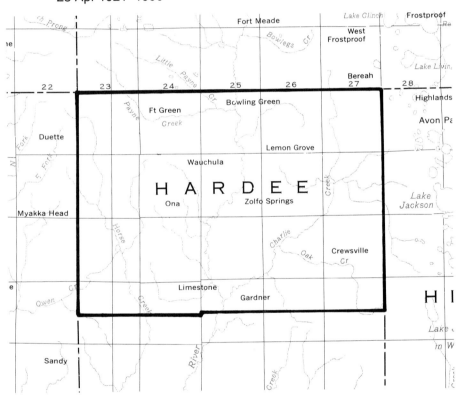

10   0   10   20   30   40 Miles

Chronology of HENDRY

Map	Date	Event	Resulting Area
❶	10 Jul 1923	HENDRY created from LEE	1,160 sq mi
❶	14 May 1925	HENDRY gained small part of Lake Okeechobee from PALM BEACH	1,160 sq mi
❶	7 Sep 1937	HENDRY gained small area from GLADES	1,160 sq mi
	29 Jul 1942	HENDRY boundaries redefined [mistake in description corrected 11 Jun 1945, no change]	
	11 Jun 1945	HENDRY boundaries clarified, correcting mistake of 29 Jul 1942 [no change]	

(Heavy line depicts historical boundary. Base map shows present-day information.)

❶ HENDRY Boundaries
10 Jul 1923 – 28 May 1963

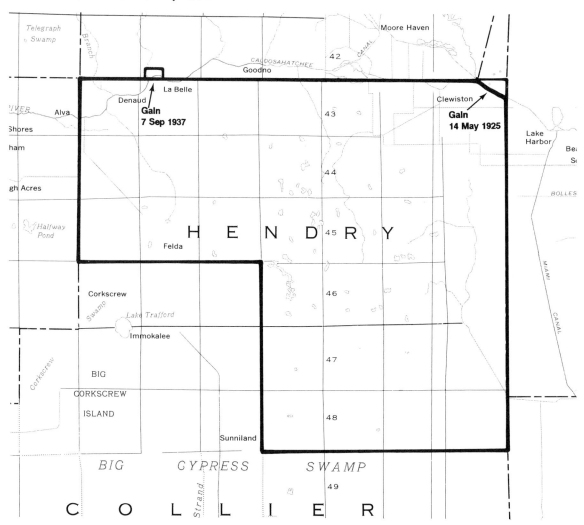

| 10 | 0 | 10 | 20 | 30 | 40 Miles |

Chronology of HENDRY

Map	Date	Event	Resulting Area
❷	29 May 1963	HENDRY gained part of Lake Okeechobee from PALM BEACH	1,160 sq mi
❷	12 Jun 1963	HENDRY gained small area from GLADES along Route 80	1,160 sq mi

(Heavy line depicts historical boundary. Base map shows present-day information.)

❷ HENDRY Boundaries
    29 May 1963–1990

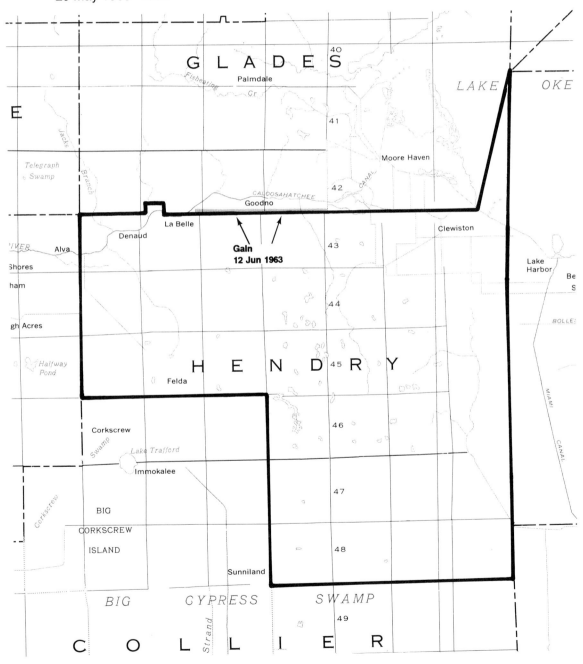

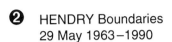

Chronology of HERNANDO

Map	Date	Event	Resulting Area
❶	24 Feb 1843	HERNANDO created from ALACHUA and HILLSBOROUGH	1,790 sq mi

(Heavy line depicts historical boundary. Base map shows present-day information.)

❶ HERNANDO Boundaries
24 Feb 1843 – 5 Mar 1844

Chronology of HERNANDO

Map	Date	Event	Resulting Area
❷	6 Mar 1844	HERNANDO gained from HILLSBOROUGH; HERNANDO renamed BENTON	1,900 sq mi

(Heavy line depicts historical boundary. Base map shows present-day information.)

❷   BENTON Boundaries
6 Mar 1844 – 31 Dec 1846

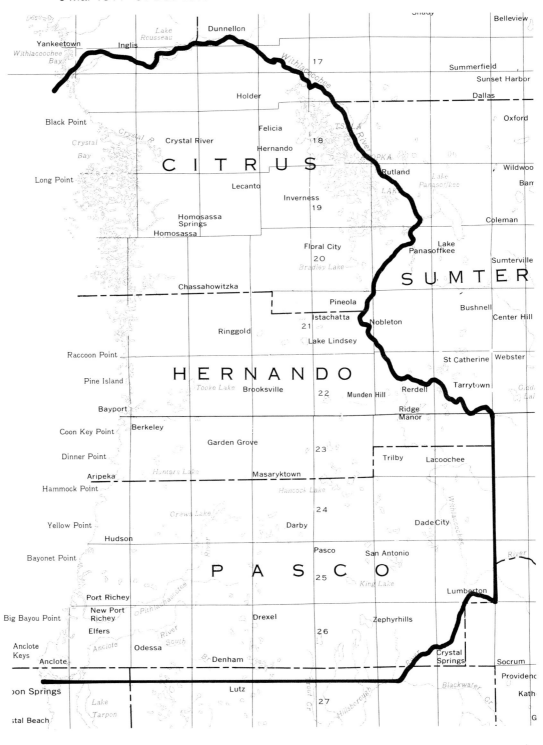

10	0	10	20	30	40 Miles

Chronology of HERNANDO

Map	Date	Event	Resulting Area
❸	1 Jan 1847	BENTON lost to HILLSBOROUGH	1,850 sq mi
	24 Dec 1850	BENTON renamed HERNANDO	

(Heavy line depicts historical boundary. Base map shows present-day information.)

❸ BENTON Boundaries
1 Jan 1847–by 1880

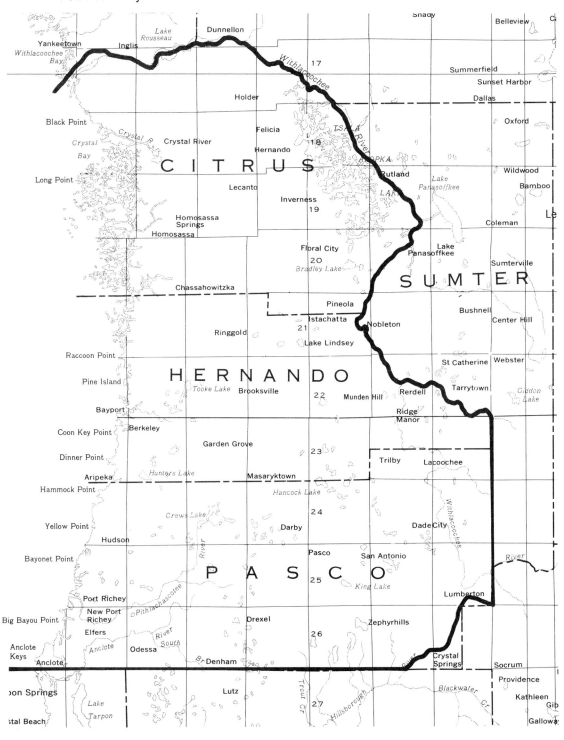

10   0   10   20   30   40 Miles

Chronology of HERNANDO

Map	Date	Event	Resulting Area
❹	by 1880	HERNANDO gained from POLK	1,880 sq mi
❹	5 Mar 1883	HERNANDO lost small area to POLK	1,880 sq mi

(Heavy line depicts historical boundary. Base map shows present-day information.)

❹ HERNANDO Boundaries
by 1880 – 1 Jun 1887

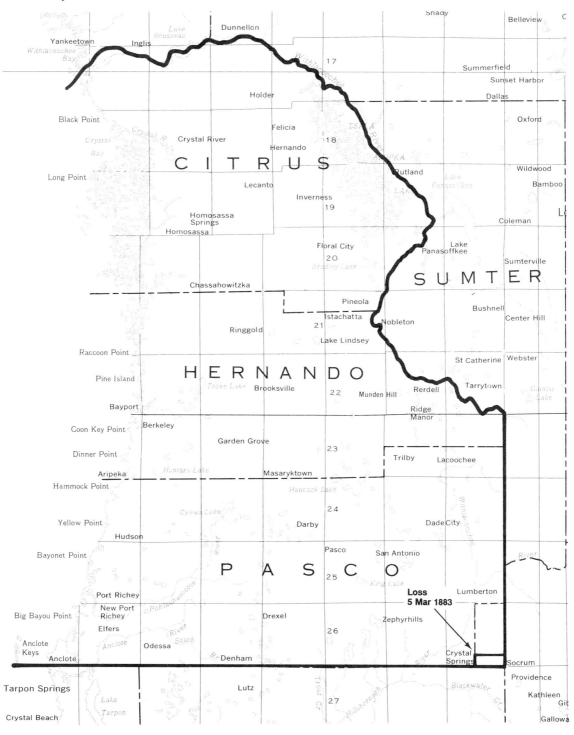

Chronology of HERNANDO

Map	Date	Event	Resulting Area
❺	2 Jun 1887	HERNANDO lost to creation of both CITRUS and PASCO	480 sq mi

(Heavy line depicts historical boundary. Base map shows present-day information.)

❺ HERNANDO Boundaries
2 Jun 1887–1990

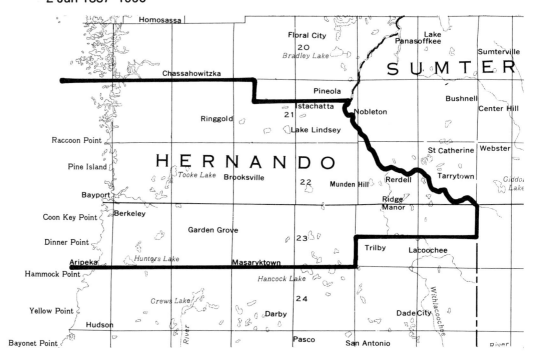

Chronology of HIGHLANDS

Map	Date	Event	Resulting Area
❶	23 Apr 1921	HIGHLANDS created from DE SOTO	1,040 sq mi
❶	13 Jun 1949	HIGHLANDS lost small area to GLADES	1,040 sq mi

(Heavy line depicts historical boundary. Base map shows present-day information.)

❶ HIGHLANDS Boundaries
23 Apr 1921–1990

Chronology of HILLSBOROUGH

Map	Date	Event	Resulting Area
❶	25 Jan 1834	HILLSBOROUGH created from ALACHUA and from non-county area (former Indian lands)	14,600 sq mi

(Heavy line depicts historical boundary. Base map shows present-day information.)

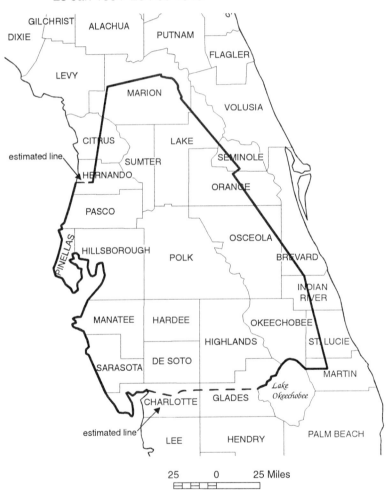

❶ HILLSBOROUGH Boundaries
25 Jan 1834–23 Feb 1843

Chronology of HILLSBOROUGH

Map	Date	Event	Resulting Area
❷	24 Feb 1843	HILLSBOROUGH lost to creation of HERNANDO	13,380 sq mi
❷	6 Mar 1844	HILLSBOROUGH lost to HERNANDO	13,290 sq mi

(Heavy line depicts historical boundary. Base map shows present-day information.)

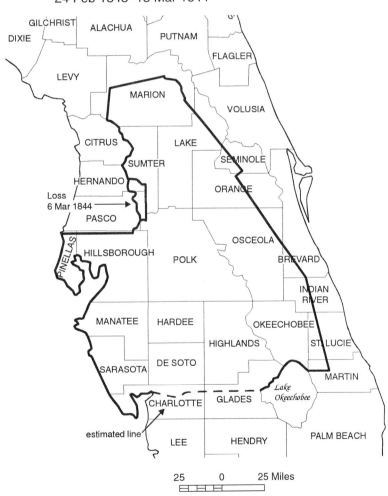

❷ HILLSBOROUGH Boundaries
24 Feb 1843–13 Mar 1844

Chronology of HILLSBOROUGH

Map	Date	Event	Resulting Area
❸	14 Mar 1844	HILLSBOROUGH lost to creation of both MARION and original ST. LUCIE (now BREVARD), and apparently lost to MOSQUITO (now ORANGE)	6,480 sq mi
❸	1 Jan 1847	HILLSBOROUGH gained from BENTON (now HERNANDO)	6,530 sq mi
❹	9 Jan 1855	HILLSBOROUGH lost to creation of MANATEE	2,900 sq mi
❺	8 Feb 1861	HILLSBOROUGH lost to creation of POLK	1,860 sq mi
❺	10 Dec 1866	HILLSBOROUGH gained small area from POLK to accommodate local resident	1,860 sq mi

(Heavy line depicts historical boundary. Base map shows present-day information.)

❸ HILLSBOROUGH Boundaries 14 Mar 1844–8 Jan 1855

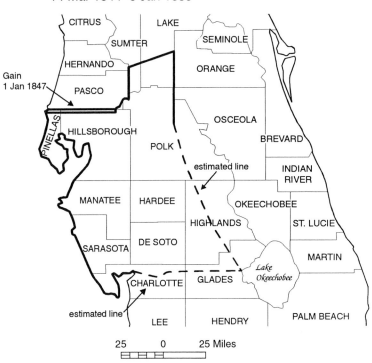

❹ HILLSBOROUGH Boundaries 9 Jan 1855–7 Feb 1861

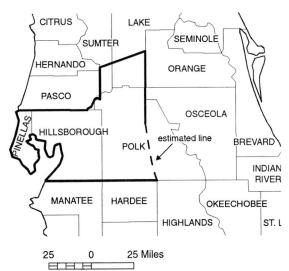

❺ HILLSBOROUGH Boundaries 8 Feb 1861–12 Dec 1866

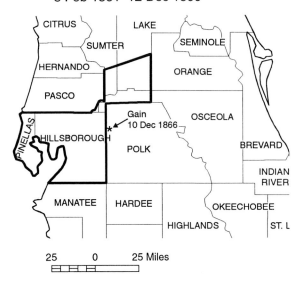

Chronology of HILLSBOROUGH

Map	Date	Event	Resulting Area
❻	13 Dec 1866	HILLSBOROUGH lost to SUMTER	1,360 sq mi

(Heavy line depicts historical boundary. Base map shows present-day information.)

❻   HILLSBOROUGH Boundaries
     13 Dec 1866–18 Feb 1874

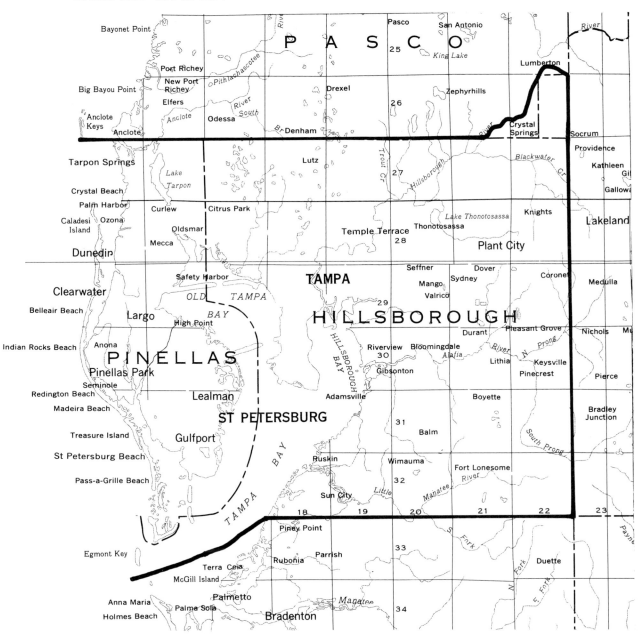

Chronology of HILLSBOROUGH

Map	Date	Event	Resulting Area
❼	19 Feb 1874	HILLSBOROUGH lost to POLK	1,330 sq mi

(Heavy line depicts historical boundary. Base map shows present-day information.)

❼ HILLSBOROUGH Boundaries
19 Feb 1874 – 13 Nov 1911

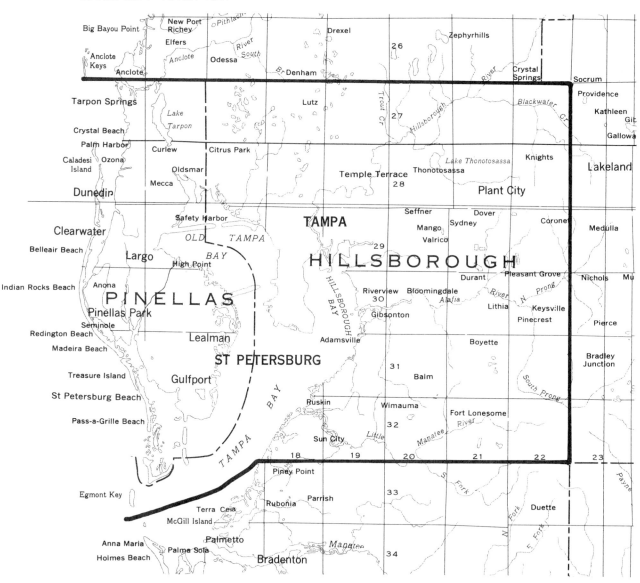

10	0	10	20	30	40 Miles

Chronology of HILLSBOROUGH

Map	Date	Event	Resulting Area
⑧	14 Nov 1911	HILLSBOROUGH lost to creation of PINELLAS	1,050 sq mi

(Heavy line depicts historical boundary. Base map shows present-day information.)

⑧ HILLSBOROUGH Boundaries
14 Nov 1911–14 May 1939

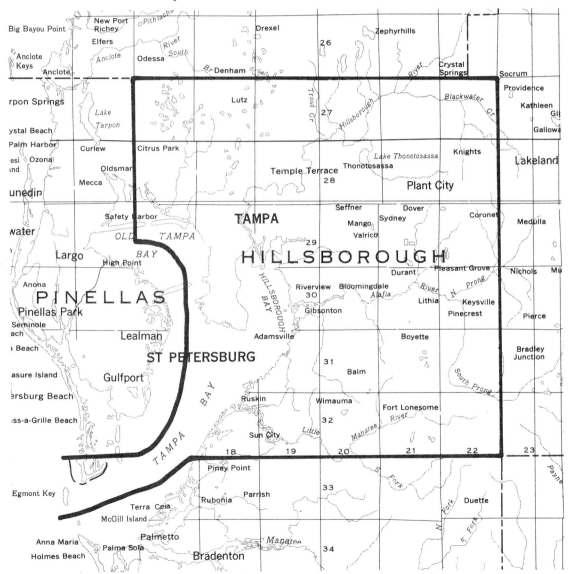

Chronology of HILLSBOROUGH

Map	Date	Event	Resulting Area
⑨	15 May 1939	HILLSBOROUGH lost small area to PINELLAS	1,050 sq mi

(Heavy line depicts historical boundary. Base map shows present-day information.)

⑨ HILLSBOROUGH Boundaries
15 May 1939–1990

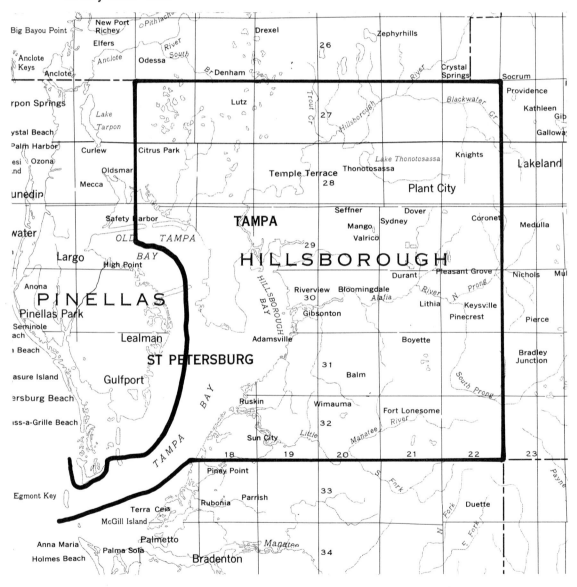

Chronology of HOLMES

Map	Date	Event	Resulting Area
❶	8 Jan 1848	HOLMES created from JACKSON and WALTON	470 sq mi
❷	8 Aug 1915	HOLMES gained from WASHINGTON	490 sq mi

(Heavy line depicts historical boundary. Base map shows present-day information.)

❶ HOLMES Boundaries
8 Jan 1848–7 Aug 1915

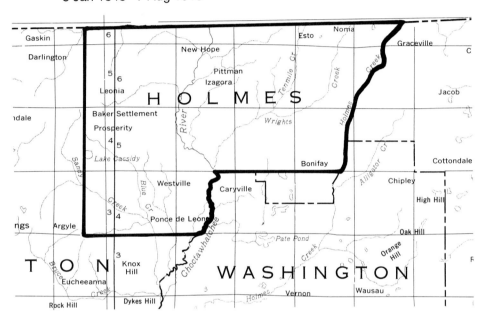

❷ HOLMES Boundaries
8 Aug 1915–1990

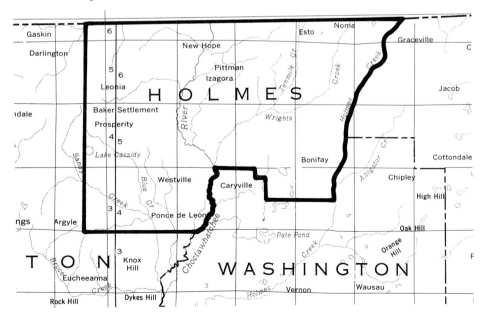

10   0   10   20   30   40 Miles

Chronology of INDIAN RIVER

Map	Date	Event	Resulting Area
❶	29 Jun 1925	INDIAN RIVER created from ST. LUCIE	500 sq mi
❶	3 Nov 1959	INDIAN RIVER gained small area from BREVARD	500 sq mi

(Heavy line depicts historical boundary. Base map shows present-day information.)

❶ INDIAN RIVER Boundaries
29 Jun 1925 – 1990

Chronology of JACKSON

Map	Date	Event	Resulting Area
❶	12 Aug 1822	JACKSON created from ESCAMBIA	11,200 sq mi
❷	24 Jun 1823	JACKSON lost to DUVAL and to creation of GADSDEN	3,890 sq mi
❸	29 Dec 1824	JACKSON gained from ESCAMBIA, lost to creation of WALTON	2,950 sq mi

(Heavy line depicts historical boundary. Base map shows present-day information.)

❶ JACKSON Boundaries
12 Aug 1822 – 23 Jun 1823

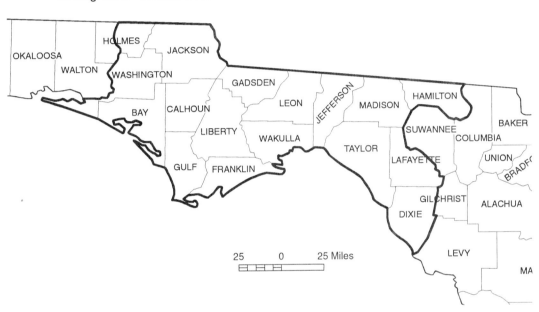

25   0   25 Miles

❷ JACKSON Boundaries
24 Jun 1823 – 28 Dec 1824

25   0   25 Miles

❸ JACKSON Boundaries
29 Dec 1824 – 8 Dec 1825

25   0   25 Miles

Chronology of JACKSON

Map	Date	Event	Resulting Area
❹	9 Dec 1825	JACKSON exchanged with WALTON, lost to creation of WASHINGTON	1,450 sq mi

(Heavy line depicts historical boundary. Base map shows present-day information.)

❹ JACKSON Boundaries
9 Dec 1825 – 11 Jan 1827

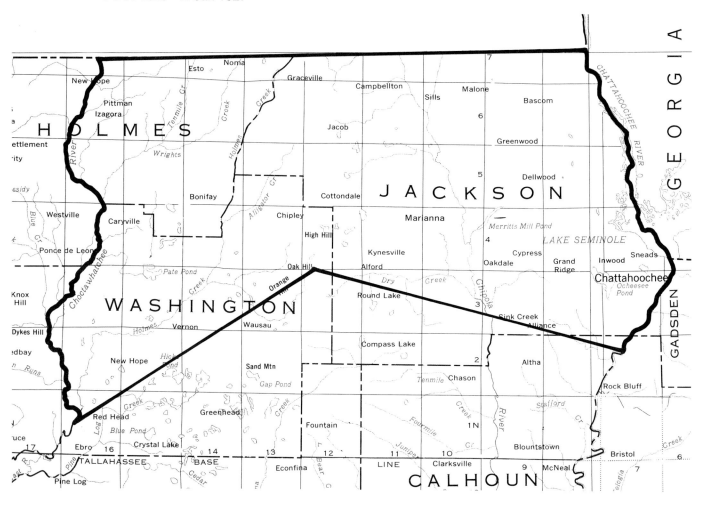

Chronology of JACKSON

Map	Date	Event	Resulting Area
❺	12 Jan 1827	JACKSON exchanged with WASHINGTON	1,100 sq mi

(Heavy line depicts historical boundary. Base map shows present-day information.)

❺ JACKSON Boundaries
12 Jan 1827–28 Oct 1828

Chronology of JACKSON

Map	Date	Event	Resulting Area
❻	29 Oct 1828	JACKSON exchanged with WASHINGTON	1,270 sq mi

(Heavy line depicts historical boundary. Base map shows present-day information.)

❻ JACKSON Boundaries
29 Oct 1828 – 8 Feb 1832

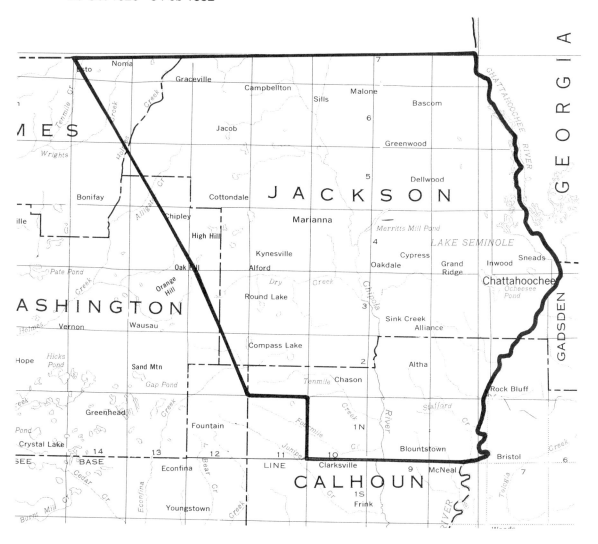

Chronology of JACKSON

Map	Date	Event	Resulting Area
❼	9 Feb 1832	JACKSON lost to creation of FAYETTE	630 sq mi

(Heavy line depicts historical boundary. Base map shows present-day information.)

❼ JACKSON Boundaries
9 Feb 1832 – 10 Feb 1832

| 10 | 0 | 10 | 20 | 30 | 40 Miles |

Chronology of JACKSON

Map	Date	Event	Resulting Area
❽	11 Feb 1832	JACKSON exchanged with WASHINGTON	770 sq mi

(Heavy line depicts historical boundary. Base map shows present-day information.)

❽ JACKSON Boundaries
11 Feb 1832 – 15 Feb 1833

Chronology of JACKSON

Map	Date	Event	Resulting Area
⑨	16 Feb 1833	JACKSON gained from FAYETTE and WASHINGTON	1,330 sq mi

(Heavy line depicts historical boundary. Base map shows present-day information.)

⑨ JACKSON Boundaries
   16 Feb 1833 – 31 Jan 1834

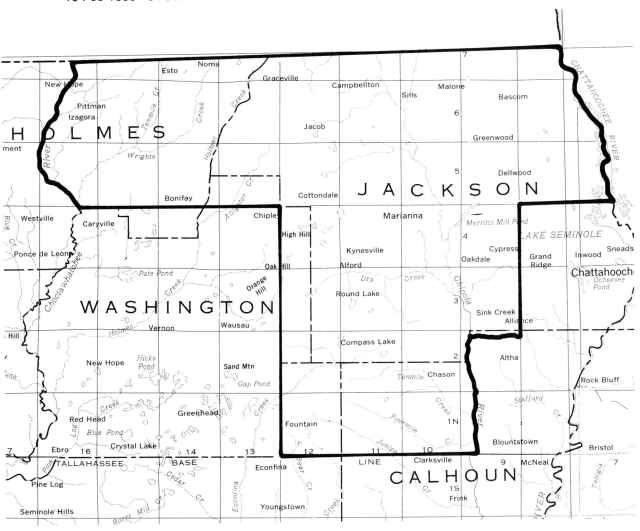

Chronology of JACKSON

Map	Date	Event	Resulting Area
⑩	1 Feb 1834	JACKSON gained all of FAYETTE; FAYETTE eliminated	1,700 sq mi

(Heavy line depicts historical boundary. Base map shows present-day information.)

⑩ JACKSON Boundaries
1 Feb 1834 – 25 Jan 1838

Chronology of JACKSON

Map	Date	Event	Resulting Area
⑪	26 Jan 1838	JACKSON lost to creation of CALHOUN	1,580 sq mi

(Heavy line depicts historical boundary. Base map shows present-day information.)

⑪   JACKSON Boundaries
26 Jan 1838 – 9 Mar 1845

10   0   10   20   30   40 Miles

Chronology of JACKSON

Map	Date	Event	Resulting Area
⑫	10 Mar 1845	JACKSON lost to CALHOUN	1,240 sq mi

(Heavy line depicts historical boundary. Base map shows present-day information.)

⑫ JACKSON Boundaries
10 Mar 1845 – 3 Jan 1847

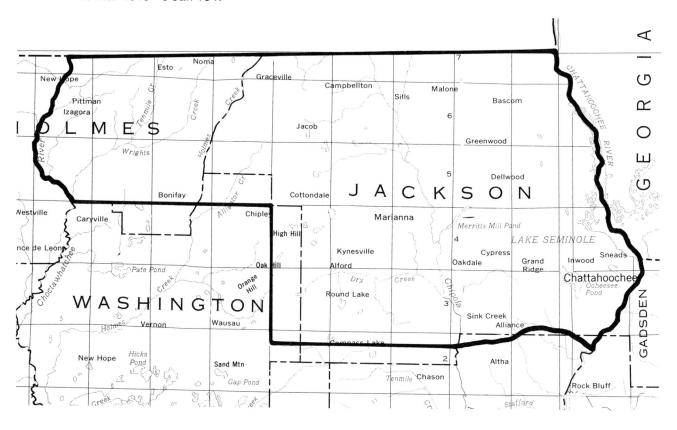

Chronology of JACKSON

Map	Date	Event	Resulting Area
⑬	4 Jan 1847	JACKSON lost to WASHINGTON	1,110 sq mi

(Heavy line depicts historical boundary. Base map shows present-day information.)

⑬ JACKSON Boundaries
4 Jan 1847–27 Dec 1847

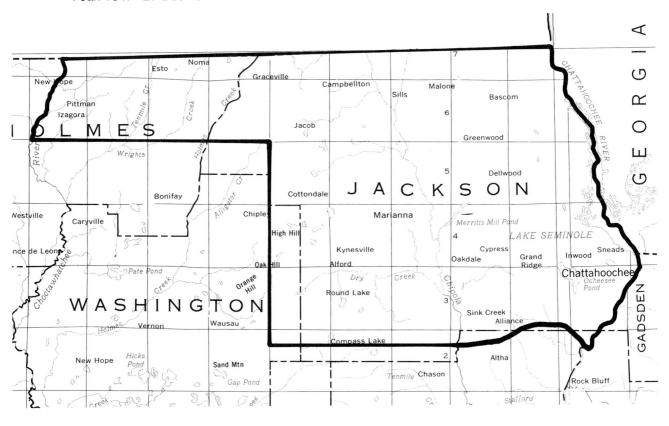

Chronology of JACKSON

Map	Date	Event	Resulting Area
⑭	28 Dec 1847	JACKSON exchanged with WASHINGTON	1,200 sq mi

(Heavy line depicts historical boundary. Base map shows present-day information.)

⑭ JACKSON Boundaries
28 Dec 1847–7 Jan 1848

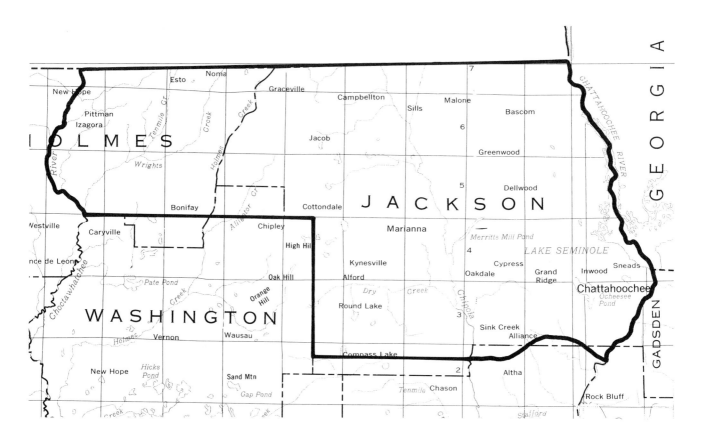

Chronology of JACKSON

Map	Date	Event	Resulting Area
⑮	8 Jan 1848	JACKSON lost to creation of HOLMES	950 sq mi

(Heavy line depicts historical boundary. Base map shows present-day information.)

⑮   JACKSON Boundaries
8 Jan 1848 – 13 Feb 1873
Feb 1875 – 30 May 1897

Chronology of JACKSON

Map	Date	Event	Resulting Area
⑯	14 Feb 1873	JACKSON gained from CALHOUN	1,020 sq mi
⑮	Feb 1875	JACKSON lost to CALHOUN	950 sq mi

(Heavy line depicts historical boundary. Base map shows present-day information.)

⑯ JACKSON Boundaries
14 Feb 1873–Feb 1875

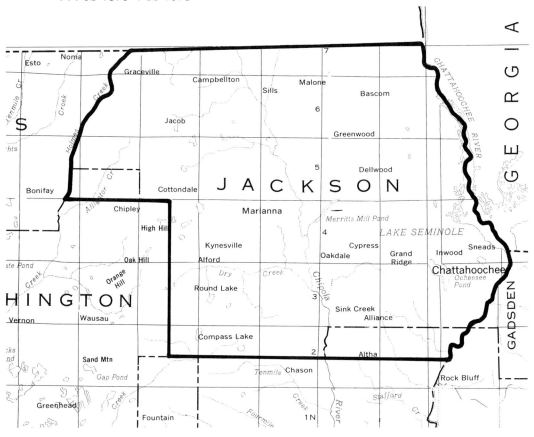

10	0	10	20	30	40 Miles

Chronology of JACKSON

Map	Date	Event	Resulting Area
⑰	31 May 1897	JACKSON exchanged with CALHOUN	980 sq mi

(Heavy line depicts historical boundary. Base map shows present-day information.)

⑰ JACKSON Boundaries
31 May 1897–7 Aug 1915

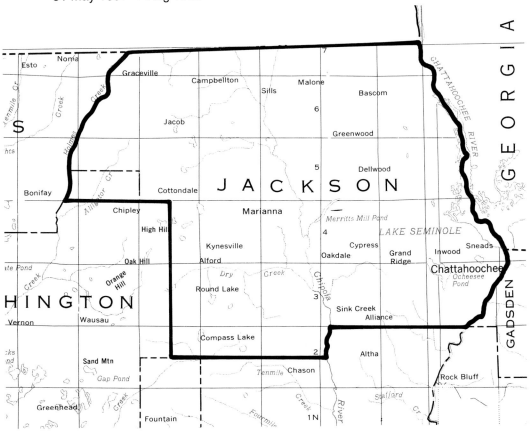

10   0   10   20   30   40 Miles

Chronology of JACKSON

Map	Date	Event	Resulting Area
⑱	8 Aug 1915	JACKSON lost to WASHINGTON	960 sq mi

(Heavy line depicts historical boundary. Base map shows present-day information.)

⑱ JACKSON Boundaries
8 Aug 1915–1990

10   0   10   20   30   40 Miles

Chronology of JEFFERSON

Map	Date	Event	Resulting Area
❶	20 Jan 1827	JEFFERSON created from LEON	4,150 sq mi
❷	26 Dec 1827	JEFFERSON lost to creation of both HAMILTON and MADISON	680 sq mi

(Heavy line depicts historical boundary. Base map shows present-day information.)

❶ JEFFERSON Boundaries
20 Jan 1827– 25 Dec 1827

25   0   25 Miles

❷ JEFFERSON Boundaries
26 Dec 1827–18 Jan 1828

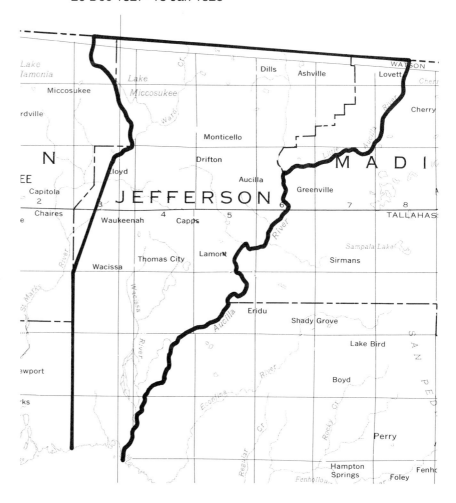

10   0   10   20   30   40 Miles

Chronology of JEFFERSON

Map	Date	Event	Resulting Area
❸	19 Jan 1828	JEFFERSON lost to LEON	670 sq mi

(Heavy line depicts historical boundary. Base map shows present-day information.)

❸ JEFFERSON Boundaries
19 Jan 1828–13 Nov 1829
13 Feb 1831–29 Jan 1832

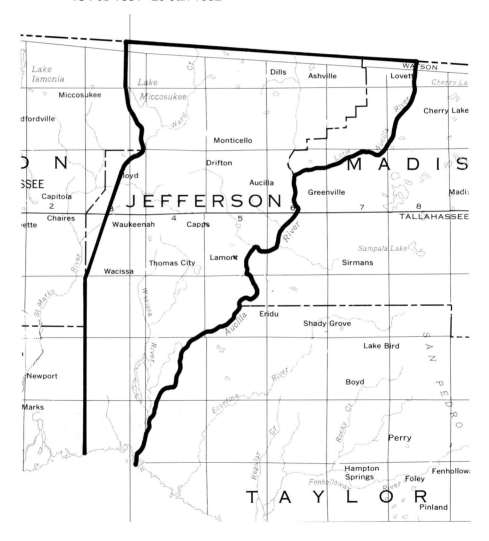

Chronology of JEFFERSON

Map	Date	Event	Resulting Area
❹	14 Nov 1829	JEFFERSON gained from LEON	790 sq mi
❸	13 Feb 1831	JEFFERSON lost to LEON	670 sq mi

(Heavy line depicts historical boundary. Base map shows present-day information.)

❹ JEFFERSON Boundaries
14 Nov 1829 – 12 Feb 1831

| 10 | 0 | 10 | 20 | 30 | 40 Miles |

Chronology of JEFFERSON

Map	Date	Event	Resulting Area
❺	30 Jan 1832	JEFFERSON gained from LEON	680 sq mi

(Heavy line depicts historical boundary. Base map shows present-day information.)

❺ JEFFERSON Boundaries
30 Jan 1832 – 8 Feb 1833

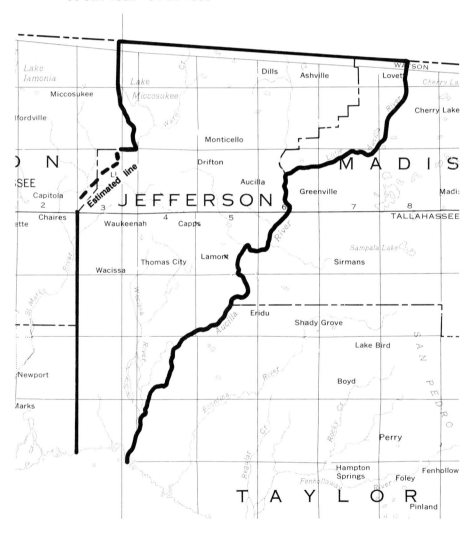

10   0   10   20   30   40 Miles

Chronology of JEFFERSON

Map	Date	Event	Resulting Area
❻	9 Feb 1833	JEFFERSON lost to MADISON	630 sq mi

(Heavy line depicts historical boundary. Base map shows present-day information.)

❻ JEFFERSON Boundaries
9 Feb 1833 – 21 Feb 1843

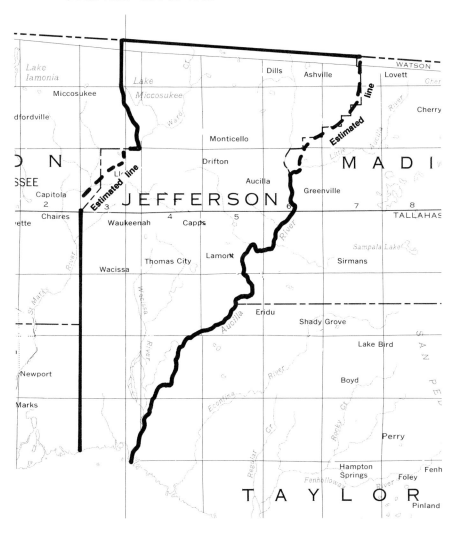

Chronology of JEFFERSON

Map	Date	Event	Resulting Area
❼	22 Feb 1843	JEFFERSON gained from MADISON	630 sq mi

(Heavy line depicts historical boundary. Base map shows present-day information.)

❼ JEFFERSON Boundaries
22 Feb 1843 – 4 Feb 1844

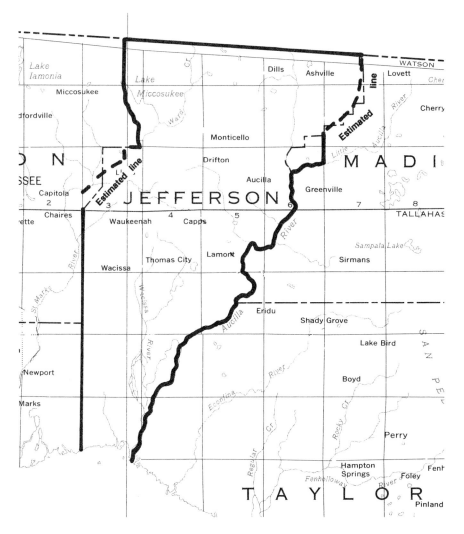

Chronology of JEFFERSON

Map	Date	Event	Resulting Area
⑧	5 Feb 1844	JEFFERSON lost to MADISON	620 sq mi

(Heavy line depicts historical boundary. Base map shows present-day information.)

⑧   JEFFERSON Boundaries
5 Feb 1844 – 10 Mar 1879

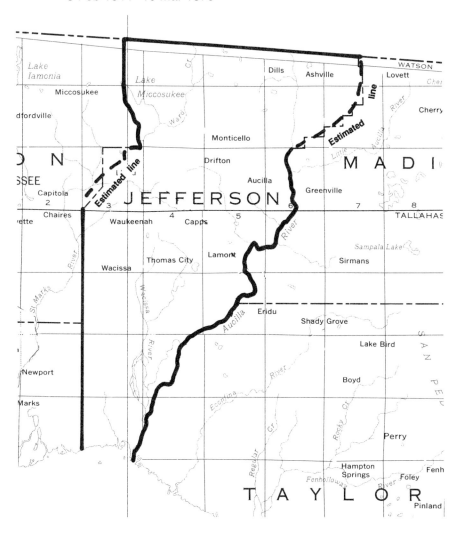

Chronology of JEFFERSON

Map	Date	Event	Resulting Area
❾	11 Mar 1879	JEFFERSON lost to LEON	610 sq mi

(Heavy line depicts historical boundary. Base map shows present-day information.)

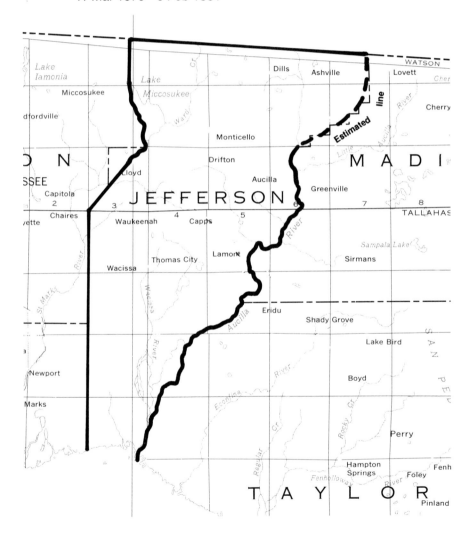

❾ JEFFERSON Boundaries
11 Mar 1879 – 6 Feb 1881

10   0   10   20   30   40 Miles

Chronology of JEFFERSON

Map	Date	Event	Resulting Area
⑩	7 Feb 1881	JEFFERSON gained from LEON	620 sq mi

(Heavy line depicts historical boundary. Base map shows present-day information.)

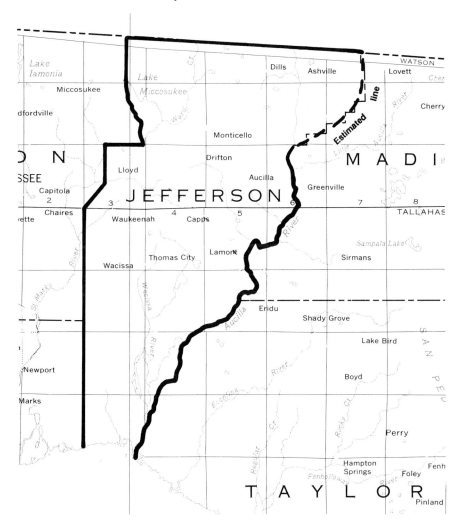

⑩ JEFFERSON Boundaries
7 Feb 1881–c. May 1923

10   0   10   20   30   40 Miles

Chronology of JEFFERSON

Map	Date	Event	Resulting Area
⑪	c. May 1923	JEFFERSON exchanged with MADISON	620 sq mi

(Heavy line depicts historical boundary. Base map shows present-day information.)

⑪ JEFFERSON Boundaries
c. May 1923–1990

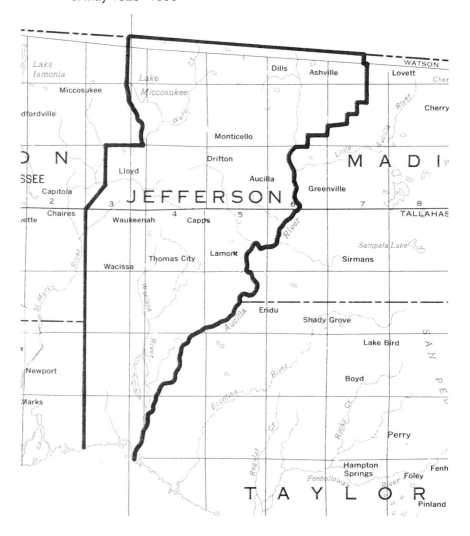

| 10 | 0 | 10 | 20 | 30 | 40 Miles |

Chronology of LAFAYETTE

Map	Date	Event	Resulting Area
❶	23 Dec 1856	LAFAYETTE created from MADISON	1,060 sq mi

(Heavy line depicts historical boundary. Base map shows present-day information.)

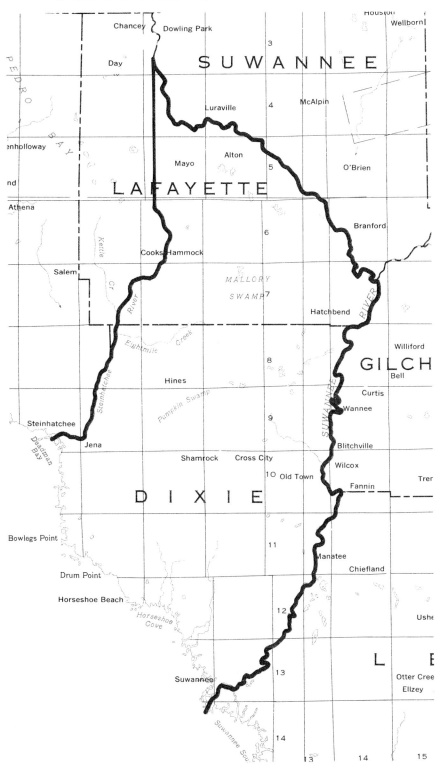

❶ LAFAYETTE Boundaries
23 Dec 1856 – 20 Dec 1858

10   0   10   20   30   40 Miles

Chronology of LAFAYETTE

Map	Date	Event	Resulting Area
❷	21 Dec 1858	LAFAYETTE gained from TAYLOR	1,280 sq mi

(Heavy line depicts historical boundary. Base map shows present-day information.)

❷ LAFAYETTE Boundaries
21 Dec 1858 – 12 Feb 1877
31 Jan 1883 – 27 May 1887

Chronology of LAFAYETTE

Map	Date	Event	Resulting Area
❸	13 Feb 1877	LAFAYETTE lost to TAYLOR	1,240 sq mi
❷	31 Jan 1883	LAFAYETTE gained from TAYLOR [mistake in description corrected 12 Feb 1885]	1,280 sq mi
	12 Feb 1885	Boundary between LAFAYETTE and TAYLOR redefined, correcting mistake of 31 Jan 1883 [no change]	
❸	28 May 1887	LAFAYETTE lost to TAYLOR	1,240 sq mi

(Heavy line depicts historical boundary. Base map shows present-day information.)

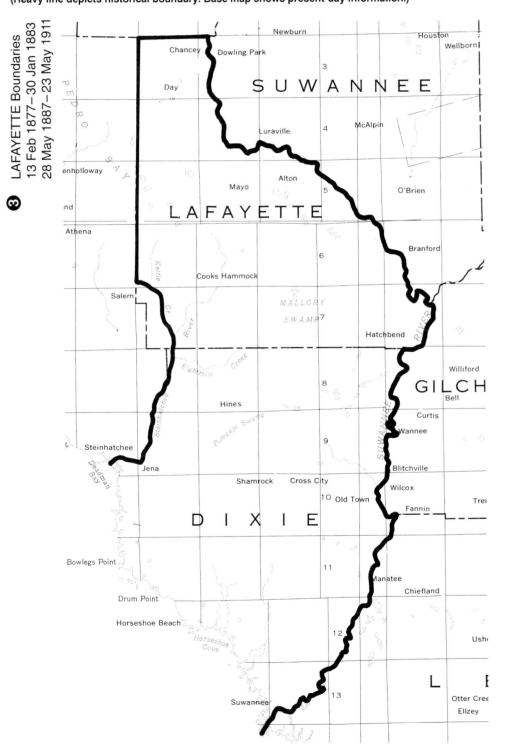

LAFAYETTE Boundaries
13 Feb 1877–30 Jan 1883
28 May 1887–23 May 1911

❸

Chronology of LAFAYETTE

Map	Date	Event	Resulting Area
❹	24 May 1911	LAFAYETTE gained from TAYLOR	1,260 sq mi

(Heavy line depicts historical boundary. Base map shows present-day information.)

❹ LAFAYETTE Boundaries
24 May 1911–24 Apr 1921

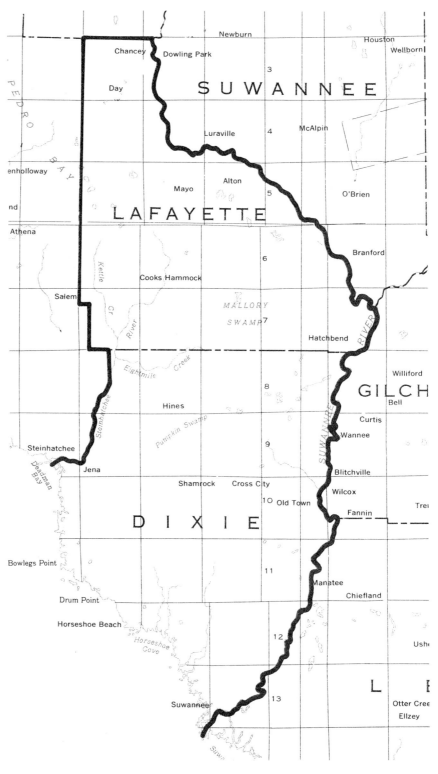

10   0   10   20   30   40 Miles

Chronology of LAFAYETTE

Map	Date	Event	Resulting Area
⑤	25 Apr 1921	LAFAYETTE lost to creation of DIXIE	560 sq mi

(Heavy line depicts historical boundary. Base map shows present-day information.)

⑤ LAFAYETTE Boundaries
25 Apr 1921–1990

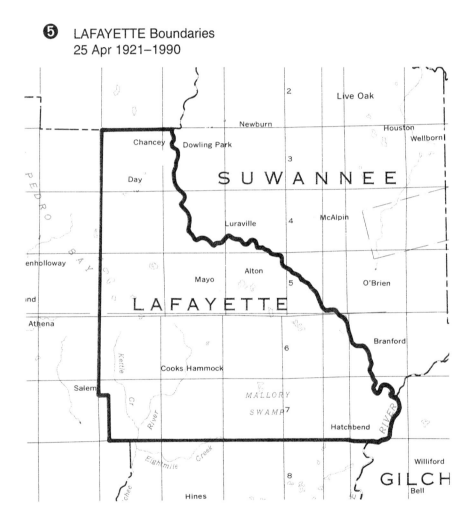

Chronology of LAKE

Map	Date	Event	Resulting Area
❶	26 Jul 1887	LAKE created from ORANGE and SUMTER	950 sq mi
❶	31 May 1889	LAKE gained small area from ORANGE	950 sq mi

(Heavy line depicts historical boundary. Base map shows present-day information.)

❶   LAKE Boundaries
26 Jul 1887– 9 Jun 1891

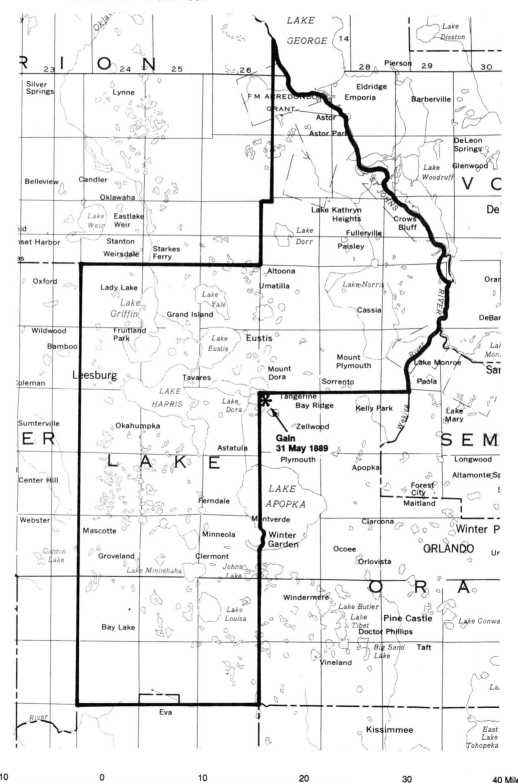

Chronology of LAKE

Map	Date	Event	Resulting Area
❷	10 Jun 1891	LAKE lost small area to POLK	950 sq mi

(Heavy line depicts historical boundary. Base map shows present-day information.)

❷   LAKE Boundaries
10 Jun 1891–1990

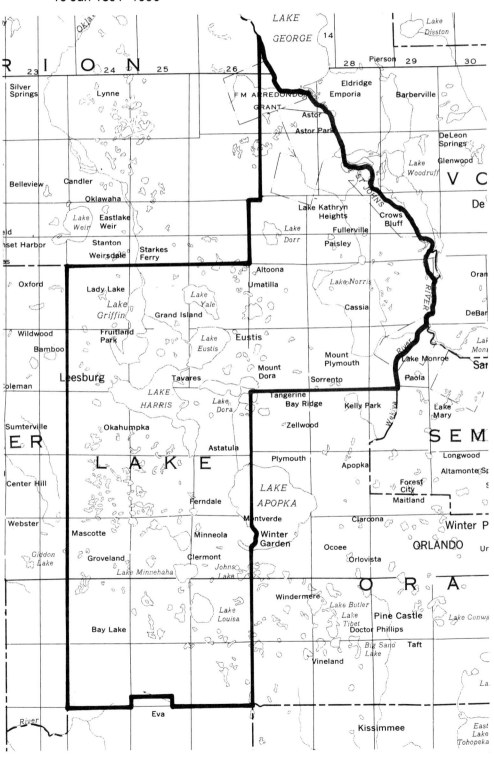

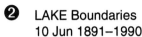

10   0   10   20   30   40 Miles

Chronology of LEE

Map	Date	Event	Resulting Area
❶	13 May 1887	LEE created from MONROE	3,960 sq mi
❷	7 Jul 1923	LEE lost to creation of COLLIER	1,960 sq mi
❸	10 Jul 1923	LEE lost to creation of HENDRY	800 sq mi

(Heavy line depicts historical boundary. Base map shows present-day information.)

❶ LEE Boundaries
13 May 1887 – 6 Jul 1923

❷ LEE Boundaries
7 Jul 1923 – 9 Jul 1923

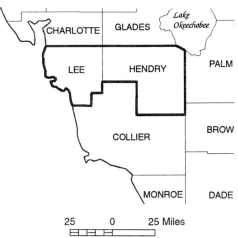

❸ LEE Boundaries
10 Jul 1923 – 1990

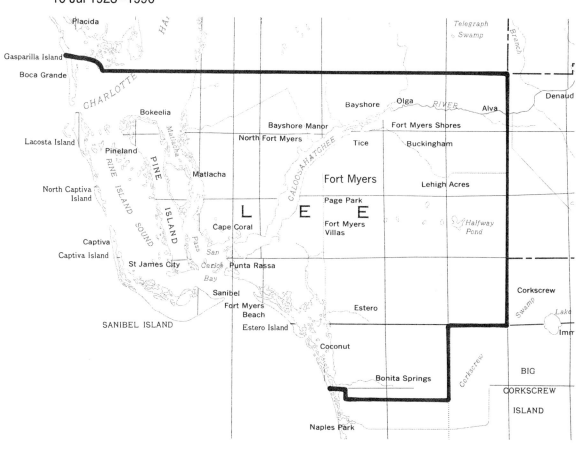

Chronology of LEON

Map	Date	Event	Resulting Area
❶	29 Dec 1824	LEON created from DUVAL and GADSDEN	5,400 sq mi

(Heavy line depicts historical boundary. Base map shows present-day information.)

❶ LEON Boundaries
29 Dec 1824–19 Jan 1827

25   0   25 Miles

Chronology of LEON

Map	Date	Event	Resulting Area
❷	20 Jan 1827	LEON lost to creation of JEFFERSON	1,270 sq mi

(Heavy line depicts historical boundary. Base map shows present-day information.)

❷ LEON Boundaries
20 Jan 1827–18 Jan 1828

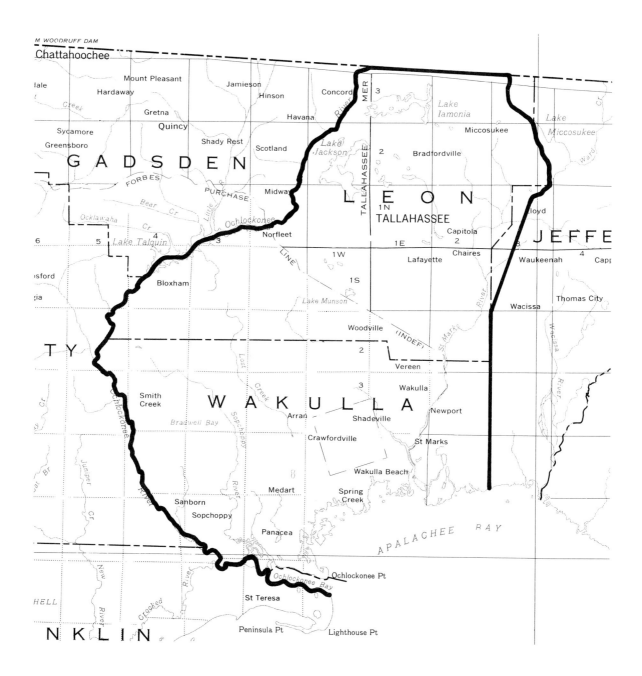

Chronology of LEON

Map	Date	Event	Resulting Area
❸	19 Jan 1828	LEON gained from JEFFERSON	1,280 sq mi

(Heavy line depicts historical boundary. Base map shows present-day information.)

❸ LEON Boundaries
19 Jan 1828–13 Nov 1829
13 Feb 1831–29 Jan 1832

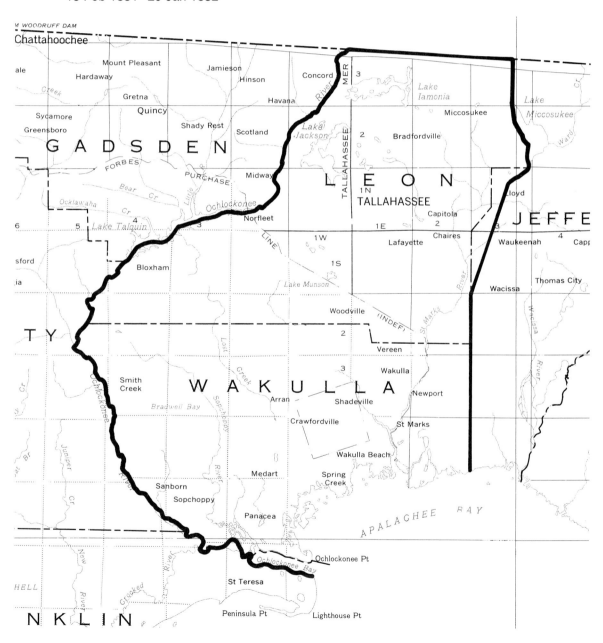

Chronology of LEON

Map	Date	Event	Resulting Area
❹	14 Nov 1829	LEON lost to JEFFERSON	1,160 sq mi
❸	13 Feb 1831	LEON gained from JEFFERSON	1,280 sq mi

(Heavy line depicts historical boundary. Base map shows present-day information.)

❹ LEON Boundaries
14 Nov 1829 – 12 Feb 1831

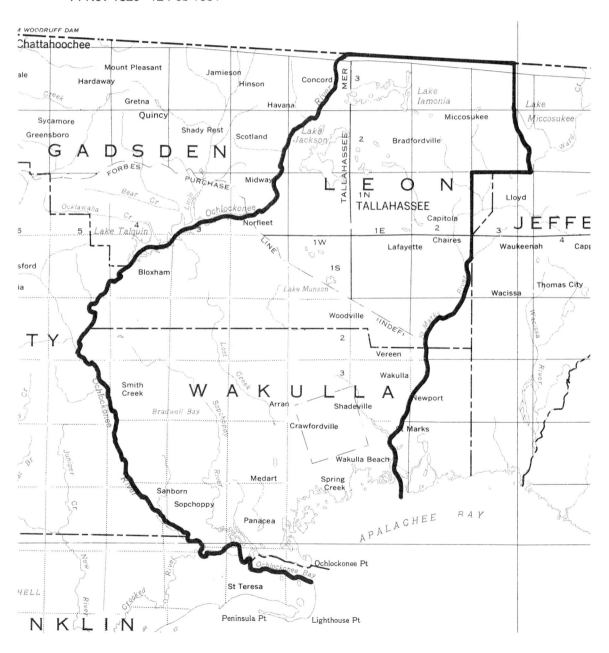

Chronology of LEON

Map	Date	Event	Resulting Area
⑤	30 Jan 1832	LEON lost to JEFFERSON	1,270 sq mi

(Heavy line depicts historical boundary. Base map shows present-day information.)

⑤ LEON Boundaries
30 Jan 1832 – 10 Mar 1843

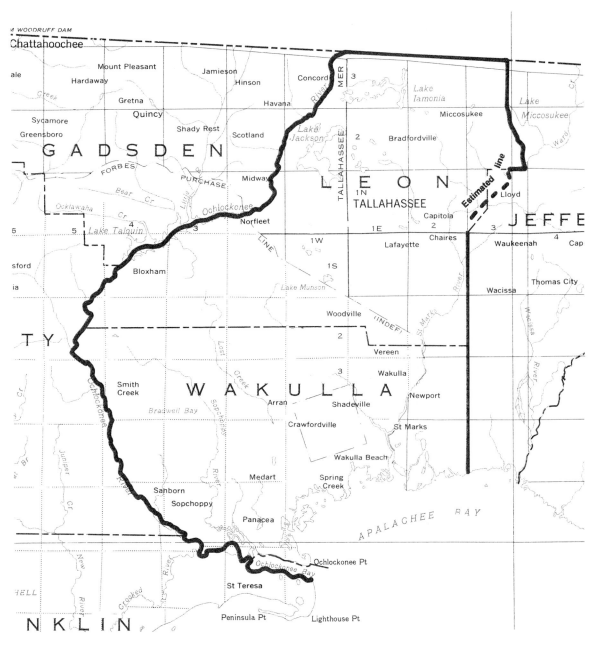

Chronology of LEON

Map	Date	Event	Resulting Area
❻	11 Mar 1843	LEON lost to creation of WAKULLA	730 sq mi
❼	6 Jan 1849	LEON lost to WAKULLA	730 sq mi

(Heavy line depicts historical boundary. Base map shows present-day information.)

❻ LEON Boundaries
11 Mar 1843 – 5 Jan 1849

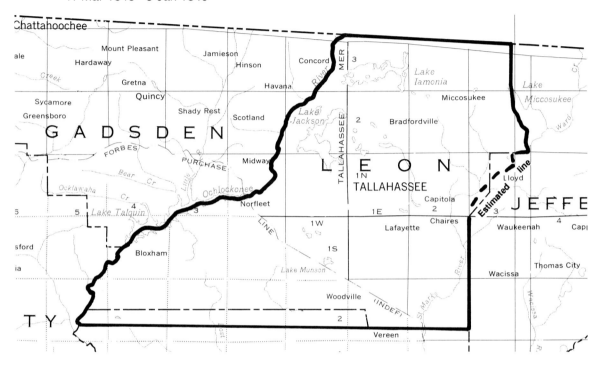

❼ LEON Boundaries
6 Jan 1849 – 21 Jan 1851

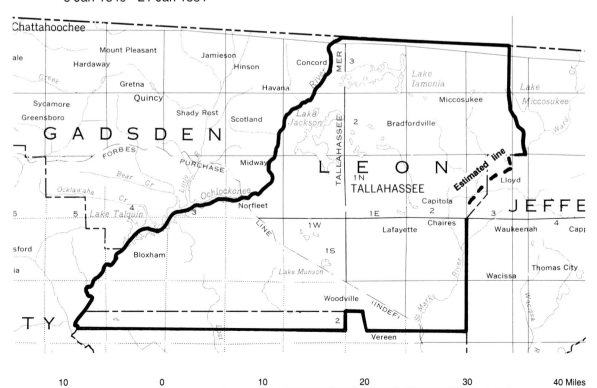

| 10 | 0 | 10 | 20 | 30 | 40 Miles |

Chronology of LEON

Map	Date	Event	Resulting Area
⑧	22 Jan 1851	LEON lost to WAKULLA	680 sq mi
⑨	11 Mar 1879	LEON gained from JEFFERSON	690 sq mi

(Heavy line depicts historical boundary. Base map shows present-day information.)

⑧ LEON Boundaries
22 Jan 1851–10 Mar 1879

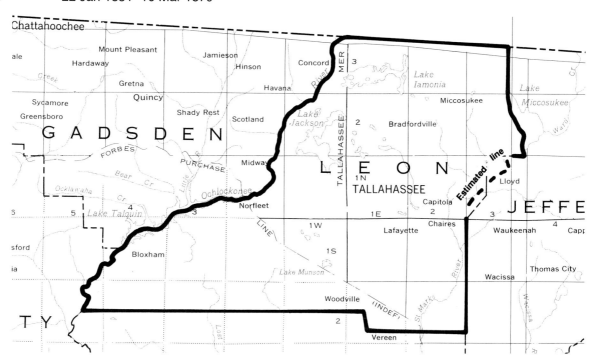

⑨ LEON Boundaries
11 Mar 1879–6 Feb 1881

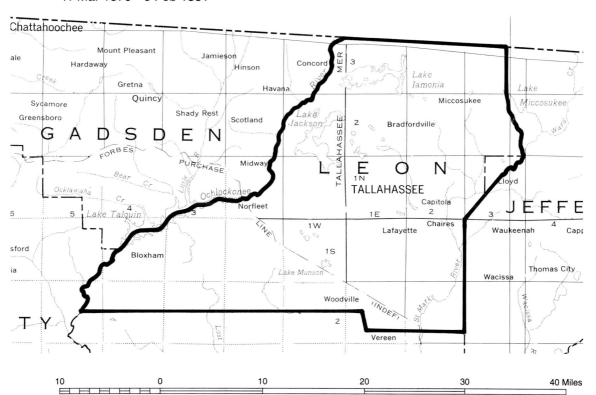

10	0	10	20	30	40 Miles

Chronology of LEON

Map	Date	Event	Resulting Area
⑩	7 Feb 1881	LEON lost to JEFFERSON	680 sq mi
	4 May 1933	LEON lost to GADSDEN when boundary shifted from west bank to middle of the Ochlockonee R. [not mapped]	

(Heavy line depicts historical boundary. Base map shows present-day information.)

⑩ LEON Boundaries
7 Feb 1881–1990

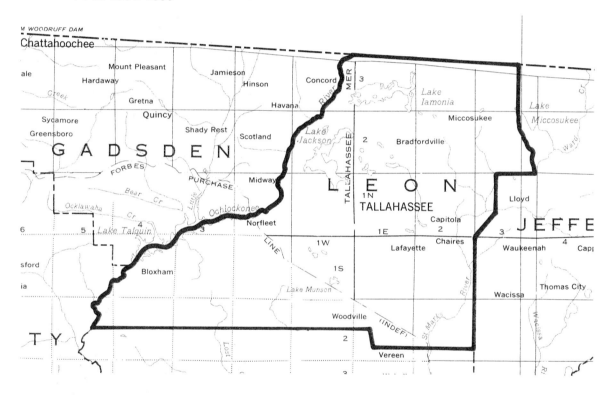

Chronology of LEVY

Map	Date	Event	Resulting Area
❶	10 Mar 1845	LEVY created from ALACHUA	920 sq mi

(Heavy line depicts historical boundary. Base map shows present-day information.)

❶ LEVY Boundaries
10 Mar 1845 – 5 Feb 1877

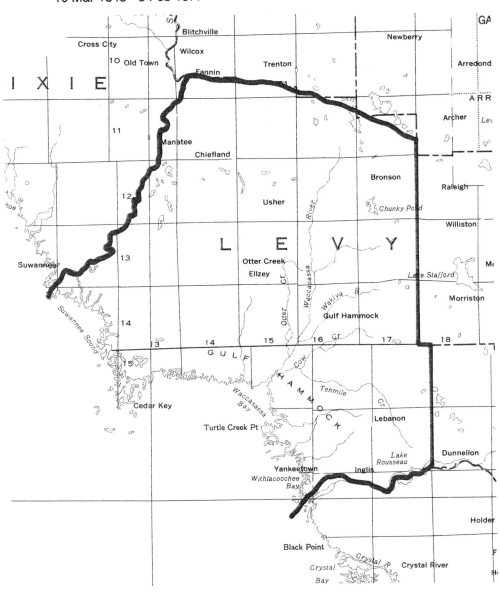

Chronology of LEVY

Map	Date	Event	Resulting Area
❷	6 Feb 1877	LEVY gained from MARION	1,090 sq mi

(Heavy line depicts historical boundary. Base map shows present-day information.)

❷ LEVY Boundaries
6 Feb 1877–2 Jun 1911

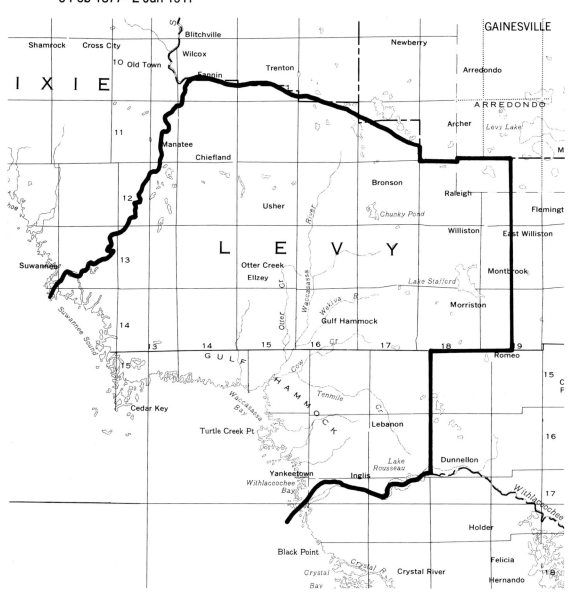

Chronology of LEVY

Map	Date	Event	Resulting Area
❸	3 Jun 1911	LEVY exchanged with ALACHUA	1,100 sq mi
❸	7 Jun 1913	LEVY gained small area from ALACHUA	1,100 sq mi
	1 Jun 1915	Legislature authorized creation of BLOXHAM from LEVY and MARION, dependent on local referendum that failed [no change; see BLOXHAM, map 1]	
	4 Jun 1925	LEVY gained small area from DIXIE when the boundary shifted from east bank to middle of the Suwannee R. [not mapped]	

(Heavy line depicts historical boundary. Base map shows present-day information.)

❸   LEVY Boundaries
3 Jun 1911–1990

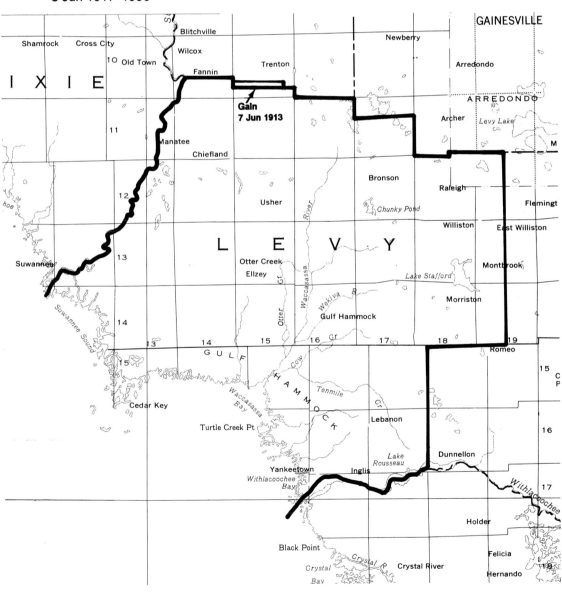

Chronology of LIBERTY

Map	Date	Event	Resulting Area
❶	15 Dec 1855	LIBERTY created from GADSDEN [mistake in description corrected 5 Jan 1859]	870 sq mi
	5 Jan 1859	LIBERTY boundaries clarified, correcting mistake of 15 Dec 1855 [no change]	

(Heavy line depicts historical boundary. Base map shows present-day information.)

❶ LIBERTY Boundaries
15 Dec 1855 – 21 Dec 1859

10   0   10   20   30   40 Miles

Chronology of LIBERTY

Map	Date	Event	Resulting Area
❷	22 Dec 1859	LIBERTY exchanged with GADSDEN	850 sq mi
❷	16 Feb 1885	LIBERTY lost narrow strip of territory all along boundary with FRANKLIN	850 sq mi

(Heavy line depicts historical boundary. Base map shows present-day information.)

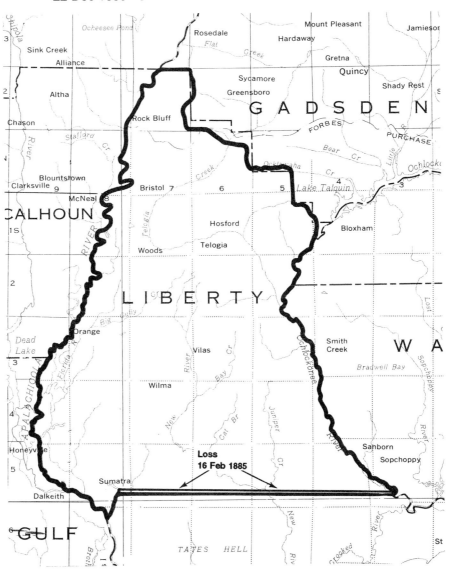

❷ LIBERTY Boundaries
22 Dec 1859 – 31 Dec 1909

Loss
16 Feb 1885

10   0   10   20   30   40 Miles

Map	Date	Event	Resulting Area
❸	1 Jan 1910	LIBERTY exchanged with GADSDEN	860 sq mi

(Heavy line depicts historical boundary. Base map shows present-day information.)

❸ LIBERTY Boundaries
1 Jan 1910 – 1990

Chronology of MADISON

Map	Date	Event	Resulting Area
❶	26 Dec 1827	MADISON created from JEFFERSON	3,000 sq mi
❶	9 Feb 1833	MADISON gained from JEFFERSON [see also JEFFERSON, map 6]	3,050 sq mi
	22 Feb 1843	MADISON lost to JEFFERSON [not mapped; see JEFFERSON, map 7]	
	5 Feb 1844	MADISON gained from JEFFERSON [not mapped; see JEFFERSON, map 8]	
❷	23 Dec 1856	MADISON lost to creation of both LAFAYETTE and TAYLOR	710 sq mi

(Heavy line depicts historical boundary. Base map shows present-day information.)

❶ MADISON Boundaries
26 Dec 1827–22 Dec 1856

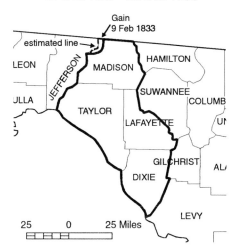

❷ MADISON Boundaries
23 Dec 1856–c. May 1923

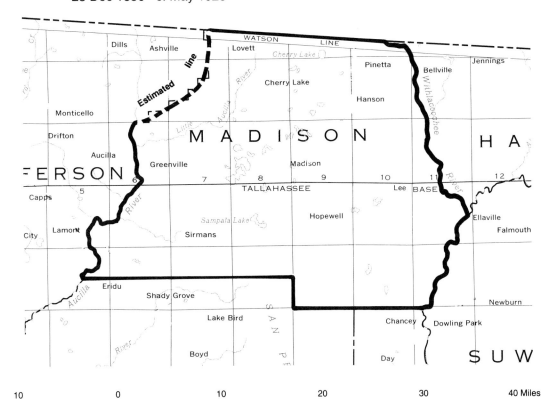

Chronology of MADISON

Map	Date	Event	Resulting Area
❸	c. May 1923	MADISON exchanged with JEFFERSON	710 sq mi

(Heavy line depicts historical boundary. Base map shows present-day information.)

❸ MADISON Boundaries
c. May 1923–1990

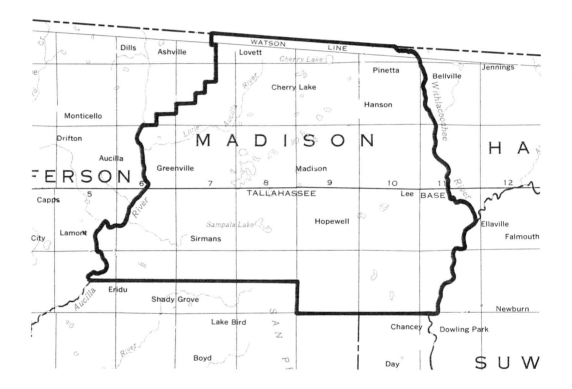

10	0	10	20	30		40 Miles

Chronology of MANATEE

Map	Date	Event	Resulting Area
❶	9 Jan 1855	MANATEE created from HILLSBOROUGH	3,630 sq mi
❷	13 Jan 1859	MANATEE gained from MONROE, exchanged with BREVARD	4,540 sq mi
❸	19 Feb 1874	MANATEE gained from BREVARD, exchanged with MONROE	5,500 sq mi
❹	21 Feb 1877	MANATEE exchanged with MONROE	5,080 sq mi

(Heavy line depicts historical boundary. Base map shows present-day information.)

❶ MANATEE Boundaries
9 Jan 1855–12 Jan 1859

❷ MANATEE Boundaries
13 Jan 1859–18 Feb 1874

❸ MANATEE Boundaries
19 Feb 1874–20 Feb 1877

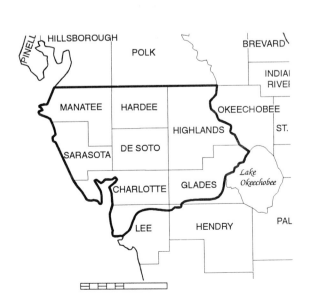

❹ MANATEE Boundaries
21 Feb 1877–18 May 1887

Chronology of MANATEE

Map	Date	Event	Resulting Area
❺	19 May 1887	MANATEE lost to creation of DE SOTO	1,320 sq mi

(Heavy line depicts historical boundary. Base map shows present-day information.)

❺ MANATEE Boundaries
19 May 1887–14 Jun 1921

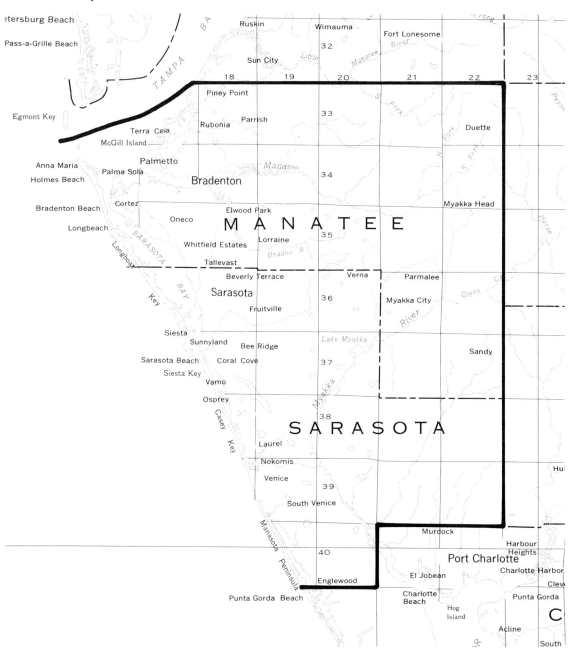

10   0   10   20   30   40 Miles

Chronology of MANATEE

Map	Date	Event	Resulting Area
❻	15 Jun 1921	MANATEE lost to creation of SARASOTA	750 sq mi

(Heavy line depicts historical boundary. Base map shows present-day information.)

❻ MANATEE Boundaries
15 Jun 1921–1990

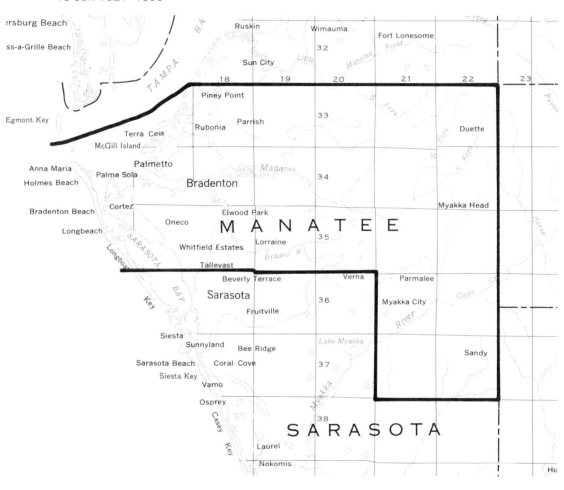

Chronology of MARION

Map	Date	Event	Resulting Area
❶	14 Mar 1844	MARION created from ALACHUA, HILLSBOROUGH, MOSQUITO (now ORANGE), and ST. JOHNS	2,720 sq mi

(Heavy line depicts historical boundary. Base map shows present-day information.)

❶ MARION Boundaries
14 Mar 1844 – 24 Dec 1846

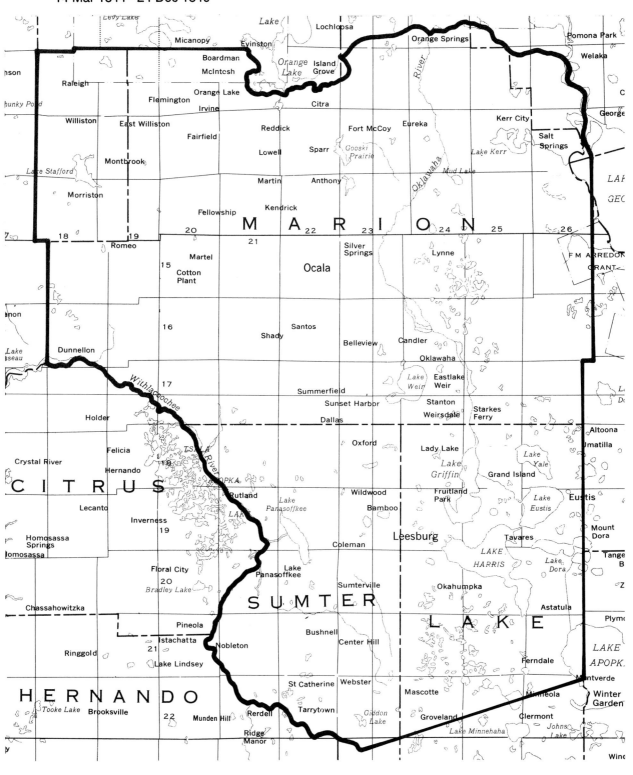

Chronology of MARION

Map	Date	Event	Resulting Area
❷	25 Dec 1846	MARION lost to ORANGE and ST. JOHNS along the St. Johns R. and Lake George	2,720 sq mi

(Heavy line depicts historical boundary. Base map shows present-day information.)

❷ MARION Boundaries
25 Dec 1846 – 29 Dec 1848

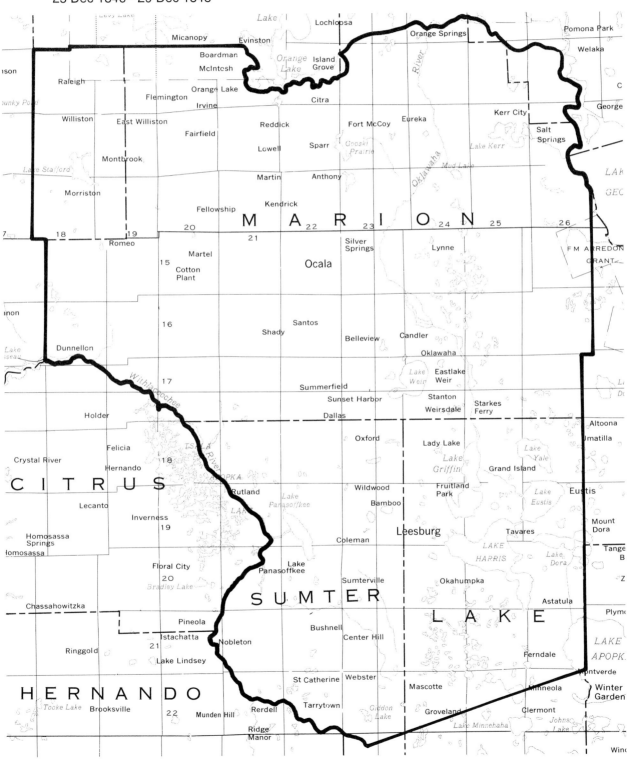

Chronology of MARION

Map	Date	Event	Resulting Area
❸	30 Dec 1848	MARION lost to ST. JOHNS	2,700 sq mi

(Heavy line depicts historical boundary. Base map shows present-day information.)

❸ MARION Boundaries
30 Dec 1848 – 7 Jan 1853

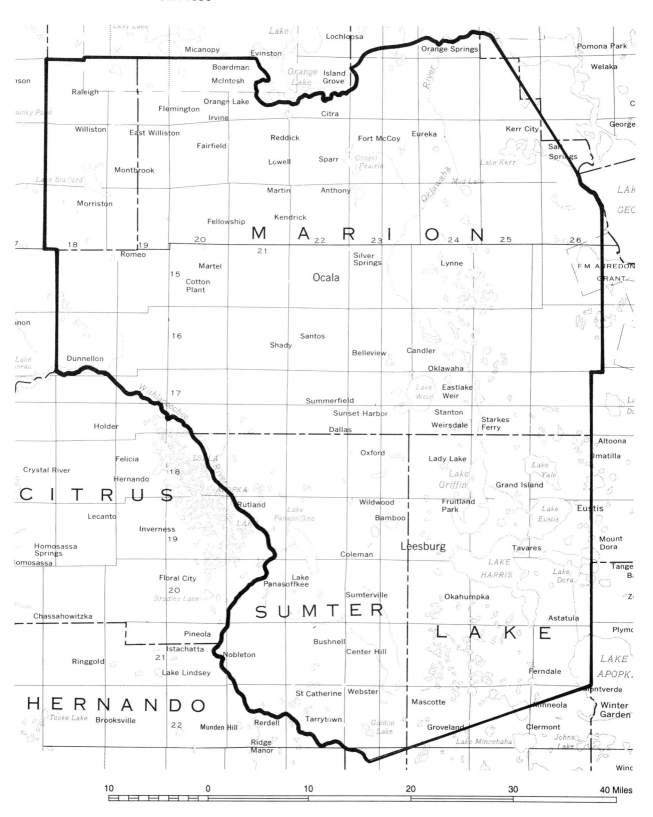

10   0   10   20   30   40 Miles

Chronology of MARION

Map	Date	Event	Resulting Area
❹	8 Jan 1853	MARION lost to creation of SUMTER	1,770 sq mi
	15 Jan 1859	MARION gained small area from SUMTER to accommodate local resident [location unknown, not mapped]	

(Heavy line depicts historical boundary. Base map shows present-day information.)

❹ MARION Boundaries
8 Jan 1853 – 5 Feb 1877

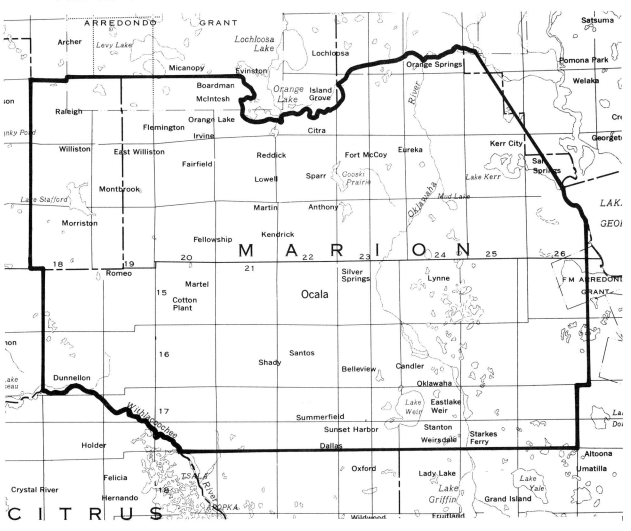

Chronology of MARION

Map	Date	Event	Resulting Area
❺	6 Feb 1877	MARION lost to LEVY	1,600 sq mi

(Heavy line depicts historical boundary. Base map shows present-day information.)

❺ MARION Boundaries
6 Feb 1877 – 27 May 1887

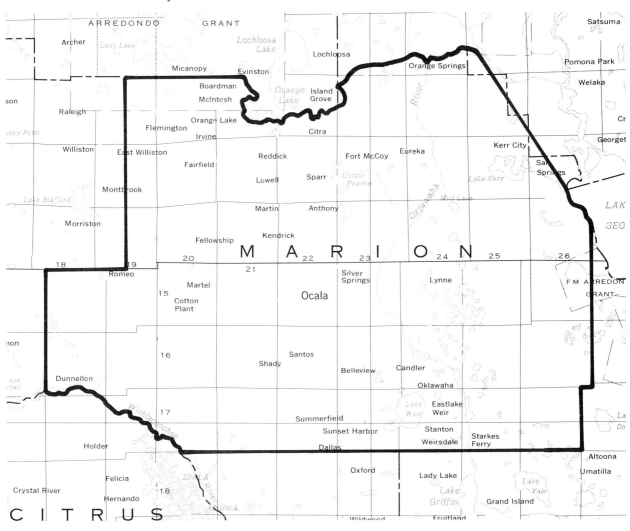

Chronology of MARION

Map	Date	Event	Resulting Area
⑥	28 May 1887	MARION exchanged with PUTNAM	1,600 sq mi
	1 Jun 1915	Legislature authorized creation of BLOXHAM from LEVY and MARION, dependent on local referendum that failed [no change; see BLOXHAM, map 1]	
⑥	c. 1973	MARION gained from ALACHUA when part of Lake Orange was drained	1,600 sq mi

(Heavy line depicts historical boundary. Base map shows present-day information.)

⑥ MARION Boundaries
28 May 1887–1990

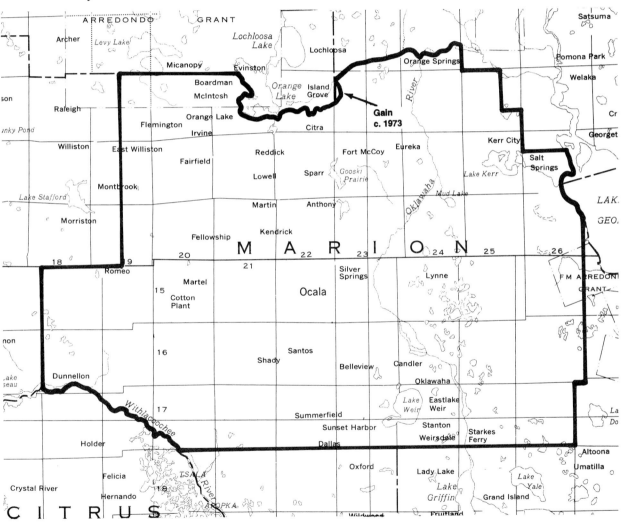

Chronology of MARTIN

Map	Date	Event	Resulting Area
❶	4 Aug 1925	MARTIN created from PALM BEACH and ST. LUCIE	560 sq mi
❷	29 May 1963	MARTIN gained part of Lake Okeechobee from PALM BEACH	560 sq mi

(Heavy line depicts historical boundary. Base map shows present-day information.)

❶ MARTIN Boundaries
4 Aug 1925 – 28 May 1963

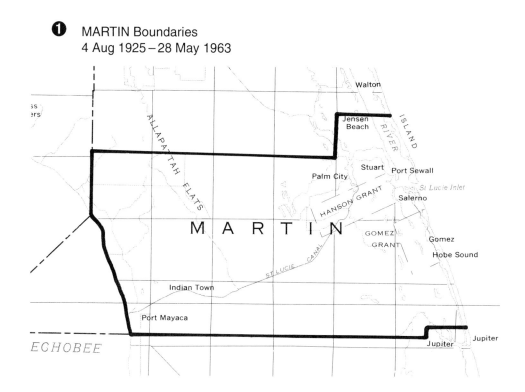

❷ MARTIN Boundaries
29 May 1963 – 1990

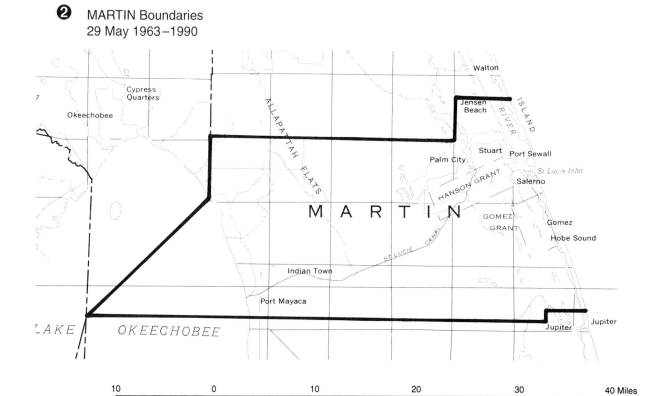

Chronology of MONROE

Map	Date	Event	Resulting Area
❶	3 Jul 1823	MONROE created from ST. JOHNS	10,000 sq mi
❷	4 Feb 1836	MONROE lost to creation of DADE	5,400 sq mi

(Heavy line depicts historical boundary. Base map shows present-day information.)

❶ MONROE Boundaries
3 Jul 1823 – 3 Feb 1836

❷ MONROE Boundaries
4 Feb 1836 – 12 Jan 1859

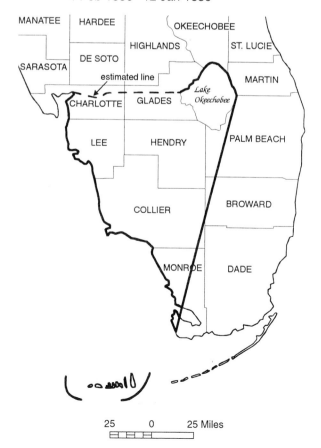

Chronology of MONROE

Map	Date	Event	Resulting Area
❸	7 Jan 1851	DADE no longer fully organized; attached to MONROE for administrative and judicial purposes	
❹	13 Jan 1859	MONROE lost to MANATEE [attachment unchanged; see map 3]	4,450 sq mi

(Heavy line depicts historical boundary. Base map shows present-day information.)

❸ MONROE Attachment
7 Jan 1851–7 Dec 1866

❹ MONROE Boundaries
13 Jan 1859–7 Dec 1866

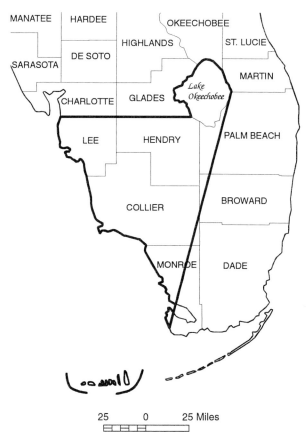

Chronology of MONROE

Map	Date	Event	Resulting Area
❺/❻	8 Dec 1866	MONROE exchanged with DADE / Area attached to MONROE enlarged due to exchange with DADE and DADE's gain from BREVARD	3,450 sq mi
❺	1872	DADE fully organized, detached from MONROE	3,450 sq mi

(Heavy line depicts historical boundary. Base map shows present-day information.)

❺ MONROE Boundaries
8 Dec 1866–18 Feb 1874

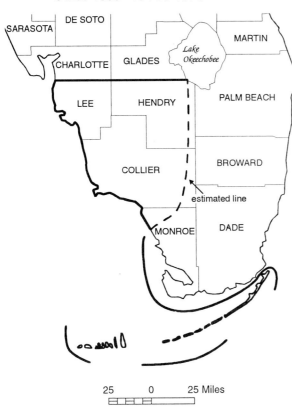

❻ MONROE Attachment
8 Dec 1866–1872

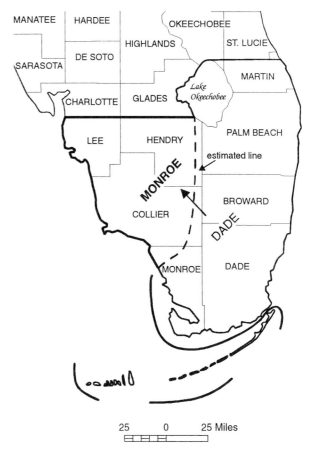

Chronology of MONROE

Map	Date	Event	Resulting Area
❼	19 Feb 1874	MONROE gained from DADE, exchanged with MANATEE	4,570 sq mi
❽	21 Feb 1877	MONROE exchanged with MANATEE	4,990 sq mi

(Heavy line depicts historical boundary. Base map shows present-day information.)

❼ MONROE Boundaries
19 Feb 1874–20 Feb 1877

25   0   25 Miles

❽ MONROE Boundaries
21 Feb 1877–12 May 1887

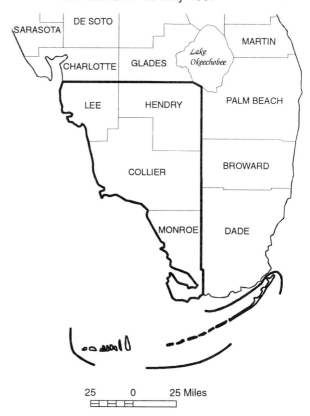

25   0   25 Miles

Chronology of MONROE

Map	Date	Event	Resulting Area
⑨/ ⑩/ ⑪	13 May 1887	MONROE lost to creation of LEE	1,030 sq mi
		(see pages 184 and 185 for lower half of map)	

(Heavy line depicts historical boundary. Base map shows present-day information.)

⑨ Northern MONROE Boundaries
13 May 1887–1990

Chronology of MONROE

Map	Date	Event	Resulting Area
⑨/⑩/⑪	13 May 1887	MONROE lost to creation of LEE	1,030 sq mi
		(see pages 183 and 185 for northern and eastern parts of map)	

(Heavy line depicts historical boundary. Base map shows present-day information.)

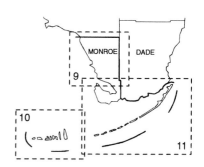

⑩ Western MONROE Boundaries
13 May 1887–1990

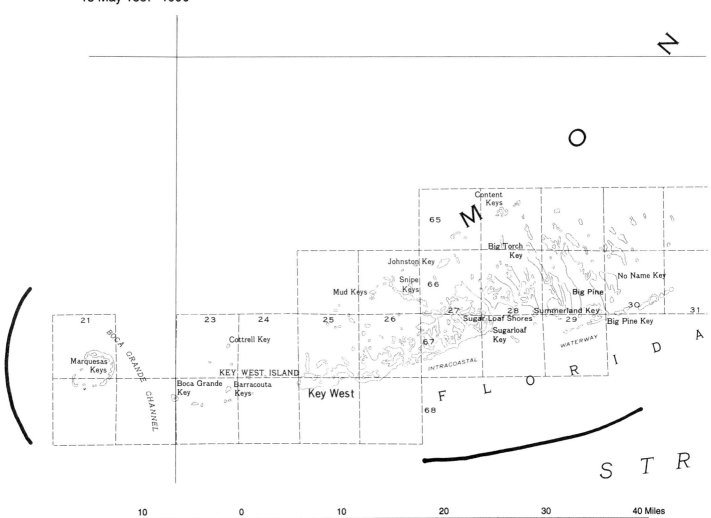

Chronology of MONROE

Map	Date	Event	Resulting Area
⑨/⑩/⑪	13 May 1887	MONROE lost to creation of LEE	1,030 sq mi
		(see pages 183 and 184 for northern and western parts of map)	
⑪	13 May 1961	MONROE lost small area to DADE	1,030 sq mi

(Heavy line depicts historical boundary. Base map shows present-day information.)

⑪ Eastern MONROE Boundaries
13 May 1887–1990

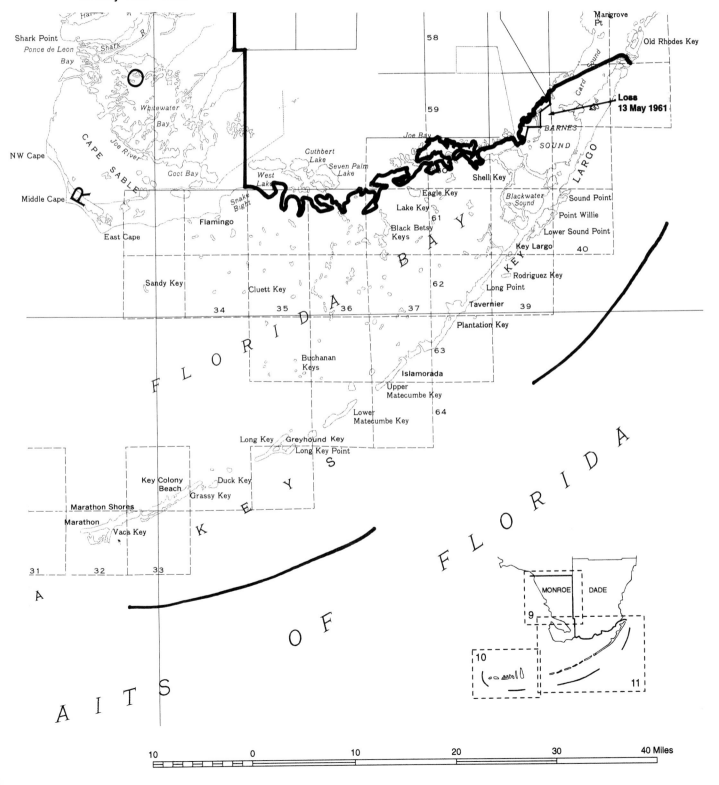

Chronology of NASSAU

Map	Date	Event	Resulting Area
❶	29 Dec 1824	NASSAU created from DUVAL	430 sq mi

(Heavy line depicts historical boundary. Base map shows present-day information.)

❶   NASSAU Boundaries
29 Dec 1824 – 29 Dec 1826

| 10 | | 0 | | 10 | | 20 | | 30 | | 40 Miles |

Chronology of NASSAU

Map	Date	Event	Resulting Area
❷	30 Dec 1826	NASSAU gained from DUVAL	670 sq mi
	23 Nov 1828	Overlap resulted when a single area was assigned to both NASSAU and DUVAL [corrected 2 Jan 1857]	

(Heavy line depicts historical boundary. Base map shows present-day information.)

❷   NASSAU Boundaries
30 Dec 1826 – 1 Jan 1857

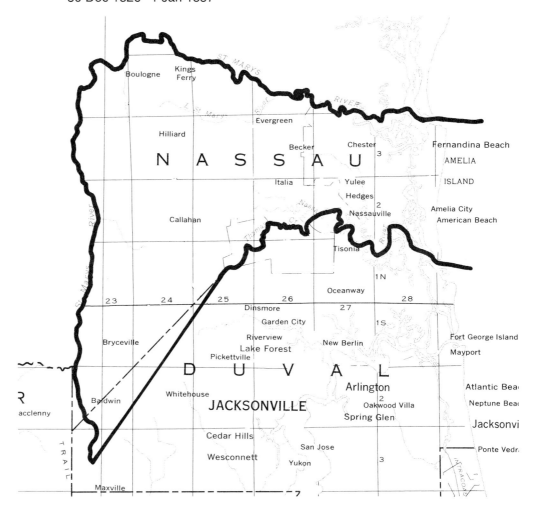

10	0	10	20	30	40 Miles

Chronology of NASSAU

Map	Date	Event	Resulting Area
❸	2 Jan 1857	1828 overlap between NASSAU and DUVAL ended; based upon its most recently defined configuration, NASSAU appeared to exchange with DUVAL	670 sq mi

(Heavy line depicts historical boundary. Base map shows present-day information.)

❸ NASSAU Boundaries
2 Jan 1857–14 Jan 1859

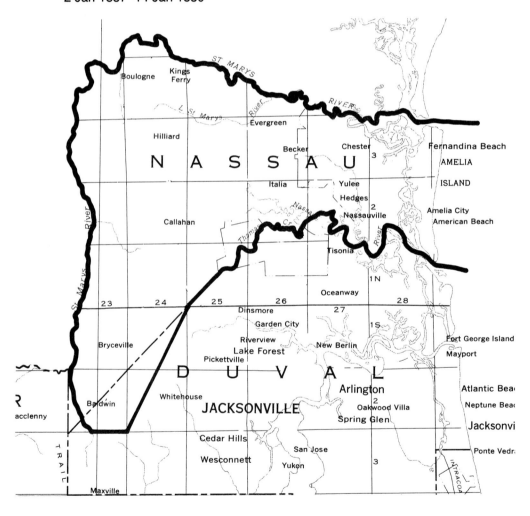

Chronology of NASSAU

Map	Date	Event	Resulting Area
❹	15 Jan 1859	NASSAU lost to DUVAL	640 sq mi

(Heavy line depicts historical boundary. Base map shows present-day information.)

❹ NASSAU Boundaries
15 Jan 1859–18 May 1911

Chronology of NASSAU

Map	Date	Event	Resulting Area
⑤	19 May 1911	NASSAU gained from BAKER	650 sq mi

(Heavy line depicts historical boundary. Base map shows present-day information.)

⑤ NASSAU Boundaries
19 May 1911–1990

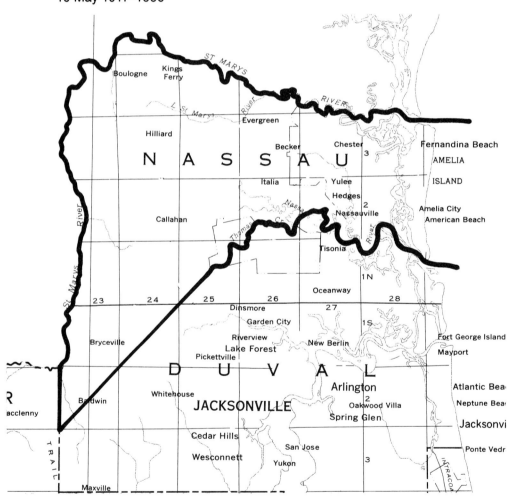

10   0   10   20   30   40 Miles

Chronology of OKALOOSA

Map	Date	Event	Resulting Area
❶	7 Sep 1915	OKALOOSA created from SANTA ROSA and WALTON	930 sq mi
❷	31 May 1947	OKALOOSA gained from ESCAMBIA	940 sq mi

(Heavy line depicts historical boundary. Base map shows present-day information.)

❶ OKALOOSA Boundaries
7 Sep 1915 – 30 May 1947

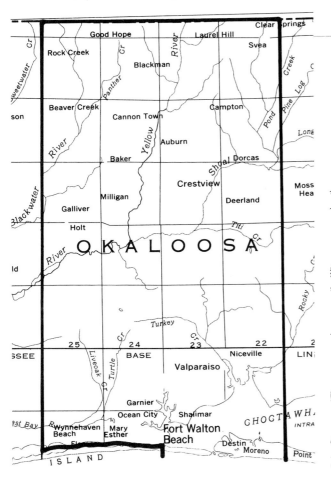

❷ OKALOOSA Boundaries
31 May 1947 – 1990

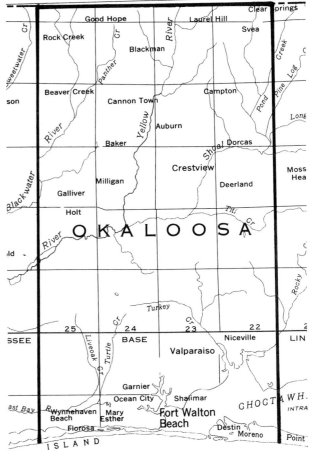

10   0   10   20   30   40 Miles

Chronology of OKEECHOBEE

Map	Date	Event	Resulting Area
❶	7 Aug 1917	OKEECHOBEE created from OSCEOLA, PALM BEACH, and ST. LUCIE	770 sq mi

(Heavy line depicts historical boundary. Base map shows present-day information.)

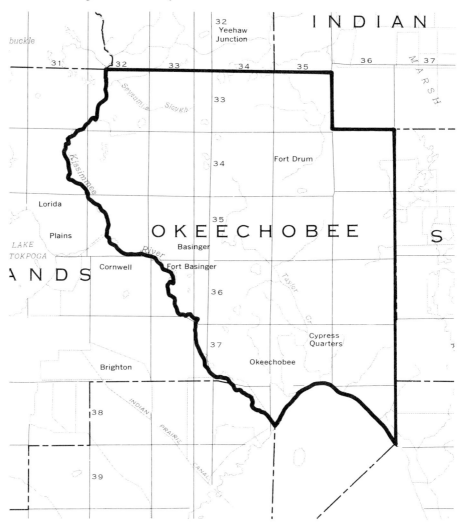

❶ OKEECHOBEE Boundaries
7 Aug 1917– 28 May 1963

10   0   10   20   30   40 Miles

Chronology of OKEECHOBEE

Map	Date	Event	Resulting Area
❷	29 May 1963	OKEECHOBEE gained part of Lake Okeechobee from PALM BEACH	770 sq mi

(Heavy line depicts historical boundary. Base map shows present-day information.)

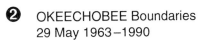

❷ OKEECHOBEE Boundaries
29 May 1963–1990

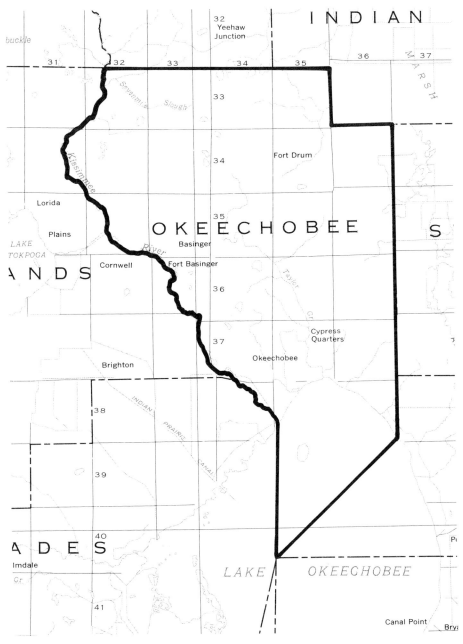

Chronology of ORANGE (created as MOSQUITO)

Map	Date	Event	Resulting Area
❶	29 Dec 1824	ORANGE created as MOSQUITO from ST. JOHNS	7,000 sq mi
❷	19 Jan 1828	MOSQUITO apparently lost to Indian lands as a result of the resurvey of the treaty line	5,800 sq mi

(Heavy line depicts historical boundary. Base map shows present-day information.)

❶ MOSQUITO Boundaries
29 Dec 1824–18 Jan 1828

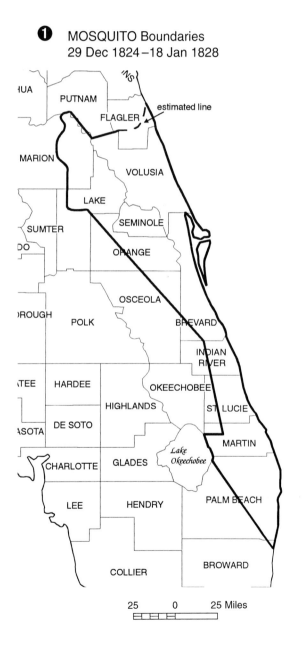

❷ MOSQUITO Boundaries
19 Jan 1828–13 Mar 1844

Chronology of ORANGE (created as MOSQUITO)

Map	Date	Event	Resulting Area
❸	14 Mar 1844	MOSQUITO apparently gained from HILLSBOROUGH, lost to creation of both MARION and original ST. LUCIE (now BREVARD)	2,600 sq mi
	30 Jan 1845	MOSQUITO renamed ORANGE	
❹	27 Feb 1845	ORANGE gained from original ST. LUCIE (now BREVARD)	4,650 sq mi
❹	25 Dec 1846	ORANGE gained small area from MARION along Lake George [see also MARION, map 2]	4,650 sq mi
❺	28 Dec 1846	ORANGE lost to original ST. LUCIE (now BREVARD)	4,250 sq mi
❻	10 Jan 1849	ORANGE exchanged with original ST. LUCIE (now BREVARD)	3,150 sq mi

(Heavy line depicts historical boundary. Base map shows present-day information.)

❸ MOSQUITO Boundaries
14 Mar 1844 – 26 Feb 1845

❹ ORANGE Boundaries
27 Feb 1845 – 27 Dec 1846

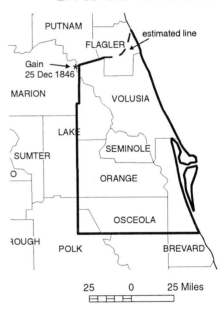

❺ ORANGE Boundaries
28 Dec 1846 – 9 Jan 1849

❻ ORANGE Boundaries
10 Jan 1849 – 28 Dec 1854

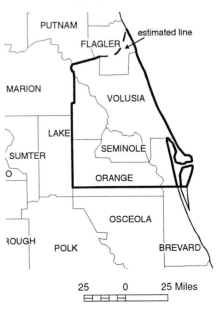

Chronology of ORANGE (created as MOSQUITO)

Map	Date	Event	Resulting Area
❼	29 Dec 1854	ORANGE lost to creation of VOLUSIA	1,500 sq mi

(Heavy line depicts historical boundary. Base map shows present-day information.)

❼ ORANGE Boundaries
29 Dec 1854 – 5 Dec 1866

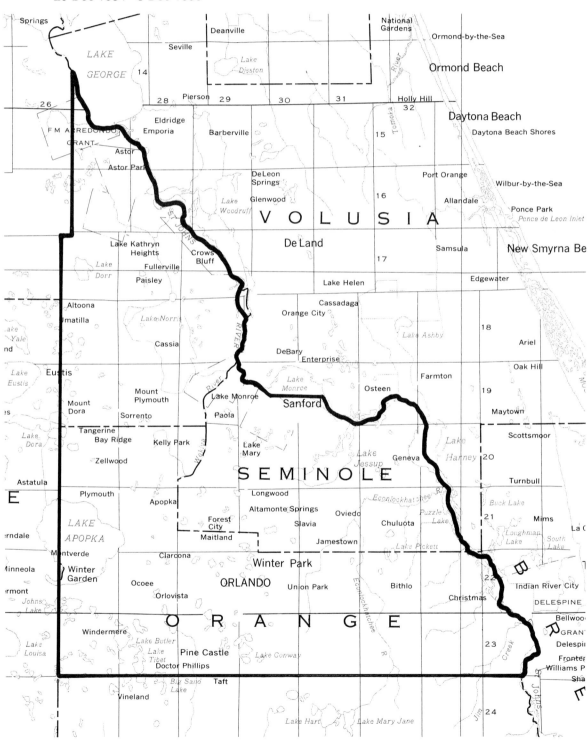

Chronology of ORANGE (created as MOSQUITO)

Map	Date	Event	Resulting Area
❽	6 Dec 1866	ORANGE gained from BREVARD	2,600 sq mi
	14 Feb 1870	Boundary between ORANGE and VOLUSIA clarified to run west of Huntoon's Island [no change]	
❾	14 Feb 1872	ORANGE gained from SUMTER	2,680 sq mi

(Heavy line depicts historical boundary. Base map shows present-day information.)

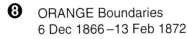

**❽ ORANGE Boundaries
6 Dec 1866–13 Feb 1872**

**❾ ORANGE Boundaries
14 Feb 1872–17 Feb 1873**

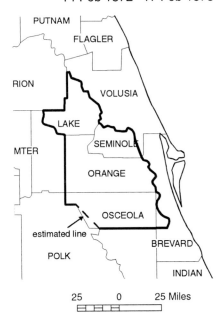

Chronology of ORANGE (created as MOSQUITO)

Map	Date	Event	Resulting Area
⑩	18 Feb 1873	ORANGE lost to BREVARD	1,910 sq mi

(Heavy line depicts historical boundary. Base map shows present-day information.)

⑩   ORANGE Boundaries
     18 Feb 1873–18 Feb 1874

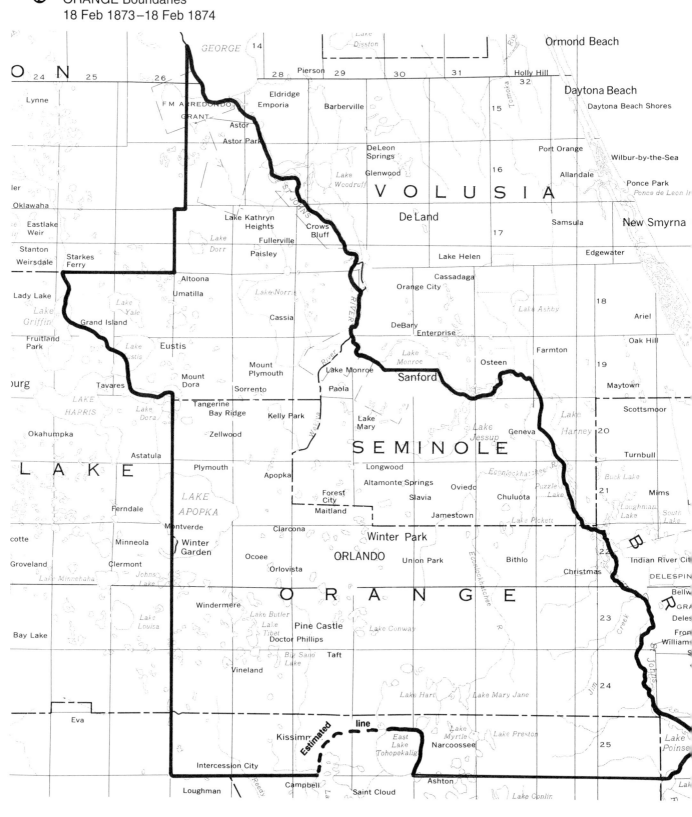

Chronology of ORANGE (created as MOSQUITO)

Map	Date	Event	Resulting Area
⑪	19 Feb 1874	ORANGE gained from BREVARD	2,000 sq mi
⑫	5 Mar 1879	ORANGE gained from POLK	2,040 sq mi

(Heavy line depicts historical boundary. Base map shows present-day information.)

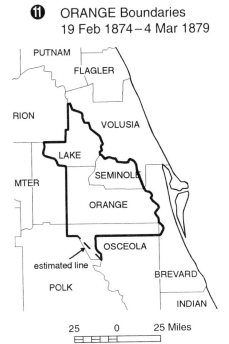

⑪ ORANGE Boundaries
19 Feb 1874 – 4 Mar 1879

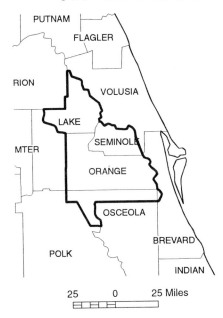

⑫ ORANGE Boundaries
5 Mar 1879 – 10 Jul 1887

Chronology of ORANGE (created as MOSQUITO)

Map	Date	Event	Resulting Area
⑬	11 Jul 1887	ORANGE lost to creation of OSCEOLA, apparently lost small area to BREVARD	1,680 sq mi

(Heavy line depicts historical boundary. Base map shows present-day information.)

⑬ ORANGE Boundaries
11 Jul 1887– 25 Jul 1887

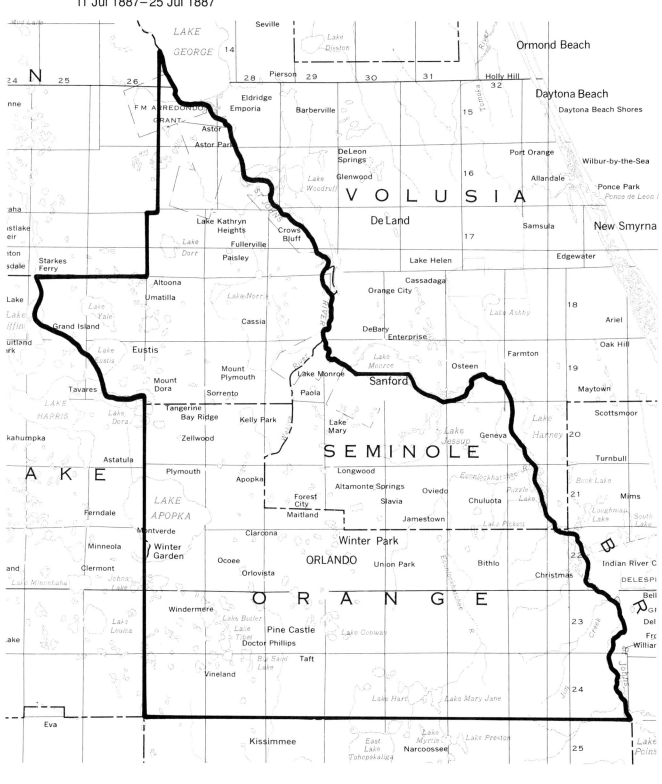

Chronology of ORANGE (created as MOSQUITO)

Map	Date	Event	Resulting Area
⑭	26 Jul 1887	ORANGE lost to creation of LAKE	1,210 sq mi
⑭	31 May 1889	ORANGE lost small area to LAKE	1,210 sq mi

(Heavy line depicts historical boundary. Base map shows present-day information.)

⑭ ORANGE Boundaries
26 Jul 1887–24 Apr 1913

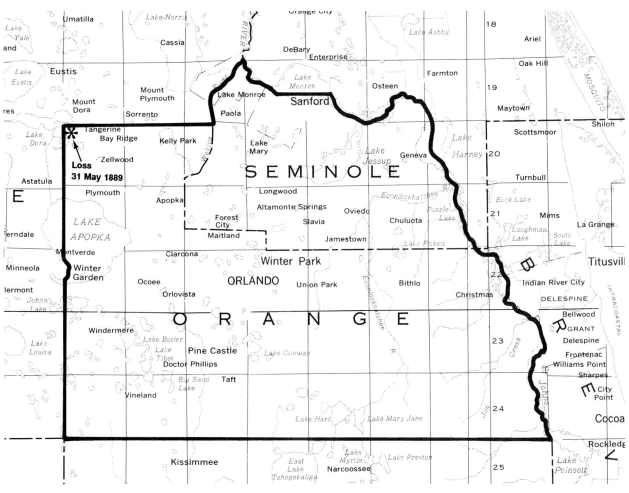

Chronology of ORANGE (created as MOSQUITO)

Map	Date	Event	Resulting Area
⑮	25 Apr 1913	ORANGE lost to creation of SEMINOLE [mistake in description corrected 22 Jun 1961]	910 sq mi
	22 Jun 1961	ORANGE boundaries redefined, correcting mistake of 25 Apr 1913 [no change]	

(Heavy line depicts historical boundary. Base map shows present-day information.)

⑮ ORANGE Boundaries
25 Apr 1913–1990

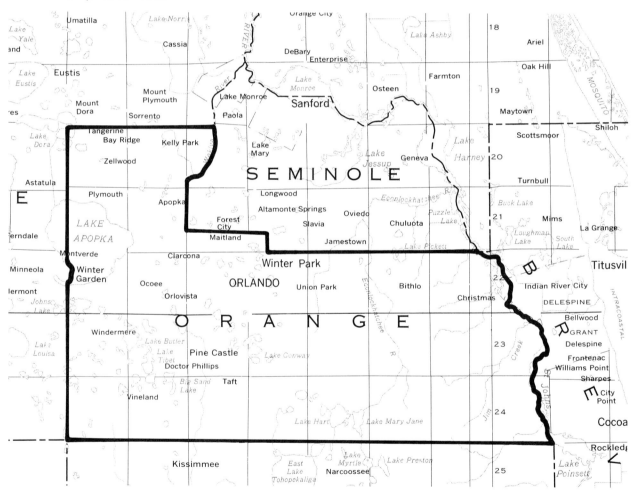

Chronology of OSCEOLA

Map	Date	Event	Resulting Area
❶	11 Jul 1887	OSCEOLA created from BREVARD and ORANGE	1,750 sq mi

(Heavy line depicts historical boundary. Base map shows present-day information.)

OSCEOLA Boundaries
11 Jul 1887–6 Aug 1917

❶

Chronology of OSCEOLA

Map	Date	Event	Resulting Area
❷	7 Aug 1917	OSCEOLA lost to creation of OKEECHOBEE	1,350 sq mi

(Heavy line depicts historical boundary. Base map shows present-day information.)

❷ OSCEOLA Boundaries
7 Aug 1917–31 Dec 1967

Chronology of OSCEOLA

Map	Date	Event	Resulting Area
❸	1 Jan 1968	OSCEOLA exchanged with POLK	1,350 sq mi

(Heavy line depicts historical boundary. Base map shows present-day information.)

❸ OSCEOLA Boundaries
1 Jan 1968–1990

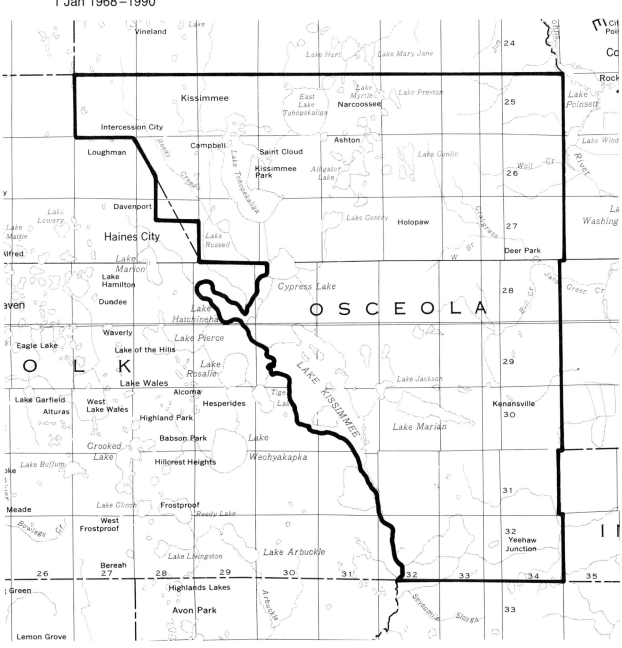

Chronology of PALM BEACH

Map	Date	Event	Resulting Area
❶	1 Jul 1909	PALM BEACH created from DADE	3,100 sq mi
❷	1 Oct 1915	PALM BEACH lost to creation of BROWARD	2,550 sq mi
❸	7 Aug 1917	PALM BEACH lost to creation of OKEECHOBEE	2,520 sq mi

(Heavy line depicts historical boundary. Base map shows present-day information.)

❶ PALM BEACH Boundaries
1 Jul 1909 – 30 Sep 1915

25   0   25 Miles

❷ PALM BEACH Boundaries
1 Oct 1915 – 6 Aug 1917

25   0   25 Miles

❸ PALM BEACH Boundaries
7 Aug 1917 – 7 May 1925

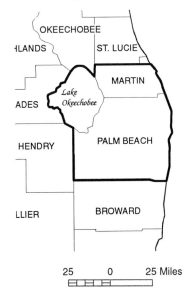

25   0   25 Miles

Chronology of PALM BEACH

Map	Date	Event	Resulting Area
❹	8 May 1925	PALM BEACH lost part of Lake Okeechobee to GLADES	2,520 sq mi
❹	14 May 1925	PALM BEACH lost small part of Lake Okeechobee to HENDRY	2,520 sq mi

(Heavy line depicts historical boundary. Base map shows present-day information.)

❹ PALM BEACH Boundaries
8 May 1925 – 3 Aug 1925

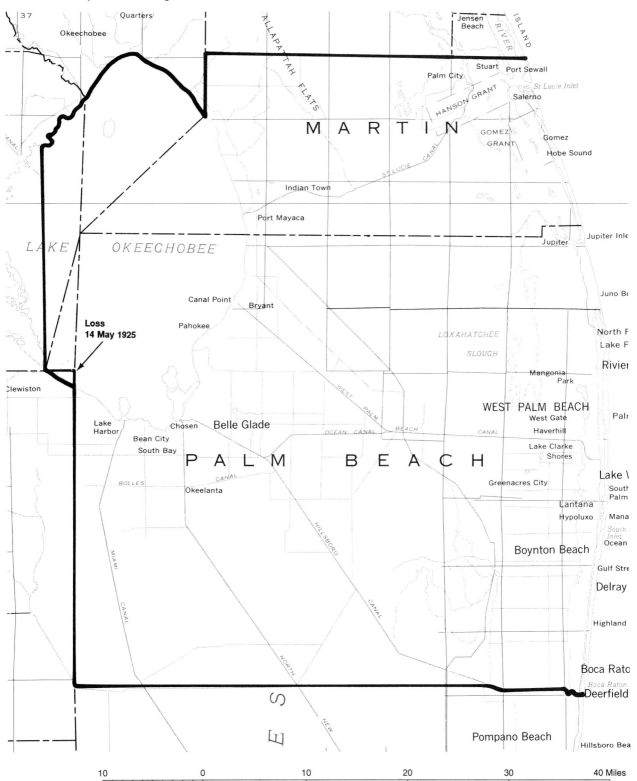

Chronology of PALM BEACH

Map	Date	Event	Resulting Area
⑤	4 Aug 1925	PALM BEACH lost to creation of MARTIN	2,000 sq mi

(Heavy line depicts historical boundary. Base map shows present-day information.)

⑤ PALM BEACH Boundaries
4 Aug 1925 – 28 May 1963

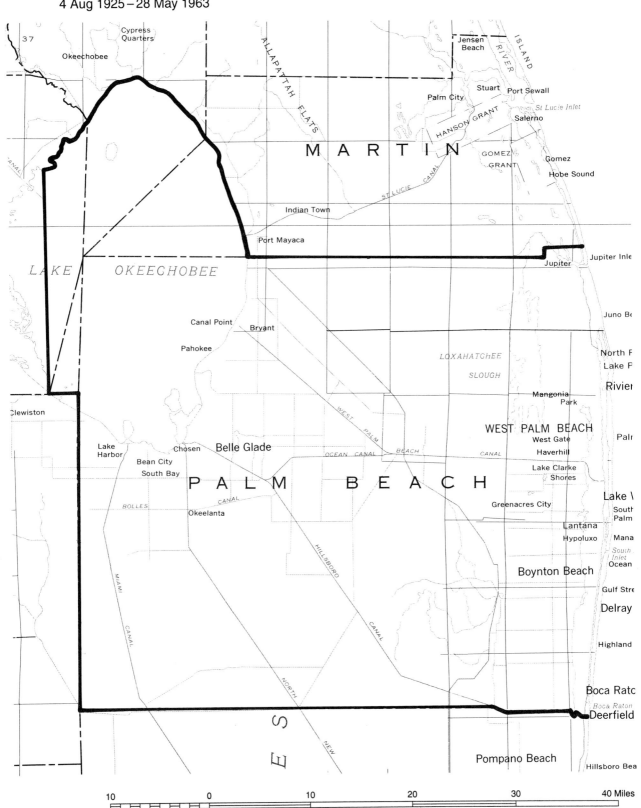

Chronology of PALM BEACH

Map	Date	Event	Resulting Area
❻	29 May 1963	PALM BEACH lost parts of Lake Okeechobee to GLADES, HENDRY, MARTIN, and OKEECHOBEE	2,000 sq mi

(Heavy line depicts historical boundary. Base map shows present-day information.)

❻ PALM BEACH Boundaries
29 May 1963–1990

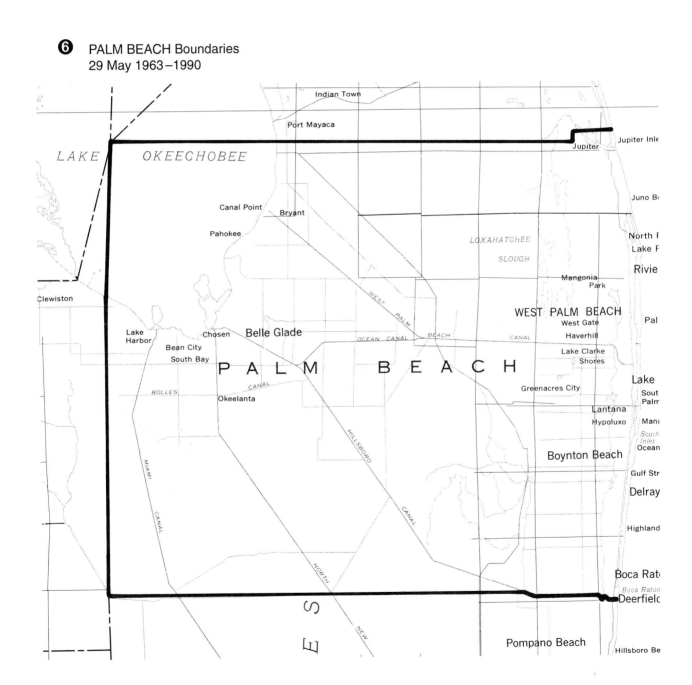

Chronology of PASCO

Map	Date	Event	Resulting Area
❶	2 Jun 1887	PASCO created from HERNANDO	760 sq mi
❷	10 Jun 1891	PASCO lost to POLK	740 sq mi
❶	29 Jul 1942	PASCO gained from POLK	760 sq mi
❷	31 Dec 1949	PASCO lost to POLK	740 sq mi

(Heavy line depicts historical boundary. Base map shows present-day information.)

❶ PASCO Boundaries
2 Jun 1887–9 Jun 1891
29 Jul 1942–30 Dec 1949

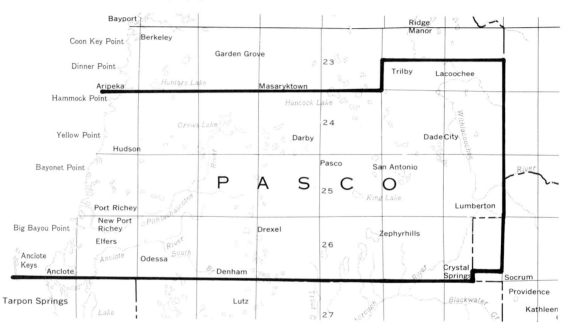

❷ PASCO Boundaries
10 Jun 1891–28 Jul 1942
31 Dec 1949–1990

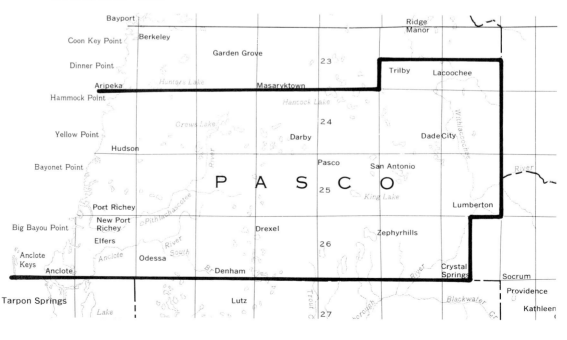

Chronology of PINELLAS

Map	Date	Event	Resulting Area
❶	14 Nov 1911	PINELLAS created from HILLSBOROUGH	280 sq mi
❷	15 May 1939	PINELLAS gained small area from HILLSBOROUGH	280 sq mi
	4 Aug 1967	PINELLAS boundary in Gulf of Mexico clarified [no change]	

(Heavy line depicts historical boundary. Base map shows present-day information.)

❶ PINELLAS Boundaries
14 Nov 1911–14 May 1939

❷ PINELLAS Boundaries
15 May 1939–1990

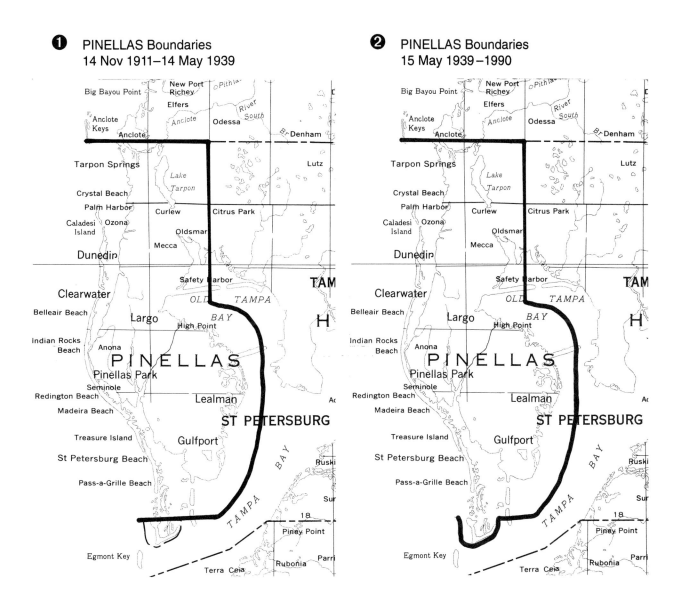

10   0   10   20   30   40 Miles

Chronology of POLK

Map	Date	Event	Resulting Area
❶	8 Feb 1861	POLK created from BREVARD and HILLSBOROUGH	1,700 sq mi
❶	10 Dec 1866	POLK lost small area to HILLSBOROUGH to accommodate local resident	1,700 sq mi

(Heavy line depicts historical boundary. Base map shows present-day information.)

❶ POLK Boundaries
8 Feb 1861– 29 Jan 1871

Chronology of POLK

Map	Date	Event	Resulting Area
❷	30 Jan 1871	POLK gained from SUMTER	1,840 sq mi

(Heavy line depicts historical boundary. Base map shows present-day information.)

❷   POLK Boundaries
30 Jan 1871–18 Feb 1874

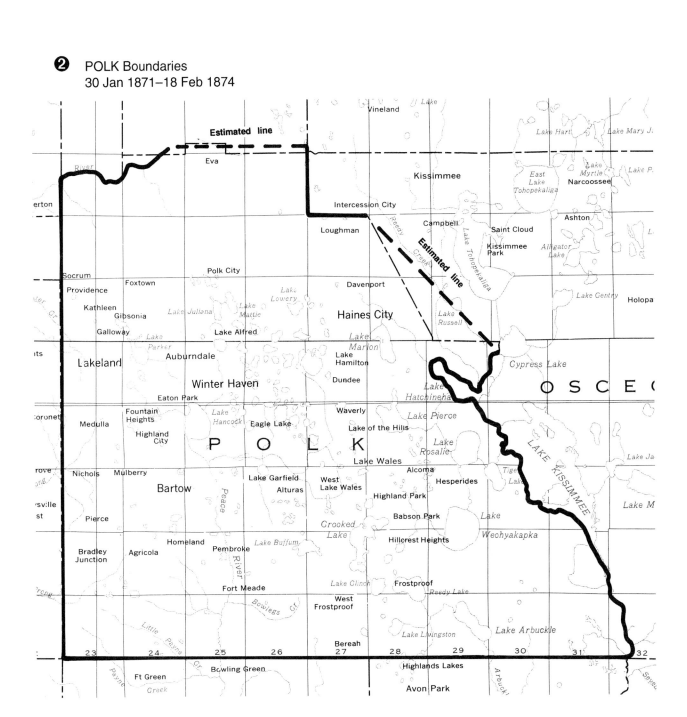

Chronology of POLK

Map	Date	Event	Resulting Area
❸	19 Feb 1874	POLK gained from HILLSBOROUGH	1,870 sq mi
❹	5 Mar 1879	POLK lost to both ORANGE and SUMTER	1,810 sq mi

(Heavy line depicts historical boundary. Base map shows present-day information.)

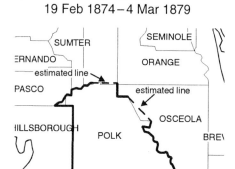

❸ POLK Boundaries
19 Feb 1874 – 4 Mar 1879

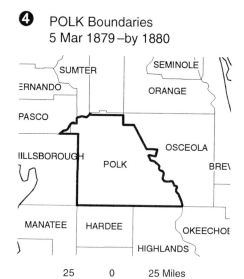

❹ POLK Boundaries
5 Mar 1879 – by 1880

Chronology of POLK

Map	Date	Event	Resulting Area
❺	by 1880	POLK lost to HERNANDO	1,780 sq mi
❺	5 Mar 1883	POLK gained small area from HERNANDO	1,780 sq mi

(Heavy line depicts historical boundary. Base map shows present-day information.)

❺   POLK Boundaries
    by 1880 – 30 May 1889

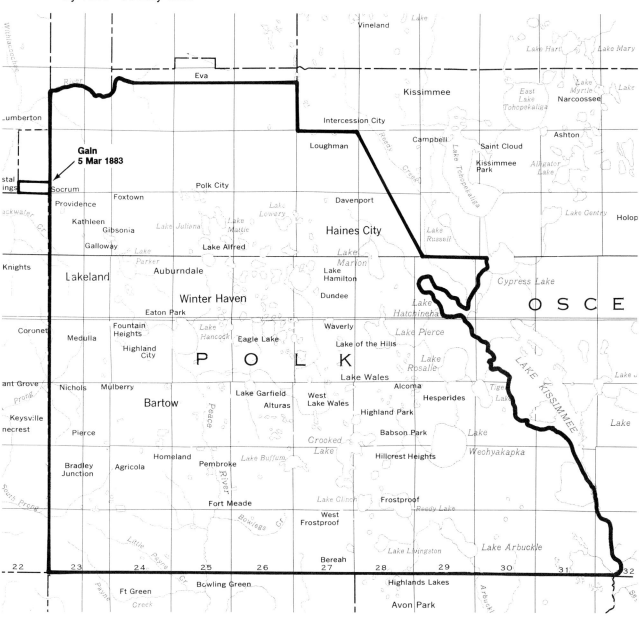

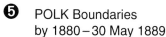

Chronology of POLK

Map	Date	Event	Resulting Area
⑥	31 May 1889	POLK gained from SUMTER	1,800 sq mi

(Heavy line depicts historical boundary. Base map shows present-day information.)

⑥ POLK Boundaries
31 May 1889 – 9 Jun 1891

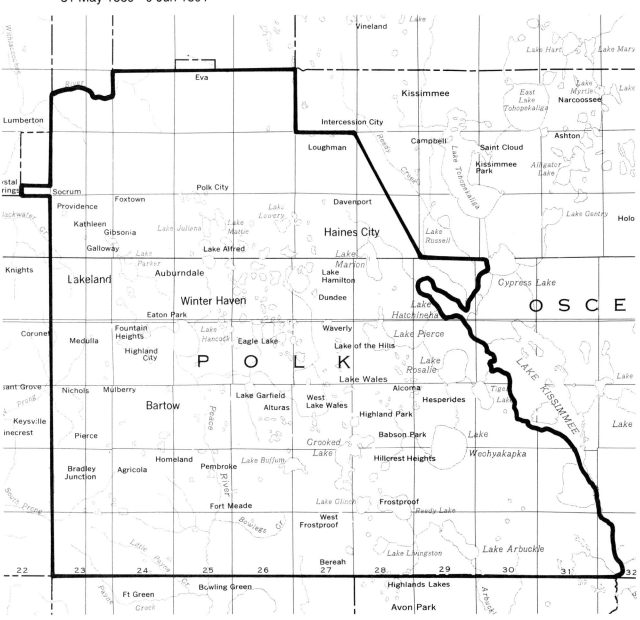

Chronology of POLK

Map	Date	Event	Resulting Area
❼	10 Jun 1891	POLK gained small area from LAKE, and gained from PASCO	1,820 sq mi
❼	29 Jul 1942	POLK lost to PASCO	1,800 sq mi
❼	31 Dec 1949	POLK gained from PASCO	1,820 sq mi

(Heavy line depicts historical boundary. Base map shows present-day information.)

❼ POLK Boundaries
10 Jun 1891– 31 Dec 1967

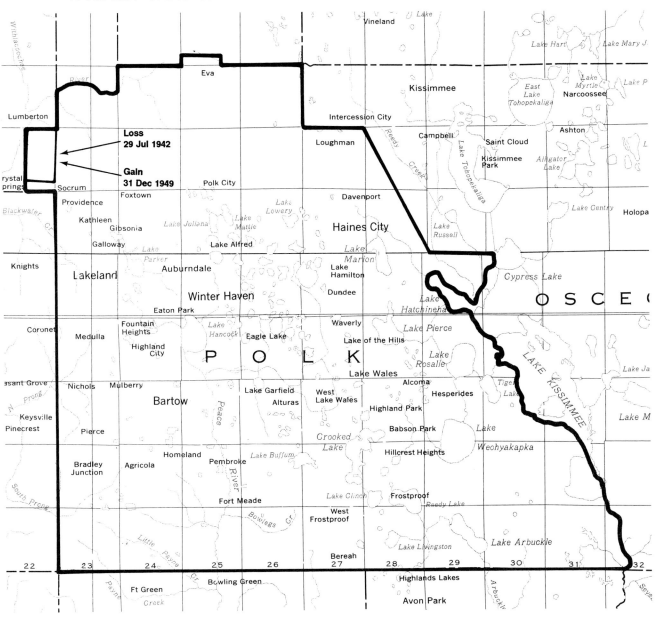

Chronology of POLK

Map	Date	Event	Resulting Area
❽	1 Jan 1968	POLK exchanged with OSCEOLA	1,820 sq mi

(Heavy line depicts historical boundary. Base map shows present-day information.)

❽ POLK Boundaries
1 Jan 1968 – 1990

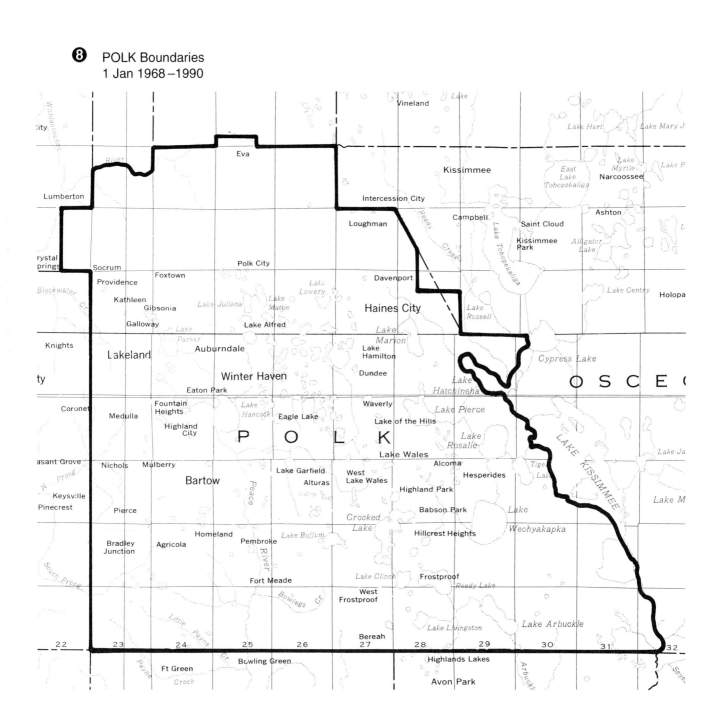

Chronology of PUTNAM

Map	Date	Event	Resulting Area
❶	13 Jan 1849	PUTNAM created from ALACHUA and ST. JOHNS	720 sq mi

(Heavy line depicts historical boundary. Base map shows present-day information.)

❶ PUTNAM Boundaries
13 Jan 1849 – 14 Jan 1859

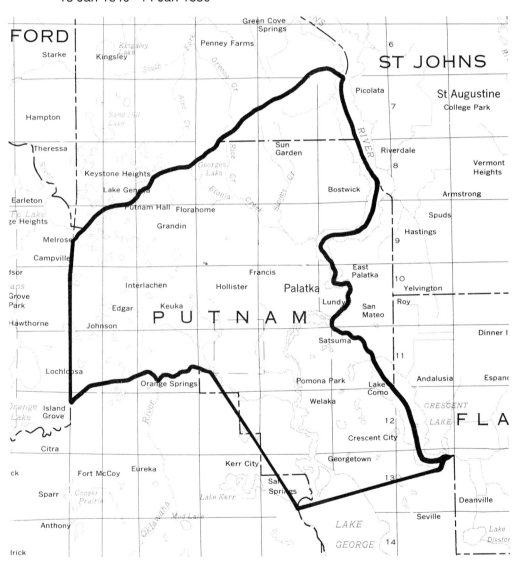

10   0   10   20   30   40 Miles

Chronology of PUTNAM

Map	Date	Event	Resulting Area
❷	15 Jan 1859	PUTNAM gained from CLAY, exchanged with ST. JOHNS in the St. Johns R. and Crescent Lake	780 sq mi

(Heavy line depicts historical boundary. Base map shows present-day information.)

❷ PUTNAM Boundaries
15 Jan 1859 – 21 Dec 1859

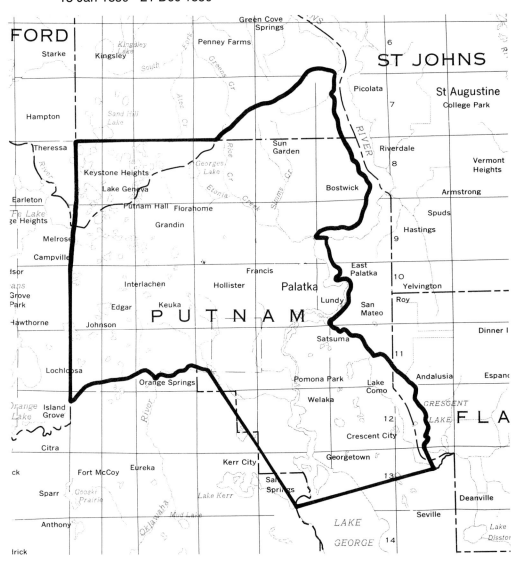

Chronology of PUTNAM

Map	Date	Event	Resulting Area
❸	22 Dec 1859	PUTNAM lost to CLAY	720 sq mi

(Heavy line depicts historical boundary. Base map shows present-day information.)

❸ PUTNAM Boundaries
22 Dec 1859 – 29 Jul 1868

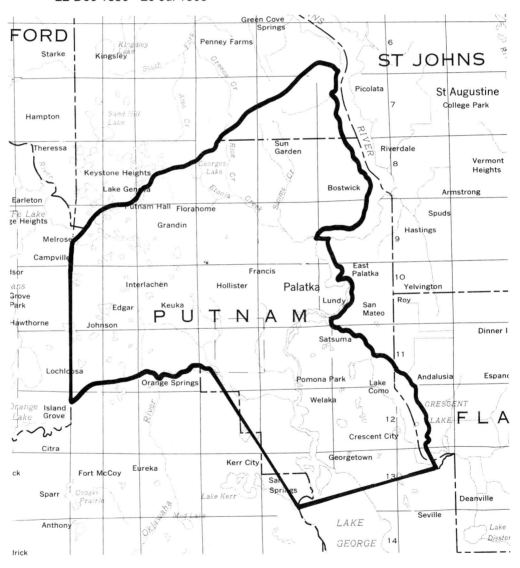

Chronology of PUTNAM

Map	Date	Event	Resulting Area
❹	30 Jul 1868	PUTNAM gained from ST. JOHNS	780 sq mi

(Heavy line depicts historical boundary. Base map shows present-day information.)

❹ PUTNAM Boundaries
30 Jul 1868 – 14 Feb 1875

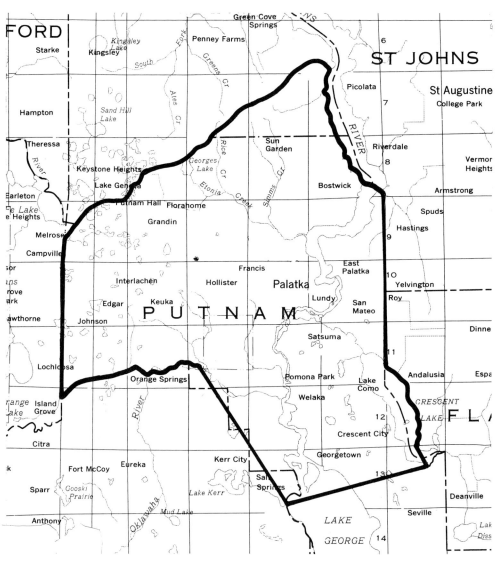

| 10 | 0 | 10 | 20 | 30 | 40 Miles |

Chronology of PUTNAM

Map	Date	Event	Resulting Area
❺	15 Feb 1875	PUTNAM exchanged with ST. JOHNS in the St. Johns R. and Crescent Lake	780 sq mi

(Heavy line depicts historical boundary. Base map shows present-day information.)

❺ PUTNAM Boundaries
   15 Feb 1875 – 25 Feb 1883

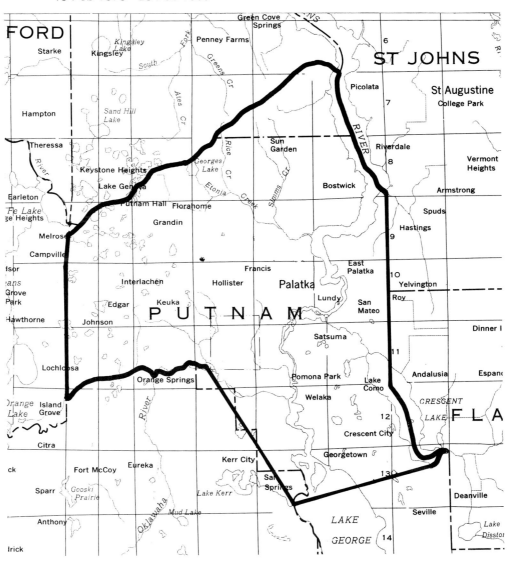

10   0   10   20   30   40 Miles

Chronology of PUTNAM

Map	Date	Event	Resulting Area
❻	26 Feb 1883	PUTNAM lost to CLAY	730 sq mi

(Heavy line depicts historical boundary. Base map shows present-day information.)

❻ PUTNAM Boundaries
26 Feb 1883 – 27 May 1887

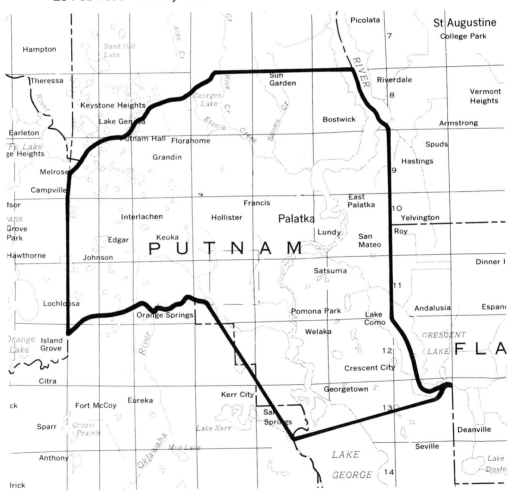

| 10 | 0 | 10 | 20 | 30 | 40 Miles |

Chronology of PUTNAM

Map	Date	Event	Resulting Area
❼	28 May 1887	PUTNAM exchanged with MARION	730 sq mi
❼	5 May 1909	PUTNAM gained small area from CLAY in the town of Melrose	730 sq mi

(Heavy line depicts historical boundary. Base map shows present-day information.)

❼ PUTNAM Boundaries
28 May 1887– 5 Jun 1927

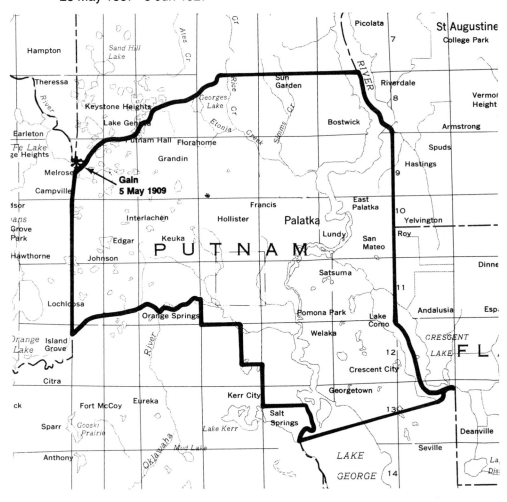

Chronology of PUTNAM

Map	Date	Event	Resulting Area
⑧	6 Jun 1927	PUTNAM gained small areas from BRADFORD and CLAY	730 sq mi
	20 Jun 1959	Boundary between PUTNAM and FLAGLER in Crescent Lake clarified [no discernible change]	
⑧	14 Jun 1984	PUTNAM lost small area to CLAY	730 sq mi

(Heavy line depicts historical boundary. Base map shows present-day information.)

⑧   PUTNAM Boundaries
6 Jun 1927–1990

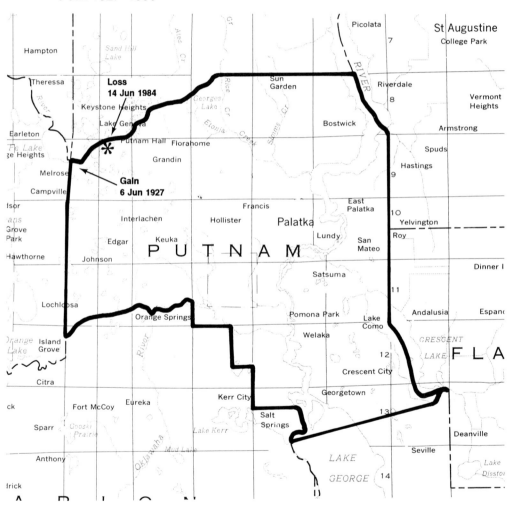

Chronology of ST. JOHNS

Map	Date	Event	Resulting Area
❶	21 Jul 1821	ST. JOHNS created from non-county area by decree of Provisional Governor Andrew Jackson	39,250 sq mi

(Heavy line depicts historical boundary. Base map shows present-day information.)

❶ ST. JOHNS Boundaries
21 Jul 1821–11 Aug 1822

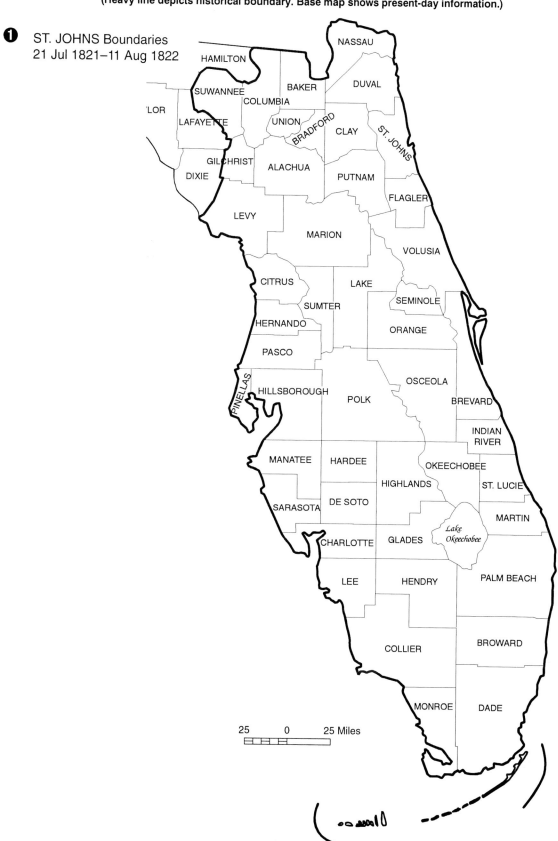

Chronology of ST. JOHNS

Map	Date	Event	Resulting Area
❷	12 Aug 1822	ST. JOHNS lost to creation of DUVAL	34,600 sq mi

(Heavy line depicts historical boundary. Base map shows present-day information.)

❷ ST. JOHNS Boundaries
12 Aug 1822 – 23 Jun 1823

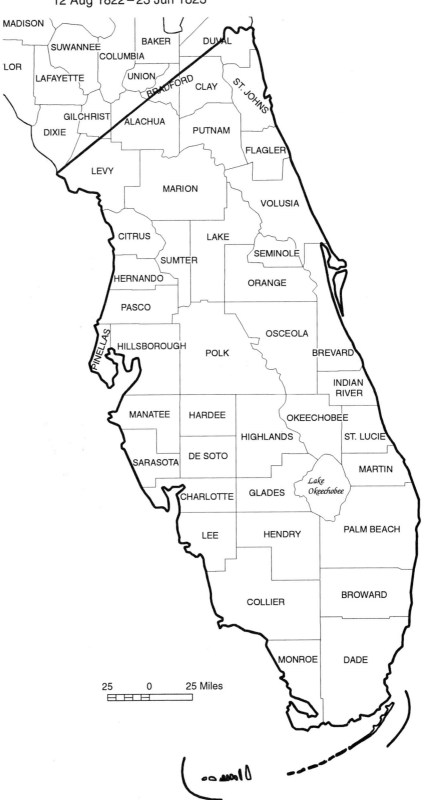

Chronology of ST. JOHNS

Map	Date	Event	Resulting Area
❸	24 Jun 1823	ST. JOHNS exchanged with DUVAL	35,150 sq mi

(Heavy line depicts historical boundary. Base map shows present-day information.)

❸ ST. JOHNS Boundaries
24 Jun 1823 – 2 Jul 1823

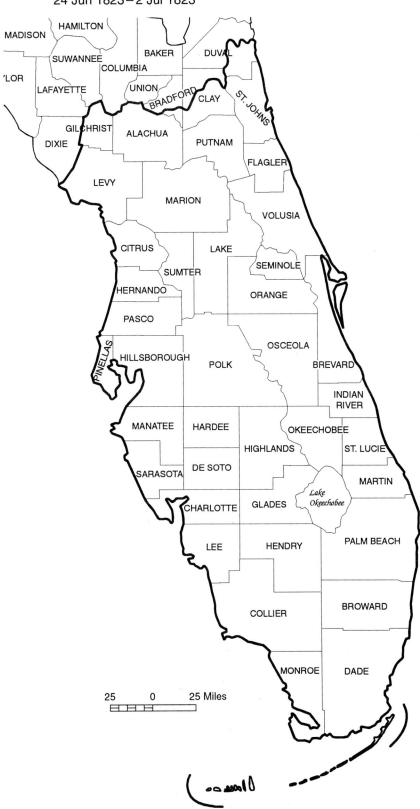

Chronology of ST. JOHNS

Map	Date	Event	Resulting Area
❹	3 Jul 1823	ST. JOHNS lost to creation of MONROE	25,150 sq mi

(Heavy line depicts historical boundary. Base map shows present-day information.)

❹ ST. JOHNS Boundaries
3 Jul 1823 – 28 Dec 1824

Chronology of ST. JOHNS

Map	Date	Event	Resulting Area
⑤	29 Dec 1824	ST. JOHNS lost to DUVAL and to creation of both ALACHUA and MOSQUITO (now ORANGE); part of ST. JOHNS reverted to non-county area (Indian land)	1,370 sq mi

(Heavy line depicts historical boundary. Base map shows present-day information.)

⑤ ST. JOHNS Boundaries
29 Dec 1824–13 Mar 1844
30 Dec 1848–12 Jan 1849

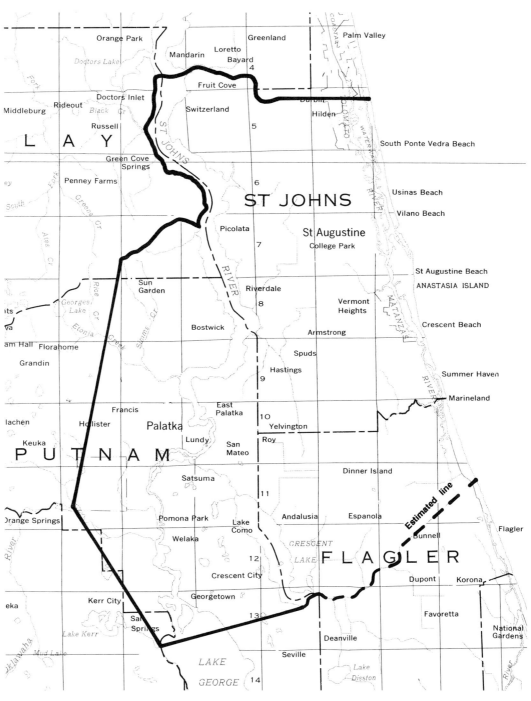

Chronology of ST. JOHNS

Map	Date	Event	Resulting Area
❻	14 Mar 1844	ST. JOHNS lost to creation of MARION	1,350 sq mi
❻	25 Dec 1846	ST. JOHNS gained from MARION along the St. Johns R. and Lake George	1,350 sq mi
❺	30 Dec 1848	ST. JOHNS gained from MARION	1,370 sq mi

(Heavy line depicts historical boundary. Base map shows present-day information.)

❻ ST. JOHNS Boundaries
14 Mar 1844 – 29 Dec 1848

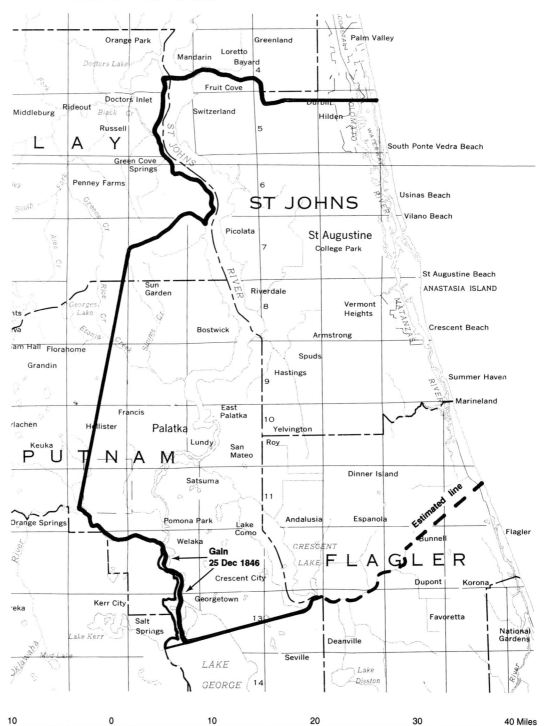

Chronology of ST. JOHNS

Map	Date	Event	Resulting Area
❼	13 Jan 1849	ST. JOHNS lost to creation of PUTNAM	900 sq mi

(Heavy line depicts historical boundary. Base map shows present-day information.)

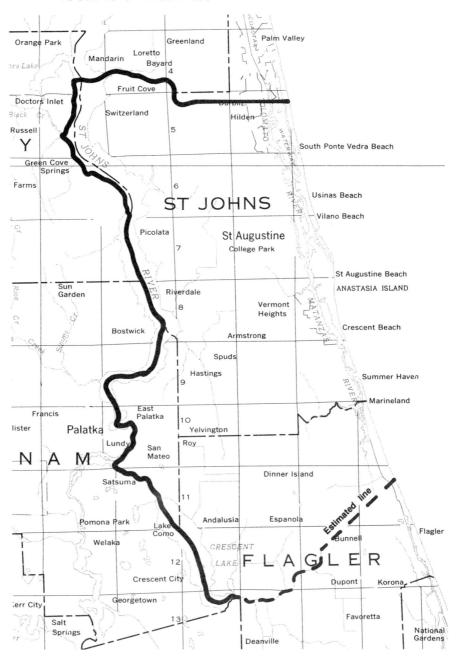

❼   ST. JOHNS Boundaries
13 Jan 1849 – 14 Jan 1859

| 10 | 0 | 10 | 20 | 30 | 40 Miles |

Chronology of ST. JOHNS

Map	Date	Event	Resulting Area
⑧	15 Jan 1859	ST. JOHNS exchanged with PUTNAM in the St. Johns R. and Crescent Lake	900 sq mi
⑧	22 Dec 1859	ST. JOHNS lost small area in the St. Johns R. to CLAY when boundary shifted from west bank to west margin of the channel	900 sq mi

(Heavy line depicts historical boundary. Base map shows present-day information.)

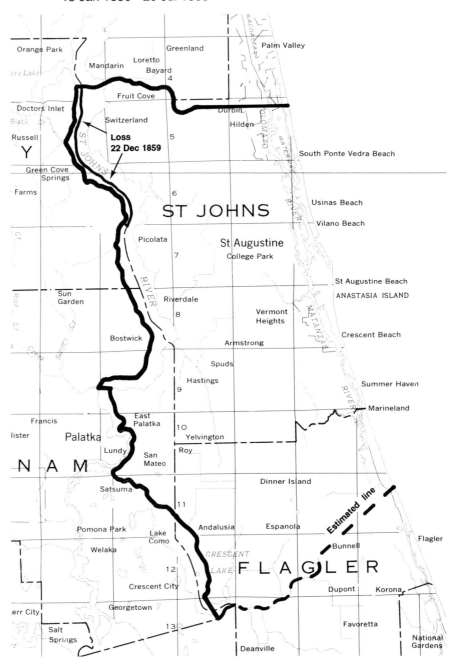

⑧ ST. JOHNS Boundaries
15 Jan 1859 – 29 Jul 1868

Chronology of ST. JOHNS

Map	Date	Event	Resulting Area
⑨	30 Jul 1868	ST. JOHNS lost to PUTNAM	840 sq mi

(Heavy line depicts historical boundary. Base map shows present-day information.)

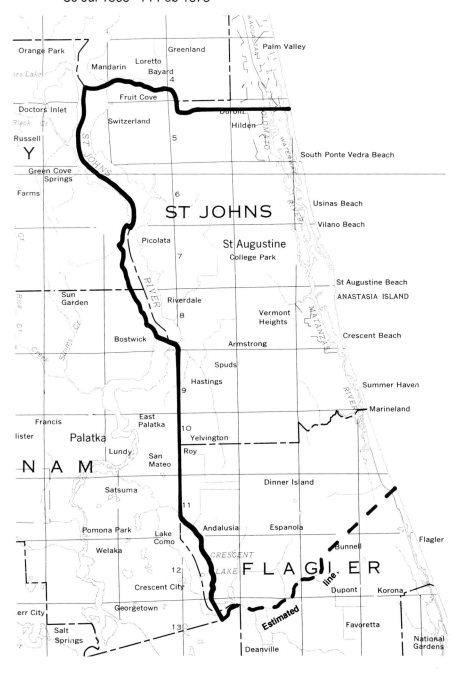

⑨ ST. JOHNS Boundaries
30 Jul 1868 – 14 Feb 1875

Chronology of ST. JOHNS

Map	Date	Event	Resulting Area
⑩	15 Feb 1875	ST. JOHNS gained from VOLUSIA, exchanged with DUVAL and PUTNAM	980 sq mi
⑩	24 May 1899	ST. JOHNS lost small area to VOLUSIA	980 sq mi
	3 Jun 1907	Boundary between ST. JOHNS and VOLUSIA clarified [no change]	

(Heavy line depicts historical boundary. Base map shows present-day information.)

⑩ ST. JOHNS Boundaries
15 Feb 1875 – 11 Jun 1917

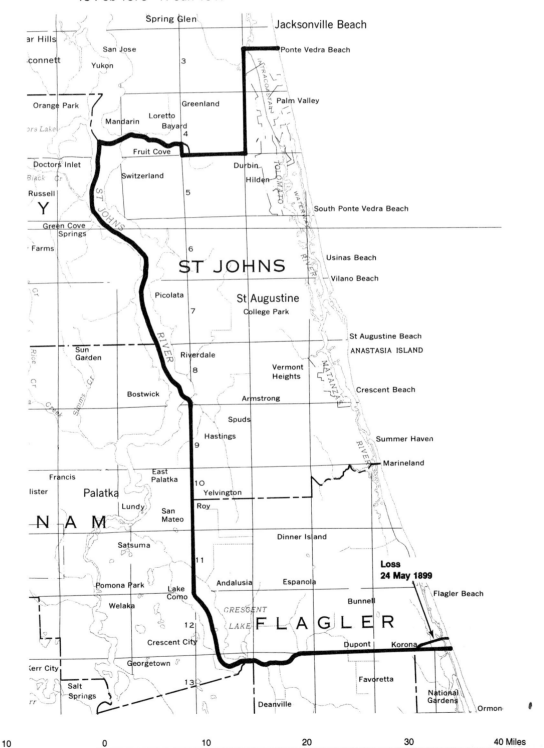

Chronology of ST. JOHNS

Map	Date	Event	Resulting Area
⑪	12 Jun 1917	ST. JOHNS lost to creation of FLAGLER	630 sq mi

(Heavy line depicts historical boundary. Base map shows present-day information.)

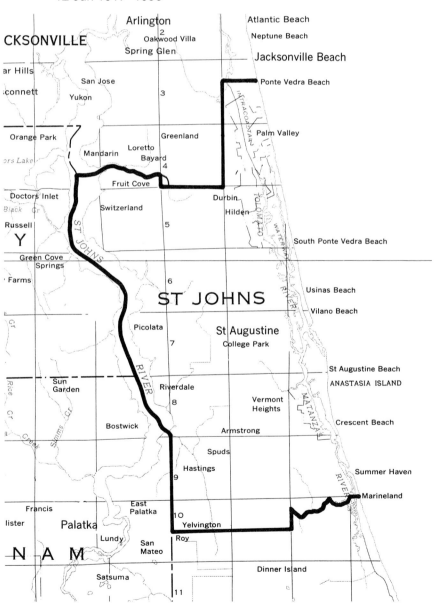

⑪   ST. JOHNS Boundaries
12 Jun 1917–1990

Chronology of ST. LUCIE

Map	Date	Event	Resulting Area
❶	1 Jul 1905	ST. LUCIE created from BREVARD	1,440 sq mi

(Heavy line depicts historical boundary. Base map shows present-day information.)

❶ ST. LUCIE Boundaries
1 Jul 1905 – 6 Aug 1917

Chronology of ST. LUCIE

Map	Date	Event	Resulting Area
❷	7 Aug 1917	ST. LUCIE lost to creation of OKEECHOBEE	1,100 sq mi

(Heavy line depicts historical boundary. Base map shows present-day information.)

❷ ST. LUCIE Boundaries
7 Aug 1917– 28 Jun 1925

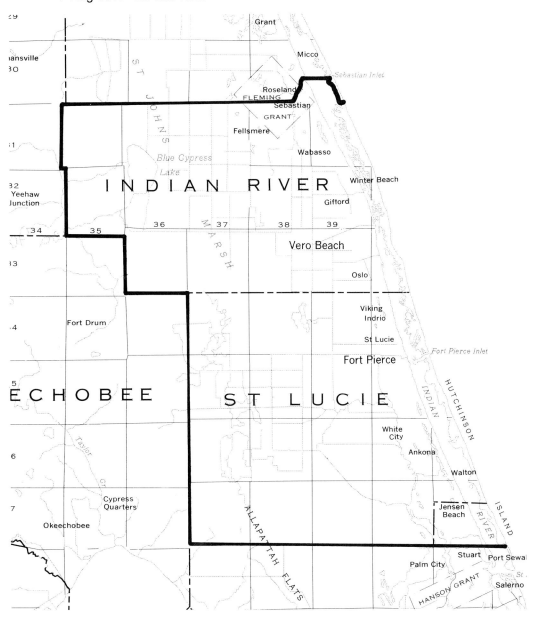

Chronology of ST. LUCIE

Map	Date	Event	Resulting Area
❸	29 Jun 1925	ST. LUCIE lost to creation of INDIAN RIVER	600 sq mi
❹	4 Aug 1925	ST. LUCIE lost to creation of MARTIN	580 sq mi

(Heavy line depicts historical boundary. Base map shows present-day information.)

❸ ST. LUCIE Boundaries
29 Jun 1925 – 3 Aug 1925

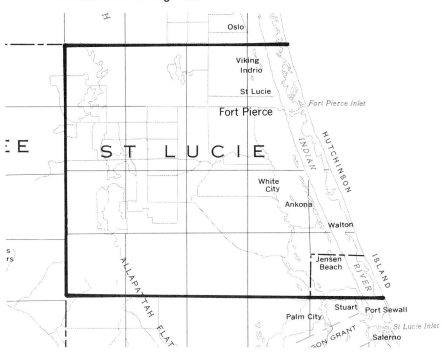

❹ ST. LUCIE Boundaries
4 Aug 1925 – 1990

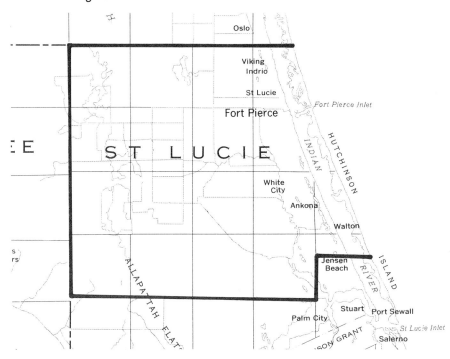

10   0   10   20   30   40 Miles

Chronology of SANTA ROSA

Map	Date	Event	Resulting Area
❶	18 Feb 1842	SANTA ROSA created from ESCAMBIA	1,470 sq mi

(Heavy line depicts historical boundary. Base map shows present-day information.)

❶ SANTA ROSA Boundaries
18 Feb 1842 – 10 Jan 1851

Chronology of SANTA ROSA

Map	Date	Event	Resulting Area
❷	11 Jan 1851	SANTA ROSA exchanged with WALTON	1,520 sq mi

(Heavy line depicts historical boundary. Base map shows present-day information.)

❷ SANTA ROSA Boundaries
11 Jan 1851–13 Jan 1853

10	0	10	20	30	40 Miles

Chronology of SANTA ROSA

Map	Date	Event	Resulting Area
❸	14 Jan 1853	SANTA ROSA gained from WALTON	1,530 sq mi

(Heavy line depicts historical boundary. Base map shows present-day information.)

❸ SANTA ROSA Boundaries
14 Jan 1853 – 6 Sep 1915

| 10 | 0 | 10 | 20 | 30 | 40 Miles |

Chronology of SANTA ROSA

Map	Date	Event	Resulting Area
❹	7 Sep 1915	SANTA ROSA lost to creation of OKALOOSA	1,020 sq mi

(Heavy line depicts historical boundary. Base map shows present-day information.)

❹ SANTA ROSA Boundaries
7 Sep 1915 – 10 Jun 1951

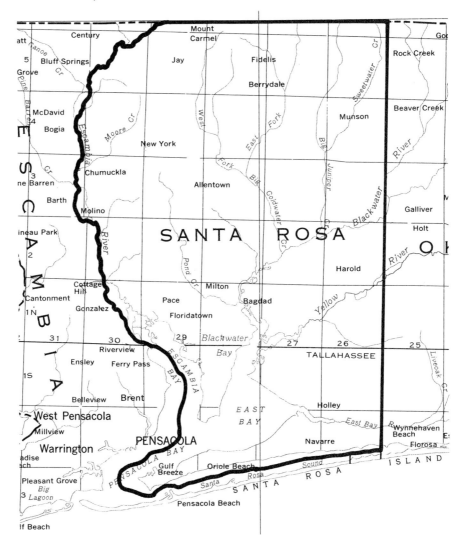

Chronology of SANTA ROSA

Map	Date	Event	Resulting Area
❺	11 Jun 1951	SANTA ROSA gained small area from ESCAMBIA	1,020 sq mi
❺	29 Jun 1957	SANTA ROSA gained small area from ESCAMBIA along the right-of-way of the toll bridge and road on Santa Rosa Sound and Island	1,020 sq mi

(Heavy line depicts historical boundary. Base map shows present-day information.)

❺ SANTA ROSA Boundaries
11 Jun 1951–1990

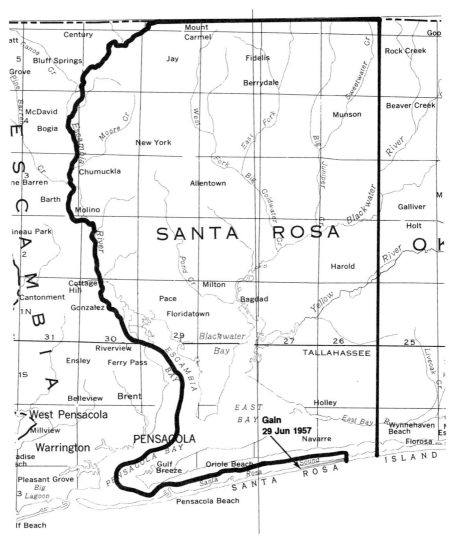

Chronology of SARASOTA

Map	Date	Event	Resulting Area
❶	15 Jun 1921	SARASOTA created from MANATEE	570 sq mi

(Heavy line depicts historical boundary. Base map shows present-day information.)

❶ SARASOTA Boundaries
15 Jun 1921–1990

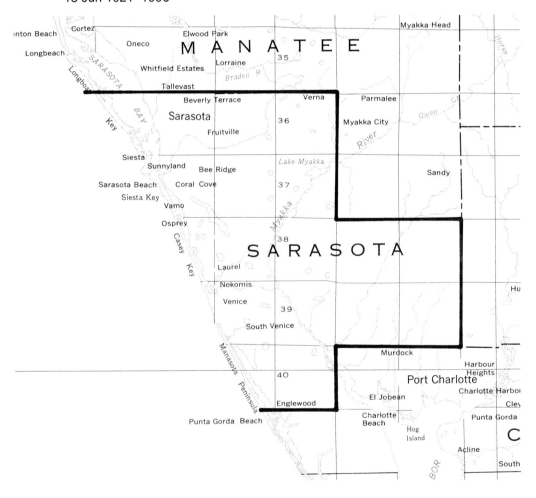

10   0   10   20   30   40 Miles

Chronology of SEMINOLE

Map	Date	Event	Resulting Area
❶	25 Apr 1913	SEMINOLE created from ORANGE [mistake in description corrected 31 May 1961]	300 sq mi
	12 Jun 1941	Part of the boundary between SEMINOLE and VOLUSIA clarified [no discernible change]	
	31 May 1961	SEMINOLE boundaries redefined, correcting mistake of 25 Apr 1913 [no change]	

(Heavy line depicts historical boundary. Base map shows present-day information.)

❶ SEMINOLE Boundaries
25 Apr 1913–1990

10	0	10	20	30	40 Miles

Chronology of SUMTER

Map	Date	Event	Resulting Area
❶	8 Jan 1853	SUMTER created from MARION	900 sq mi
	15 Jan 1859	SUMTER lost small area to MARION to accommodate local resident [location unknown, not mapped]	

(Heavy line depicts historical boundary. Base map shows present-day information.)

❶ SUMTER Boundaries
8 Jan 1853–12 Dec 1866

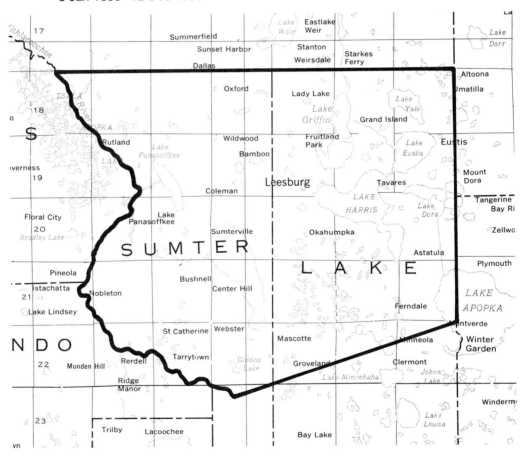

| 10 | 0 | 10 | 20 | 30 | 40 Miles |

Chronology of SUMTER

Map	Date	Event	Resulting Area
❷	13 Dec 1866	SUMTER gained from HILLSBOROUGH	1,400 sq mi

(Heavy line depicts historical boundary. Base map shows present-day information.)

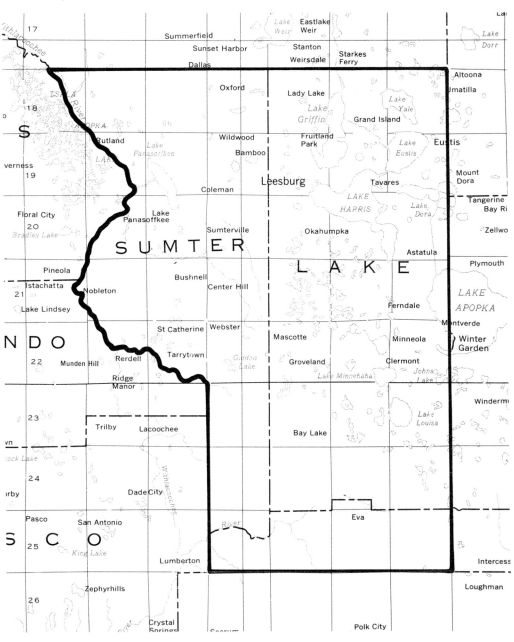

❷   SUMTER Boundaries
13 Dec 1866 – 29 Jan 1871

10   0   10   20   30   40 Miles

Chronology of SUMTER

Map	Date	Event	Resulting Area
❸	30 Jan 1871	SUMTER lost to POLK	1,260 sq mi

(Heavy line depicts historical boundary. Base map shows present-day information.)

❸   SUMTER Boundaries
30 Jan 1871–13 Feb 1872

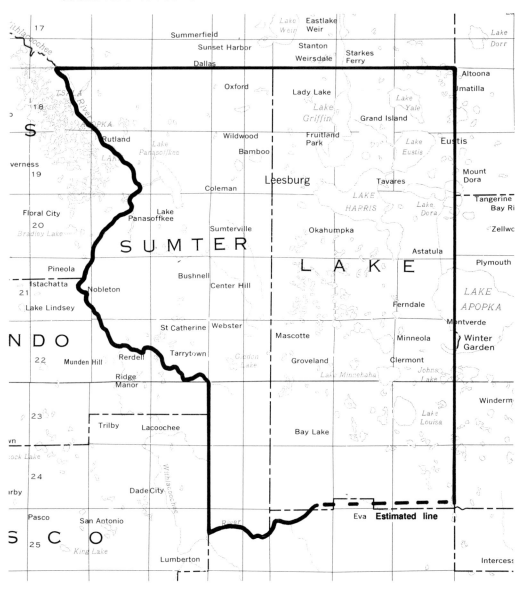

10	0	10	20	30	40 Miles

Chronology of SUMTER

Map	Date	Event	Resulting Area
❹	14 Feb 1872	SUMTER lost to ORANGE	1,180 sq mi

(Heavy line depicts historical boundary. Base map shows present-day information.)

❹ SUMTER Boundaries
14 Feb 1872 – 4 Mar 1879

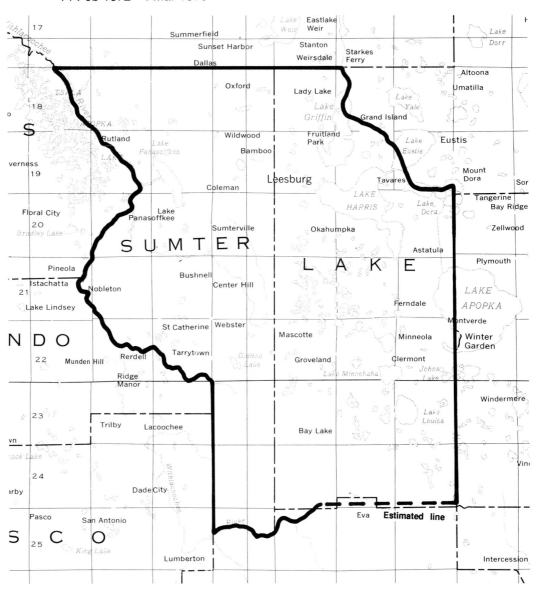

Chronology of SUMTER

Map	Date	Event	Resulting Area
5	5 Mar 1879	SUMTER gained from POLK	1,200 sq mi

(Heavy line depicts historical boundary. Base map shows present-day information.)

5 SUMTER Boundaries
5 Mar 1879 – 25 Jul 1887

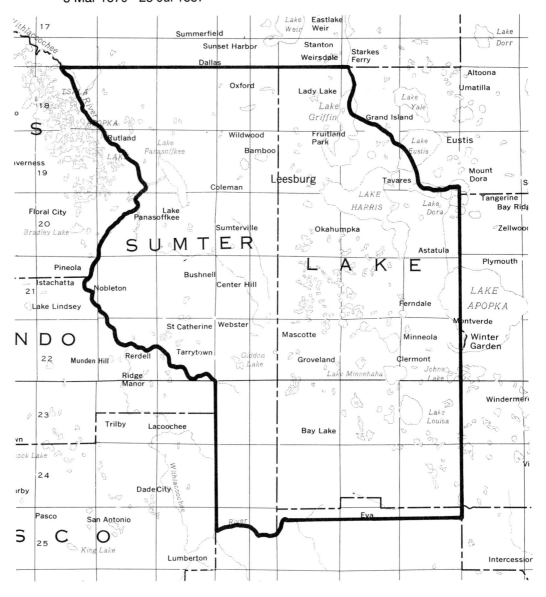

Chronology of SUMTER

Map	Date	Event	Resulting Area
⑥	26 Jul 1887	SUMTER lost to creation of LAKE	580 sq mi

(Heavy line depicts historical boundary. Base map shows present-day information.)

⑥ SUMTER Boundaries
26 Jul 1887– 30 May 1889

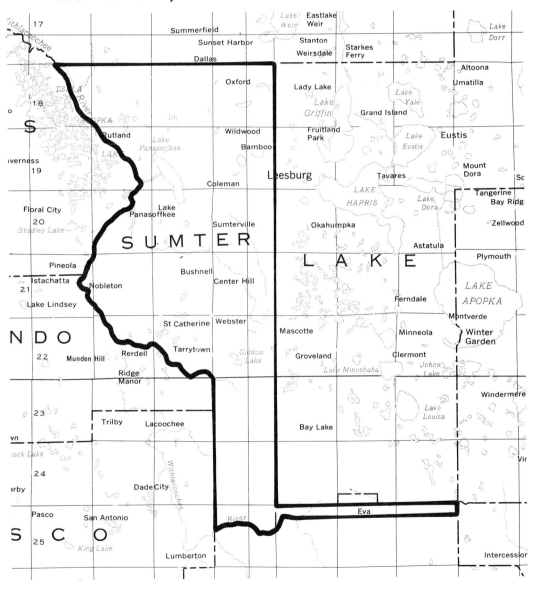

Chronology of SUMTER

Map	Date	Event	Resulting Area
❼	31 May 1889	SUMTER lost to POLK	560 sq mi

(Heavy line depicts historical boundary. Base map shows present-day information.)

❼ SUMTER Boundaries
31 May 1889–1990

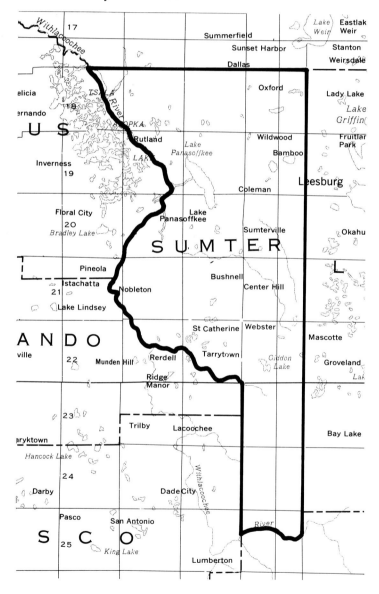

| 10 | 0 | 10 | 20 | 30 | 40 Miles |

Chronology of SUWANNEE

Map	Date	Event	Resulting Area
❶	c. Feb 1859	SUWANNEE created from COLUMBIA	750 sq mi

(Heavy line depicts historical boundary. Base map shows present-day information.)

❶ SUWANNEE Boundaries
    c. Feb 1859 – 11 Dec 1859

10   0   10   20   30   40 Miles

Chronology of SUWANNEE

Map	Date	Event	Resulting Area
❷	12 Dec 1859	SUWANNEE lost to COLUMBIA	700 sq mi
❷	27 Nov 1863	SUWANNEE gained small area from COLUMBIA so as to include entire town of Wellborn in SUWANNEE	700 sq mi

(Heavy line depicts historical boundary. Base map shows present-day information.)

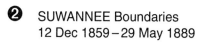

❷ SUWANNEE Boundaries
12 Dec 1859 – 29 May 1889

10   0   10   20   30   40 Miles

Chronology of SUWANNEE

Map	Date	Event	Resulting Area
❸	30 May 1889	SUWANNEE exchanged with COLUMBIA	700 sq mi

(Heavy line depicts historical boundary. Base map shows present-day information.)

❸ SUWANNEE Boundaries
30 May 1889–1990

Chronology of TAYLOR

Map	Date	Event	Resulting Area
❶	23 Dec 1856	TAYLOR created from MADISON	1,250 sq mi

(Heavy line depicts historical boundary. Base map shows present-day information.)

❶ TAYLOR Boundaries
23 Dec 1856 – 20 Dec 1858

Chronology of TAYLOR

Map	Date	Event	Resulting Area
❷	21 Dec 1858	TAYLOR lost to LAFAYETTE	1,030 sq mi

(Heavy line depicts historical boundary. Base map shows present-day information.)

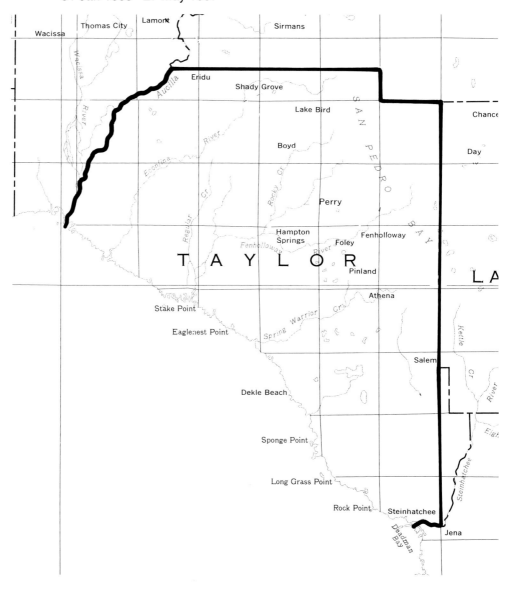

❷ TAYLOR Boundaries
21 Dec 1858–12 Feb 1877
31 Jan 1883–27 May 1887

10   0   10   20   30   40 Miles

Chronology of TAYLOR

Map	Date	Event	Resulting Area
❸	13 Feb 1877	TAYLOR gained from LAFAYETTE	1,070 sq mi
❷	31 Jan 1883	TAYLOR lost to LAFAYETTE [mistake in description corrected 12 Feb 1885]	1,030 sq mi
	12 Feb 1885	Boundary between TAYLOR and LAFAYETTE redefined, correcting mistake of 31 Jan 1883 [no change]	
❸	28 May 1887	TAYLOR gained from LAFAYETTE	1,070 sq mi

(Heavy line depicts historical boundary. Base map shows present-day information.)

❸ TAYLOR Boundaries
13 Feb 1877–30 Jan 1883
28 May 1887–23 May 1911

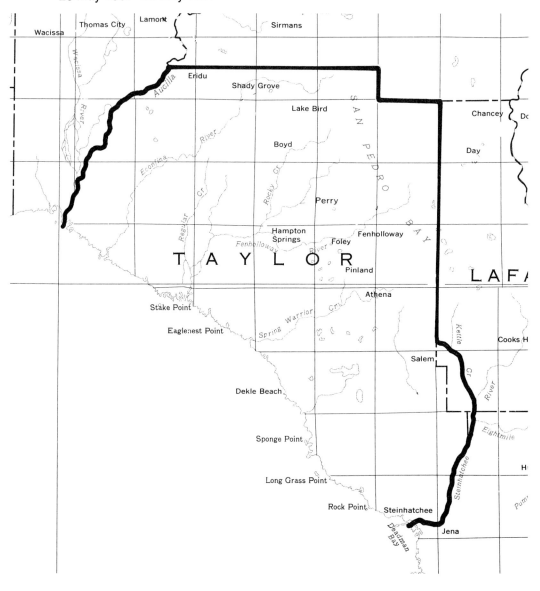

Chronology of TAYLOR

Map	Date	Event	Resulting Area
❹	24 May 1911	TAYLOR lost to LAFAYETTE	1,050 sq mi

(Heavy line depicts historical boundary. Base map shows present-day information.)

❹ **TAYLOR Boundaries**
24 May 1911–1990

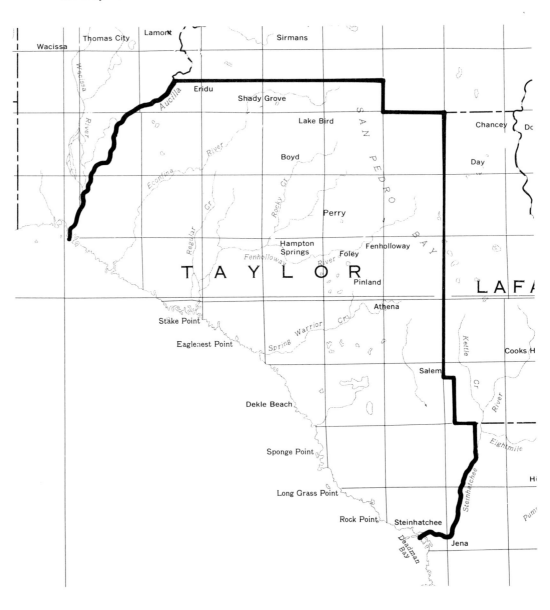

| 10 | 0 | 10 | 20 | 30 | 40 Miles |

Chronology of UNION

Map	Date	Event	Resulting Area
❶	1 Oct 1921	UNION created from BRADFORD	250 sq mi

(Heavy line depicts historical boundary. Base map shows present-day information.)

❶ UNION Boundaries
1 Oct 1921–1990

| 10 | 0 | 10 | 20 | 30 | 40 Miles |

Chronology of VOLUSIA

Map	Date	Event	Resulting Area
❶	29 Dec 1854	VOLUSIA created from ORANGE	1,650 sq mi
	14 Feb 1870	Boundary between VOLUSIA and ORANGE clarified to run west of Huntoon's Island [no change]	
❷	15 Feb 1875	VOLUSIA lost to ST. JOHNS	1,570 sq mi

(Heavy line depicts historical boundary. Base map shows present-day information.)

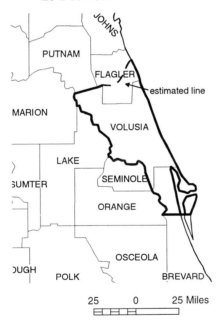

❶ VOLUSIA Boundaries
29 Dec 1854–14 Feb 1875

❷ VOLUSIA Boundaries
15 Feb 1875–10 Mar 1879

Chronology of VOLUSIA

Map	Date	Event	Resulting Area
❸	11 Mar 1879	VOLUSIA lost to BREVARD	1,270 sq mi
❸	24 May 1899	VOLUSIA gained small area from ST. JOHNS	1,270 sq mi
	3 Jun 1907	Boundary between VOLUSIA and ST. JOHNS clarified [no change]	

(Heavy line depicts historical boundary. Base map shows present-day information.)

❸   VOLUSIA Boundaries
11 Mar 1879 – 11 Jun 1917

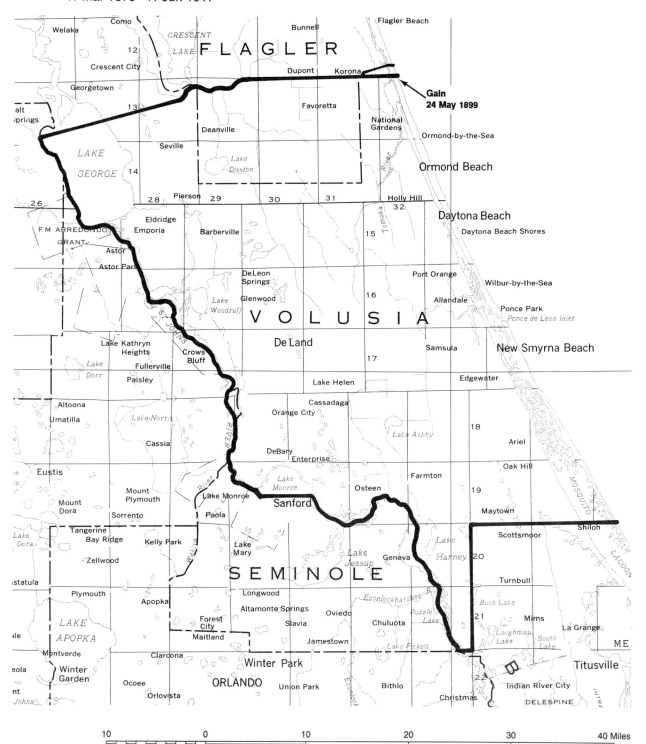

| 10 | 0 | 10 | 20 | 30 | 40 Miles |

Chronology of VOLUSIA

Map	Date	Event	Resulting Area
❹	12 Jun 1917	VOLUSIA lost to creation of FLAGLER	1,110 sq mi
	12 Jun 1941	Part of the boundary between VOLUSIA and SEMINOLE clarified [no discernible change]	
	14 Jun 1967	VOLUSIA boundaries redefined [no change]	
	24 Jun 1983	VOLUSIA boundaries redefined [no change]	

(Heavy line depicts historical boundary. Base map shows present-day information.)

❹ VOLUSIA Boundaries
12 Jun 1917–1990

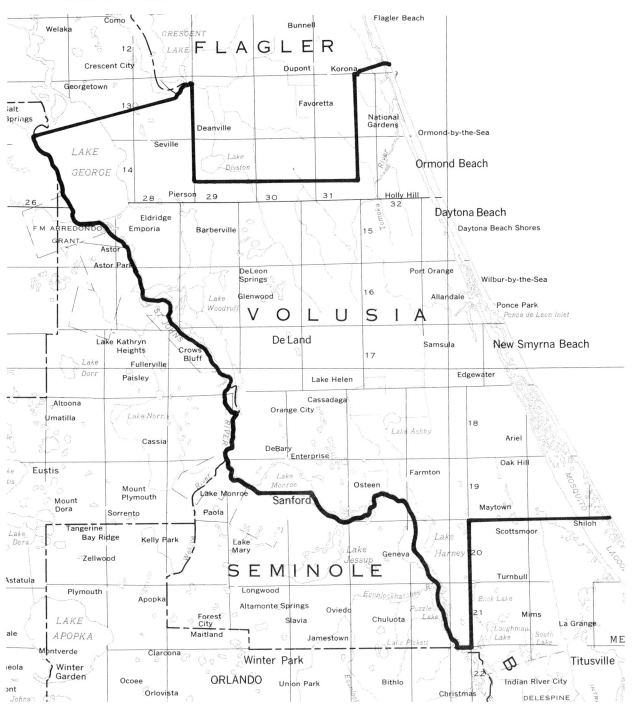

Chronology of WAKULLA

Map	Date	Event	Resulting Area
❶	11 Mar 1843	WAKULLA created from LEON	550 sq mi
❷	6 Jan 1849	WAKULLA gained from LEON	550 sq mi
❷	13 Jan 1851	WAKULLA lost to FRANKLIN when boundary shifted from west bank to east bank of Ochlockonee R.	550 sq mi

(Heavy line depicts historical boundary. Base map shows present-day information.)

❶ WAKULLA Boundaries
11 Mar 1843–5 Jan 1849

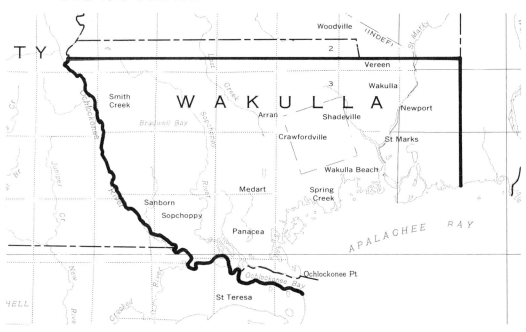

❷ WAKULLA Boundaries
6 Jan 1849–21 Jan 1851

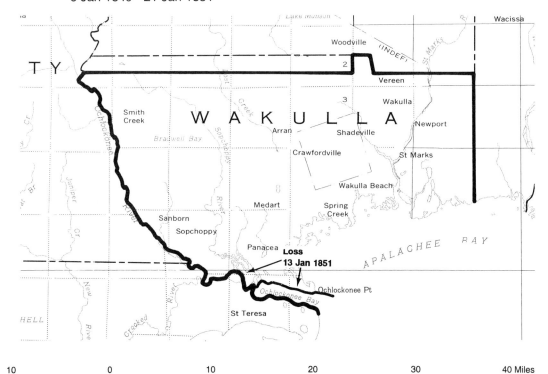

Chronology of WAKULLA

Map	Date	Event	Resulting Area
❸	22 Jan 1851	WAKULLA gained from LEON	600 sq mi
❸	1 Oct 1986	WAKULLA gained from FRANKLIN when boundary shifted from east bank to middle of Ochlockonee R. and Bay	600 sq mi

(Heavy line depicts historical boundary. Base map shows present-day information.)

❸ WAKULLA Boundaries
22 Jan 1851–1990

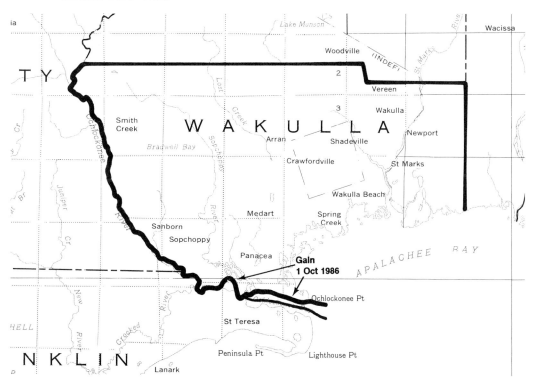

Chronology of WALTON

Map	Date	Event	Resulting Area
❶	29 Dec 1824	WALTON created from ESCAMBIA and JACKSON	2,400 sq mi

(Heavy line depicts historical boundary. Base map shows present-day information.)

❶ WALTON Boundaries
29 Dec 1824 – 8 Dec 1825

Chronology of WALTON

Map	Date	Event	Resulting Area
❷	9 Dec 1825	WALTON gained from ESCAMBIA, exchanged with JACKSON, lost to creation of WASHINGTON	1,690 sq mi

(Heavy line depicts historical boundary. Base map shows present-day information.)

❷   WALTON Boundaries
9 Dec 1825 – 7 Jan 1848

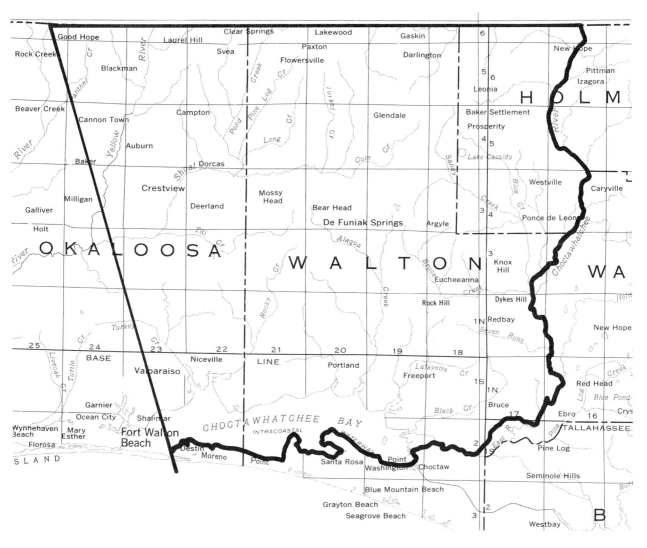

Chronology of WALTON

Map	Date	Event	Resulting Area
❸	8 Jan 1848	WALTON lost to creation of HOLMES	1,460 sq mi

(Heavy line depicts historical boundary. Base map shows present-day information.)

❸ WALTON Boundaries
8 Jan 1848–10 Jan 1851

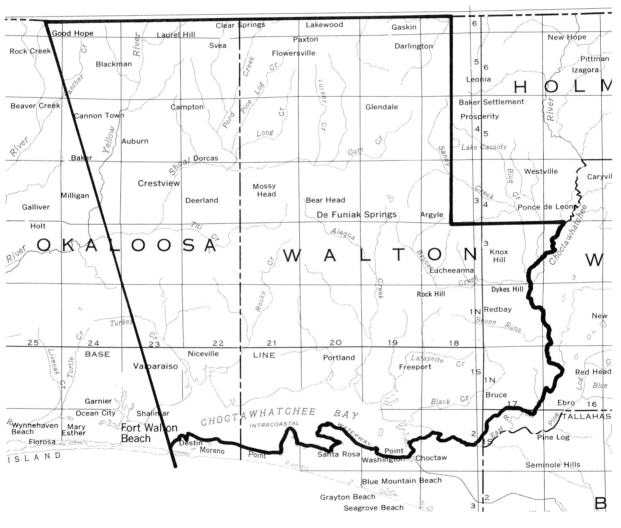

Chronology of WALTON

Map	Date	Event	Resulting Area
❹	11 Jan 1851	WALTON gained part of Santa Rosa I. from ESCAMBIA, exchanged with SANTA ROSA	1,400 sq mi

(Heavy line depicts historical boundary. Base map shows present-day information.)

❹ WALTON Boundaries
11 Jan 1851–13 Jan 1853

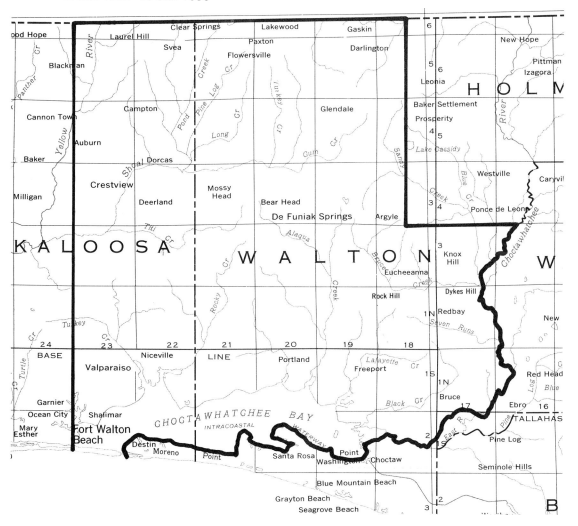

Chronology of WALTON

Map	Date	Event	Resulting Area
❺	14 Jan 1853	WALTON lost to SANTA ROSA	1,390 sq mi
	27 Jan 1881	WALTON granted concurrent jurisdiction with WASHINGTON over the waters of Choctawhatchee Bay [not mapped]	

(Heavy line depicts historical boundary. Base map shows present-day information.)

❺ WALTON Boundaries
14 Jan 1853–16 May 1913

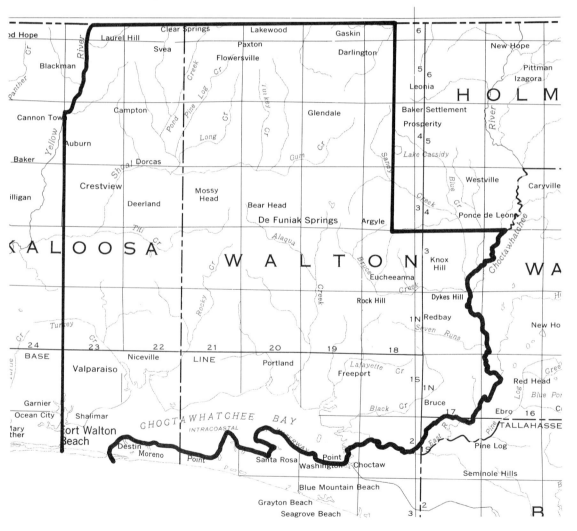

Chronology of WALTON

Map	Date	Event	Resulting Area
❻	17 May 1913	WALTON gained from WASHINGTON	1,500 sq mi

(Heavy line depicts historical boundary. Base map shows present-day information.)

❻ WALTON Boundaries
17 May 1913 – 6 Sep 1915

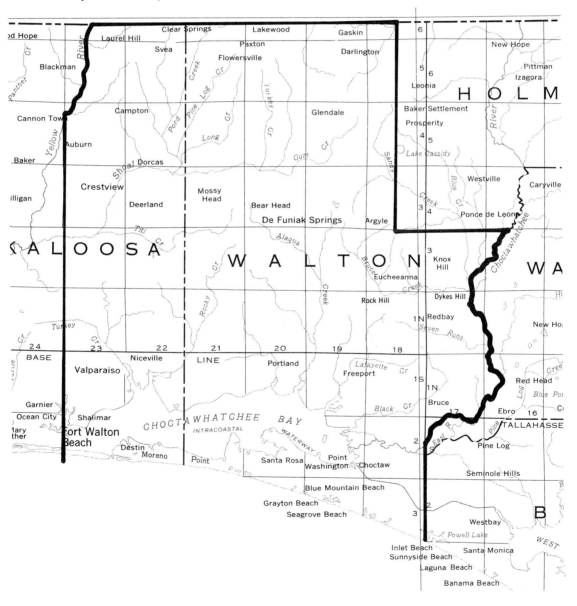

Chronology of WALTON

Map	Date	Event	Resulting Area
❼	7 Sep 1915	WALTON lost to creation of OKALOOSA	1,070 sq mi

(Heavy line depicts historical boundary. Base map shows present-day information.)

❼ WALTON Boundaries
7 Sep 1915 – 1990

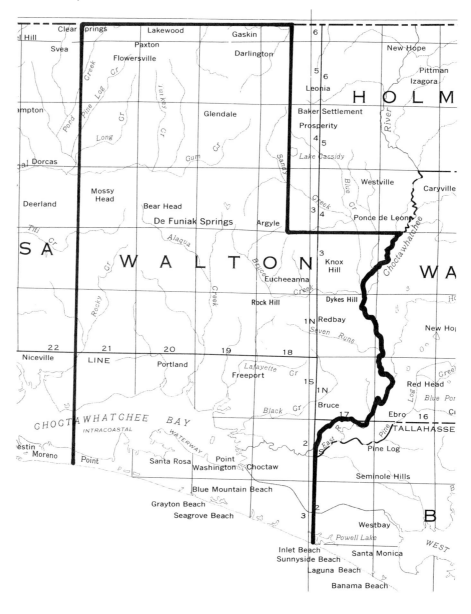

10   0   10   20   30   40 Miles

Chronology of WASHINGTON

Map	Date	Event	Resulting Area
❶	9 Dec 1825	WASHINGTON created from JACKSON and WALTON	2,600 sq mi
❷	12 Jan 1827	WASHINGTON exchanged with JACKSON	2,900 sq mi
❸	29 Oct 1828	WASHINGTON exchanged with JACKSON	2,700 sq mi
❹	8 Feb 1832	WASHINGTON lost to creation of FRANKLIN	2,260 sq mi

(Heavy line depicts historical boundary. Base map shows present-day information.)

❶ WASHINGTON Boundaries
9 Dec 1825 – 11 Jan 1827

❷ WASHINGTON Boundaries
12 Jan 1827 – 28 Oct 1828

❸ WASHINGTON Boundaries
29 Oct 1828 – 7 Feb 1832

❹ WASHINGTON Boundaries
8 Feb 1832 – 10 Feb 1832

Chronology of WASHINGTON

Map	Date	Event	Resulting Area
❺	11 Feb 1832	WASHINGTON exchanged with JACKSON	2,120 sq mi
❻	16 Feb 1833	WASHINGTON lost to FAYETTE and JACKSON	1,850 sq mi
❼	26 Jan 1838	WASHINGTON apparently gained small area from FRANKLIN, lost to creation of CALHOUN	1,710 sq mi
❽	25 Feb 1840	WASHINGTON exchanged with CALHOUN	1,510 sq mi

(Heavy line depicts historical boundary. Base map shows present-day information.)

❺ WASHINGTON Boundaries
11 Feb 1832–15 Feb 1833

25   0   25 Miles

❻ WASHINGTON Boundaries
16 Feb 1833–25 Jan 1838

25   0   25 Miles

❼ WASHINGTON Boundaries
26 Jan 1838–24 Feb 1840

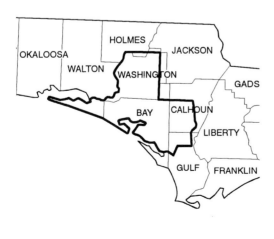

25   0   25 Miles

❽ WASHINGTON Boundaries
25 Feb 1840–3 Jan 1847

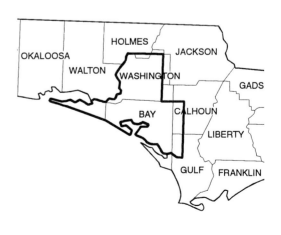

25   0   25 Miles

Chronology of WASHINGTON

Map	Date	Event	Resulting Area
⑨	4 Jan 1847	WASHINGTON gained from JACKSON	1,660 sq mi
⑩	28 Dec 1847	WASHINGTON exchanged with JACKSON	1,570 sq mi
⑪	14 Feb 1873	WASHINGTON gained from CALHOUN [mistake in description corrected 2 Jun 1893]	1,600 sq mi
	27 Jan 1881	WASHINGTON granted concurrent jurisdiction with WALTON over the waters of Choctawhatchee Bay [not mapped]	
	2 Jun 1893	WASHINGTON boundaries redefined, correcting mistake of 14 Feb 1873 [no change]	
⑫	4 Jun 1897	WASHINGTON exchanged with CALHOUN	1,430 sq mi

(Heavy line depicts historical boundary. Base map shows present-day information.)

⑨ WASHINGTON Boundaries
4 Jan 1847–27 Dec 1847

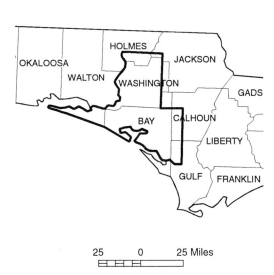

25 0 25 Miles

⑩ WASHINGTON Boundaries
28 Dec 1847–13 Feb 1873

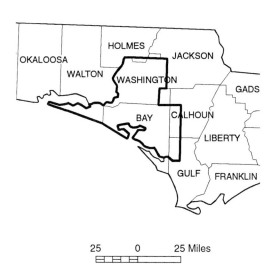

25 0 25 Miles

⑪ WASHINGTON Boundaries
14 Feb 1873–3 Jun 1897

25 0 25 Miles

⑫ WASHINGTON Boundaries
4 Jun 1897–16 May 1913

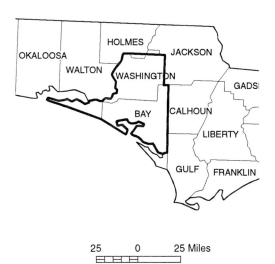

25 0 25 Miles

Chronology of WASHINGTON

Map	Date	Event	Resulting Area
⑬	17 May 1913	WASHINGTON lost to WALTON	1,320 sq mi

Heavy line depicts historical boundary. Base map shows present-day information.)

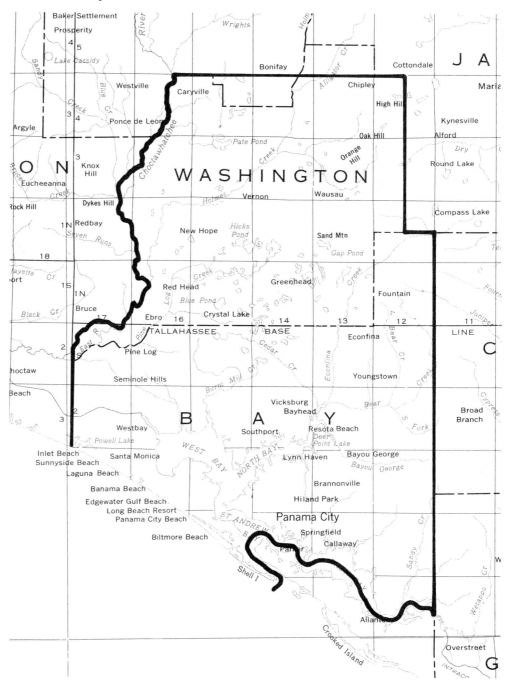

⑬ WASHINGTON Boundaries
17 May 1913 – 30 Jun 1913

Chronology of WASHINGTON

Map	Date	Event	Resulting Area
⑭	1 Jul 1913	WASHINGTON lost to creation of BAY	600 sq mi
⑮	8 Aug 1915	WASHINGTON gained from JACKSON, lost to HOLMES	600 sq mi

(Heavy line depicts historical boundary. Base map shows present-day information.)

⑭ WASHINGTON Boundaries
1 Jul 1913–7 Aug 1915

⑮ WASHINGTON Boundaries
8 Aug 1915–1990

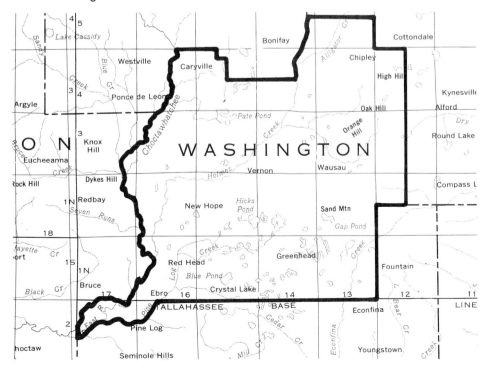

10   0   10   20   30   40 Miles

Territorial, State, and Federal Censuses in Florida

Date	Census
by 1 Aug 1825	Territorial census [not mapped]. Statistics for 3 of 11 counties (Dubester, 7; Dodd); names for LEON only (Dodd).
1 Jun 1830	Federal census. Statistics and names.
1 Jun 1837	Territorial census authorized, but not taken (Harper, 43).
1 Apr 1838	Territorial census. Statistics for 17 of 20 counties (U.S. Congress, House Doc. 206, p. 25); no names.
1 Jun 1840	Federal census. Statistics and names.
after 24 Jul 1845	Census for statehood. Statistics for 17 of 26 counties (Dubester, 7); no names.
1 Jun 1850	Federal census. Statistics and names.
by 1 Sep 1855	State census. Statistics for all counties except DUVAL (Dubester, 8); some names at Florida State Archives and Florida State Library, Tallahassee.
1 Jun 1860	Federal census. Statistics and names for all counties except HERNANDO.
by 1 Sep 1867	State census. Statistics and some names at Florida State Archives, Tallahassee.
1 Jun 1870	Federal census. Statistics and names.
1 Apr 1875	State census [not mapped]. No statistics; names for ALACHUA only at Florida State Archives, Tallahassee.
1 Jun 1880	Federal census. Statistics and names.
1 Jun 1885	Special federal census. Statistics (Dubester, 8); names on National Archives Microfilm Publication M845 for all counties except ALACHUA, CLAY, COLUMBIA, and NASSAU.
2 Jun 1890	Federal census. Statistics; no names.
1 Jul 1895	State census. Statistics (Dubester, 8); some names at Florida State Library, Tallahassee.
1 Jun 1900	Federal census. Statistics and names.
1 Jul 1905	State census. Statistics (Dubester, 8); no names.
15 Apr 1910	Federal census. Statistics and names.
1 Jul 1915	State census. Statistics (Dubester, 9); no names. Statistics for BROWARD were included, although the county was not officially organized until 1 October 1915.
1 Jan 1920	Federal census. Statistics and names.
15 Feb 1925	State census. Statistics (Dubester, 9); no names.
1 Apr 1930	Federal census. Statistics; names not available until 2002.
8 Apr 1935	State census. Statistics (Dubester, 10); names at Florida State Archives, Tallahassee.
1 Apr 1940	Federal census. Statistics; names not available until 2012.

Date	Census
8 Apr 1945	State census. Statistics (Dubester, 10); names at Florida State Archives, Tallahassee.
1 Apr 1950	Federal census. Statistics; names not available until 2022.
1 Apr 1960	Federal census. Statistics; names not available until 2032.
1 Apr 1970	Federal census. Statistics; names not available until 2042.
1 Apr 1980	Federal census. Statistics; names not available until 2052.
1 Apr 1990	Federal census. Statistics; names not available until 2062.

Census Outline
Maps for Florida

Florida Territory—Federal Census 1830

ESCAMBIA

WALTON

JACKSON

WASHINGTON

GADSDEN

LEON

JEFFERSON

MADISON

HAMILTON

ALACHUA

area overlapped
by DUVAL
and NASSAU

NASSAU

DUVAL

ST. JOHNS

estimated line

MOSQUITO

Non-county
(Indian Terr.)

estimated line

Lake
Okeechobee

MONROE

25   0   25 Miles

Florida Territory—Territorial Census 1838

ESCAMBIA

WALTON

JACKSON

WASHINGTON

GADSDEN

CALHOUN

FRANKLIN

LEON

MADISON

JEFFERSON

estimated line

estimated line

HAMILTON

COLUMBIA

area overlapped
by DUVAL
and NASSAU

NASSAU

DUVAL

ST. JOHNS

estimated line

ALACHUA

MOSQUITO

estimated line

HILLSBOROUGH

estimated line

Lake
Okeechobee

MONROE

DADE

25   0   25 Miles

Florida Territory—Federal Census 1840

ESCAMBIA

WALTON

JACKSON

WASHINGTON

GADSDEN

CALHOUN

FRANKLIN

LEON

estimated line

MADISON

JEFFERSON

estimated line

HAMILTON

COLUMBIA

area overlapped
by DUVAL
and NASSAU

NASSAU

DUVAL

ALACHUA

ST. JOHNS

estimated line

MOSQUITO

estimated line

HILLSBOROUGH

estimated line

Lake
Okeechobee

MONROE

DADE

25   0   25 Miles

Florida—State Census 1845

Florida—Federal Census 1850

Florida—State Census 1855

ESCAMBIA

SANTA ROSA

WALTON

HOLMES

JACKSON

WASHINGTON

CALHOUN

GADSDEN

LEON

estimated line

WAKULLA

JEFFERSON

estimated line

MADISON

FRANKLIN

HAMILTON

COLUMBIA

estimated line

area overlapped
by DUVAL
and NASSAU

NASSAU

DUVAL

estimated line

ST. JOHNS

ALACHUA

PUTNAM

estimated line

LEVY

MARION

VOLUSIA

SUMTER

ORANGE

HERNANDO

HILLSBOROUGH

BREVARD

MANATEE

estimated line

Lake
Okeechobee

MONROE

DADE

25   0   25 Miles

Florida—Federal Census 1860

ESCAMBIA
SANTA ROSA
WALTON
HOLMES
JACKSON
GADSDEN
estimated line
WASHINGTON
LEON
JEFFERSON
MADISON
HAMILTON
NASSAU
CALHOUN
LIBERTY
WAKULLA
TAYLOR
SUWANNEE
COLUMBIA
NEW RIVER
DUVAL
FRANKLIN
LAFAYETTE
ALACHUA
CLAY
ST. JOHNS
estimated line
LEVY
PUTNAM
MARION
VOLUSIA
SUMTER
ORANGE
HERNANDO
estimated line
HILLSBOROUGH
BREVARD
MANATEE
Lake Okeechobee
MONROE
DADE

25   0   25 Miles

Florida—State Census 1867

Florida—Federal Census 1870

Florida—Federal Census 1880

estimated line

25   0   25 Miles

Florida—Special Federal Census 1885

estimated line

25   0   25 Miles

Florida—Federal Census 1890

Florida—State Census 1895

25   0   25 Miles

Florida—Federal Census 1900

Florida—State Census 1905

Florida—Federal Census 1910

Florida—State Census 1915

Florida—Federal Census 1920

Florida—State Census 1925

25   0   25 Miles

Florida—State and Federal Censuses 1930–1940

25   0   25 Miles

Florida—State Census 1945

ESCAMBIA
SANTA ROSA
OKALOOSA
HOLMES
JACKSON
WALTON
WASHINGTON
GADSDEN
NASSAU
BAY
CALHOUN
LEON
JEFFERSON
HAMILTON
DUVAL
LIBERTY
WAKULLA
MADISON
BAKER
GULF
FRANKLIN
TAYLOR
SUWANNEE
COLUMBIA
LAFAYETTE
UNION
CLAY
ST. JOHNS
GILCHRIST
BRADFORD
DIXIE
ALACHUA
PUTNAM
FLAGLER
LEVY
MARION
VOLUSIA
CITRUS
LAKE
SEMINOLE
SUMTER
HERNANDO
ORANGE
PASCO
OSCEOLA
PINELLAS
HILLSBOROUGH
POLK
BREVARD
INDIAN RIVER
MANATEE
HARDEE
OKEECHOBEE
ST. LUCIE
HIGHLANDS
SARASOTA
DE SOTO
MARTIN
Lake Okeechobee
CHARLOTTE
GLADES
PALM BEACH
LEE
HENDRY
BROWARD
COLLIER
MONROE
DADE

25   0   25 Miles

Florida—Federal Censuses 1950–1960

25   0   25 Miles

Florida—Federal Censuses 1970–1990

25   0   25 Miles

Bibliography

American State Papers: Documents, Legislative and Executive, of the Congress of the United States: 8, Public Lands. 9, Claims. 9 vols. 1832–1861. Reprint. Greenville, S.C.: Southern Historical Press, 1994. Indexed by McMullin (below).

"Annexation of West Florida to Alabama." *Gulf States Historical Magazine* 1 (1902–1903): 445–451. Consists of letters by Charles Tait, John Williams Walker, and John H. Chaplin.

Atlas of Florida, Containing Sectional Maps of Each County: Showing Land Surveys, Roads, Railroads, Canals, Drainage and Other Valuable Information. 1926. Reprint. Melbourne, Fla.: Living Pictures, [1980].

"Battle of Bloxham . . . Marion's Private 'War.'" *Ocala Star-Banner.* 4 July 1976, p. 90. Newspaper article on the failed attempt to create Bloxham County in 1915.

Bemis, Samuel Flagg. *Pinckney's Treaty: America's Advantage from Europe's Distress, 1783–1800.* Rev. ed. New Haven, Conn.: Yale University Press, 1960.

Bloodworth, Bertha E., and Alton C. Morris. *Places in the Sun: The History and Romance of Florida Place-Names.* Gainesville: University of Florida, 1978.

Boyd, Mark F. "First American Road in Florida: Papers Relating to the Survey and Construction of the Pensacola–St. Augustine Highway." *Florida Historical Society Quarterly* 14 (1935): 72–106, 138–192.

Bruff, J. Goldsborough. *State of Florida, Compiled in the Bureau of Topographical Engineers from the Best Authorities* [map]. Washington, D.C., 1846.

Burns, Francis P. "West Florida and the Louisiana Purchase: An Examination into the Question of Whether It Was Included in the Territory Ceded by the Treaty of 1803." *Louisiana Historical Quarterly* 15 (1932): 391–416.

Callahan, James Morton. *Neutrality of the American Lakes and Anglo-American Relations.* Johns Hopkins University Studies in Historical and Political Science, ser. 16, nos. 1–4, ed. Herbert B. Adams. Baltimore: Johns Hopkins Press, 1898.

Cappon, Lester J., Barbara Bartz Petchenik, and John Hamilton Long, eds. *Atlas of Early American History: The Revolutionary Era, 1760–1790.* Princeton, N.J.: Princeton University Press, 1976. Section on boundaries is thoroughly documented.

Carswell, Elba Wilson. *Tempestuous Triangle: Historical Notes on Washington County, Florida.* Chipley, Fla.: Washington County School Board, 1974.

Cline, Howard F. *Provisional Historical Gazeteer* [sic], *with Locational Notes on Florida Colonial Communities, 1700–1823, and 16 Maps, 3 Figures.* 1964. Reprinted as *Florida Indians II.* New York: Garland Publishing, 1974. A technical report prepared for the U.S. Department of Justice, Land Claims Division, Indian Lands Section.

Cotterill, R. S. "National Land System in the South: 1803–1812." *Mississippi Valley Historical Review* 16 (1929–1930): 495–506.

Cox, Isaac Joslin. *West Florida Controversy, 1798–1813: A Study in American Diplomacy.* Baltimore: Johns Hopkins Press, 1918.

Cubberly, Frederick. "Florida against Georgia: A Story of the Boundary Dispute." *Florida Historical Society Quarterly* 3 (1924): 20–28.

Darby, William. *Memoir on the Geography, and Natural and Civil History of Florida, Attended by a Map of That Country, Connected with the Adjacent Places: And an Appendix, Containing the Treaty of Cession, and Other Papers Relative to the Subject.* Philadelphia, 1821.

De Vorsey, Louis, Jr. *Indian Boundary in the Southern Colonies, 1763–1775.* Chapel Hill: University of North Carolina Press, 1961.

De Vorsey, Louis, Jr., ed. *De Brahm's Report of the General Survey in the Southern District of North America.* Columbia: University of South Carolina Press, 1971.

Dodd, Dorothy. "Florida Census of 1825." *Florida Historical Quarterly* 22 (1943): 34–40.

Dubester, Henry J. *State Censuses: An Annotated Bibliography of Censuses of Population Taken after the Year 1790 by States and Territories of the United States.* 1948. Reprint. New York: Burt Franklin, 1969. The standard guide for its subject.

Ellicott, Andrew. *Journal of Andrew Ellicott, Late Commissioner on Behalf of the United States during Part of the Year 1796, the Years 1797, 1798, 1799, and Part of the Year 1800: For Determining the Boundary between the United States and Possessions of His Catholic Majesty in America, Containing Occasional Remarks on the Situation, Soil, Rivers, Natural Productions, and Diseases of the Different Countries on the Ohio, Mississippi, and Gulf of Mexico.* Philadelphia, 1803.

Filby, P. William, comp. *American and British Genealogy and Heraldry: A Selected List of Books.* 3d ed. Boston: New England Historic Genealogical Society, 1983.

Filby, P. William, comp. *American and British Genealogy and Heraldry: 1982–1985 Supplement.* Boston: New England Historic Genealogical Society, 1987.

Filby, P. William, comp. *Bibliography of American County Histories.* Baltimore: Genealogical Publishing Co., 1985.

Fitzgerald, Joseph H., ed. *Changing Perceptions: Mapping the Shape of Florida, 1502–1982.* Miami: Historical Association of Southern Florida, 1984. Catalogue of a special exhibition at the Historical Museum of Southern Florida, 22 September–18 November 1984.

Florida. *Acts and Resolutions Adopted by the Legislature.* Tallahassee, 1845–. Cited as Fla. Laws.

Florida. *Florida Statutes.* Jacksonville, et al. 1892–. Cited as Fla. Stat.

Florida Department of Agriculture. *Sectional Map of Florida.* Buffalo, N.Y.: J. W. Clement Co., Matthews-Northrup Works, 1935.

Florida Statutes Annotated (West). St. Paul, Minn.: West Publishing Co., 1988.

Florida Supreme Court. *Florida Reports.* 160 vols. 1846–1948. Reports of cases heard before the Supreme Court of Florida. Cited as Fla. Rpts.

Florida Territory. *Acts and Resolutions of the Legislative Council.* 1st–23d assemblies, August 1822–January 1845. Pensacola and Tallahassee, 1823–1845. The session laws of Florida Territory. Cited as Fla. Terr. Acts.

Florida Territory. *Compilation of the Public Acts of the Legislative Council of the Territory of Florida Passed prior to 1840.* Compiled by John P. Duval. Tallahassee, 1839.

Florida Works Progress Administration. *Creation of Counties in Florida, 1820–1936.* [Unpublished single sheet, n.d.].

"From Pensacola to St. Augustine in 1827: A Journey of the Rt. Rev. Michael Portier." *Florida Historical Quarterly* 26 (1947): 135–166.

Fuller, Hubert Bruce. *Purchase of Florida: Its History and Diplomacy.* Cleveland: Burrows Brothers Co., 1906.

George, Paul S., ed. *Guide to the History of Florida.* New York: Greenwood Press, 1989.

Grismer, Karl H. *History of St. Petersburg, Historical and Biographical.* St. Petersburg, Fla.: Tourist News Publishing Co., [1924].

Grismer, Karl H. *Story of Sarasota: The History of the City and County of Sarasota, Florida.* Sarasota, Fla.: M. E. Russell, 1946.

Harper, Roland M. "Ante-Bellum Census Enumerations in Florida." *Florida Historical Society Quarterly* 6 (1927): 42–52.

Harris, Michael H., comp. *Florida History: A Bibliography.* Metuchen, N.J.: Scarecrow Press, 1972.

Hilliard, Sam Bowers. *Atlas of Antebellum Southern Agriculture.* Baton Rouge: Louisiana State University Press, 1984.

Hinsdale, B. A. "Establishment of the First Southern Boundary of the United States." In *Annual Report of the American Historical Association for the Year 1893,* 329–366. Washington, D.C., 1894.

Historical Records Survey, Florida. *Okaloosa County (Crestview).* Inventory of the County Archives of Florida, no. 46. Jacksonville: Historical Records Survey, 1939. Cited as HRS Fla., *Okaloosa.*

Historical Records Survey, Florida. *Pinellas County (Clearwater).* Inventory of the County Archives of Florida, no. 54. Jacksonville: Florida Historical Records Survey Project, 1940. Cited as HRS Fla., *Pinellas.*

Historical Records Survey, Florida. "Record of Acts of the Legislative Council of the Territory of Florida and General Assembly of the State of Florida Relating to County Boundaries, 1821–1937." 1937. Typescript. Florida Historical Records Survey Project, 1936–1942. Florida State Library, Tallahassee.

Historical Records Survey, Florida. *Spanish Land Grants in Florida.* Tallahassee: Florida State Library Board, 1940–1941.

History of Florida, Past and Present, Historical and Biographical. 3 vols. Chicago: Lewis Publishing Co., 1923.

Holmes, Jack D. L. "Southern Boundary Commission, the Chattahoochee River, and the Florida Seminoles, 1799." *Florida Historical Quarterly* 44 (1966): 312–341.

Hudson, F. M. "Beginnings in Dade County." *Tequesta* 1, no. 3 (July 1943): 1–35.

Hutchinson, Janet, comp. *History of Martin County [Florida].* Hutchinson Island, Fla.: Martin County Historical Society, 1975.

Johnson, Cecil. *British West Florida, 1763–1783.* Yale Historical Publications, Miscellany 42. New Haven, Conn.: Yale University Press, 1943.

Kane, Joseph Nathan. *American Counties: Origins of Names, Dates of Creation and Organization, Area, Population, Historical Data, and Published Sources.* 3d ed. Metuchen, N.J.: Scarecrow Press, 1972.

Lainhart, Ann S. *State Census Records.* [Baltimore]: Genealogical Publishing Co., 1992.

Le Baron, J. Francis. *Duval County, Fla.* [map]. 2d ed. Jacksonville, 1898.

Le Baron, J. Francis. *Map of Brevard County, Florida.* Jacksonville, 1885.

Long, John H. "Case Study in Utilizing Computer Technology: The Atlas of Historical County Boundaries." *Perspectives: American Historical Association Newsletter* 30, no. 3 (March 1992): 16–17. Describes how computers have been employed early in the making of this atlas.

McCarthy, Kevin M. *History of Gilchrist County [Florida].* N.p.: Historical Committee of the Trenton Women's Club, 1986.

[McCraw, Jamon]. *Florida Historical Index: Every Historical Platt [sic] Site in Florida, by Its Township, Range, and Section.* N.p., 1986. Revised edition of McCraw's *Florida Historical Sites Unlimited.* 1976.

MacDonald, Grace E., comp. *Check-List of Session Laws.* New York: H. W. Wilson Co., 1936. Complemented by Pollack (below), this guide lists all state session laws through 1935.

MacDonald, Grace E., comp. *Check-List of Statutes of States of the United States of America, Including Revisions, Compilations, Digests, Codes and Indexes.* Providence, R.I.: Oxford Press, 1937. The most complete guide to state codes through 1937.

McGroarty, William Buckner. "Major Andrew Ellicott and His Historic Border Lines." *Virginia Magazine of History and Biography* 58 (1950): 98–110.

McIver, Stuart B. *Fort Lauderdale and Broward County: An Illustrated History.* Woodland Hills, Calif.: Windsor Publications, 1983.

McMullin, Phillip W., ed. *Grassroots of America: A Computerized Index to the American State Papers: Land Grants and Claims (1789–1837) with Other Aids to Research.* 1972. Reprint. Greenville, S.C.: Southern Historical Press, 1994. An index to the *Public Lands* and *Claims* series of the *American State Papers.*

Map of Polk County Florida, Compiled from U.S. Land Office, Private Surveys and Other Authentic Sources. Jacksonville, 1883.

"Map of the State of Florida to Accompany the Florida Annual for 1884." New York, 1884.

Marks, Henry S., ed. "Boundary Disputes in the Republic of West Florida in 1810." *Louisiana History* 12 (1971): 355–365.

Martin, Sidney Walter. *Florida during the Territorial Days.* Athens: University of Georgia Press, 1944.

Martin, Sidney Walter. "Public Domain in Territorial Florida." *Journal of Southern History* 10 (1944): 174–187.

Mitchell, S. Augustus. *Map of Florida.* [Philadelphia], 1852. Included as map number 21 in many editions of Mitchell's *New Universal Atlas.* Philadelphia, 1852.

Morris, Allen. *Florida Place Names.* Coral Gables, Fla.: University of Miami Press, 1974.

Mowat, Charles Loch. *East Florida as a British Province, 1763–1784.* University of California Publications in History, vol. 32. Berkeley and Los Angeles: University of California Press, 1943.

Opdyke, John B. *Alachua County [Florida]: A Sesquicentennial Tribute.* Gainesville: Alachua County Historical Commission, 1974.

Parry, Clive, ed. *Consolidated Treaty Series.* 231 vols. Dobbs Ferry, N.Y.: Oceana Publications, 1969–1981.

Paullin, Charles O. *Atlas of the Historical Geography of the United States.* Edited by John K. Wright. Washington, D.C., and New York: Carnegie Institution of Washington and American Geographical Society of New York, 1932. Excellent section on international and interstate boundary disputes.

Pollack, Ervin H., comp. *Supplement with Bibliographical Notes, Emendations, and Additions to the Check List of Session Laws, Compiled by Grace E. MacDonald.* Preliminary ed. Boston: National Association of State Libraries, 1941. Fills gaps in MacDonald's 1936 compilation (above) to produce the most complete list of state session laws through 1935.

Rabenhorst, Thomas D., and Carville V. Earle, eds. *Historical U.S. County Outline Map Collection, 1840–1980.* Baltimore: Department of Geography, University of Maryland (Baltimore County), 1984. A portfolio of redrawn federal maps; no supporting text or documentation.

Rand, McNally, and Company. "Florida [map]." In *Rand, McNally and Co.'s Business Atlas Containing Large Scale Maps of Each State and Territory of the United States, the Provinces of Canada, West India Islands, Etc., Etc. Together with a Complete Reference Map of the World.* Chicago, 1880.

Rand, McNally, and Company. *1972 Commercial Atlas and Marketing Guide.* Chicago: Rand, McNally, and Company, 1972.

Rand, McNally, and Company. *1973 Commercial Atlas and Marketing Guide.* Chicago: Rand, McNally, and Company, 1973.

Read, William A. *Florida Place-Names of Indian Origin and Seminole Personal Names.* Louisiana State University Studies, no. 11. Baton Rouge: Louisiana State University Press, 1934.

Report of the Commissioners Appointed in Pursuance of an Act for the Amicable Settlement of Limits with the State of Georgia, and Authorizing the Establishment of a Government in the

Mississippi Territory. Published by order of the House of Representatives. Washington, D.C., 1803.

Rowland, Dunbar, ed. *Mississippi Provincial Archives, 1763–1766: English Dominion.* Nashville: Brandon Printing Co., 1911. Only volume published in a projected multivolume series.

Royce, Charles C., comp. "Indian Land Cessions in the United States." Part 2 of *Eighteenth Annual Report of the Bureau of American Ethnology, 1896–1897.* Washington, D.C., 1899. The standard authority in its field; state maps detail all Indian land-cession treaties with the federal government.

Schene, Michael G. "History of Volusia County, Florida." Ph.D. diss., Florida State University, 1976.

Sealock, Richard B., Margaret M. Sealock, and Margaret S. Powell. *Bibliography of Place-Name Literature: United States and Canada.* 3d ed. Chicago: American Library Association, 1982.

Searcy, I. G. *Map of Florida Constructed Principally from Authentic Documents in the Land Office at Tallahassee.* Tallahassee and Baltimore, 1829.

Servies, James A., comp. *Bibliography of West Florida.* Rev. ed. 4 vols. Pensacola, Fla.: James A. Servies, 1978.

Shofner, Jerrell H. *Jackson County, Florida—A History.* Marianna, Fla.: Jackson County Heritage Association, 1985.

Shortt, Adam, and Arthur G. Doughty, eds. *Documents Relating to the Constitutional History of Canada.* Vol. 1, *1759–1791.* Canadian Archives, Sessional Paper no. 18. Ottawa, 1907. Contains full text of King George III's Proclamation of 1763, including boundary descriptions.

Simpson, J. Clarence. *Provisional Gazetteer of Florida Place-Names of Indian Derivation, Either Obsolescent or Retained Together with Others of Recent Application.* Florida Geological Survey Special Publication no. 1. Tallahassee: Florida State Board of Conservation, 1956.

Sinko, Peggy Tuck. *Guide to Local and Family History at the Newberry Library.* Salt Lake City: Ancestry Publishing, 1987.

Stanley, J. Randall. *History of Jackson County [Florida].* N.p.: Jackson County Historical Society, 1950.

Stephenson, Richard W., comp. *Land Ownership Maps: A Checklist of Nineteenth Century United States County Maps in the Library of Congress.* Washington, D.C.: Library of Congress, 1967. Most of the maps listed here have been reproduced on microfiche by the Library of Congress.

Sterkx, Henry Eugene, and Brooks Thompson. "Philemon Thomas and the West Florida Revolution." *Florida Historical Quarterly* 39 (1961), 378–386.

Swindler, William F., ed. *Sources and Documents of United States Constitutions.* 10 vols. Dobbs Ferry, N.Y.: Oceana Publications, 1973–1979. The most complete and up-to-date compilation for the states.

Tebeau, Charlton W. *History of Florida.* Coral Gables, Fla.: University of Miami Press, 1971.

Territorial Papers of the United States. Vols. 1–26 edited by Clarence E. Carter; vols. 27–28 edited by John P. Bloom. Washington, D.C.: Government Printing Office, 1934–1975. Cited as *Terr. Papers U.S.*

Thompson, Leslie A. *Manual or Digest of the Statute Law of the State of Florida, Including Law of the United States Relative to the Government of Florida.* Boston, 1847.

Thorndale, William, and William Dollarhide. *Map Guide to the U.S. Federal Censuses, 1790–1920.* Baltimore: Genealogical Publishing Co., 1987. An atlas of well-designed county outline maps for each state, accompanied by a bibliography and an explanation of methodology.

United States. *Statutes at Large of the United States of America, 1789–1873.* 17 vols. Boston: Little, Brown, 1845–1874. Cited as U.S. Stat.

U.S. Congress, House. *Apalachicola River, Fla.* 64th Congress, 2d sess., 1916–1917. House Document 1725. Serial 7147.

U.S. Congress, House. "Census of the Territory of Florida, 1838." In *Florida.* 27th Congress, 2d sess., 1841–1842. House Document 206, p. 25. Serial 404.

U.S. Congress, Senate. *Documents and Other Papers Relating to the Boundary Line between the States of Georgia and Florida.* 33d Congress, 2d sess., 1854–1855. Senate Misc. Document 25. Serial 773.

U.S. Engineer Department. *Map of the Seat of War in Florida. Compiled by Order of Bvt. Brigr. Genl. Z. Taylor, Principally from the Surveys and Reconnaissances of the Officers of the U.S. Army, by Capt. John Mackay and Lieut. J. E. Blake, U.S. Topographical Engineers.* Washington, D.C., 1839.

U.S. General Land Office. "Plat Exhibiting the State of the Surveys in the State of Florida, with References." In *Annual Report of the Commissioner of the General Land Office.* 29th Congress, 1st sess., 1845–1846. Senate Document 16. Serial 472.

Upchurch, John C. "Aspects of the Development and Exploration of the Forbes Purchase." *Florida Historical Quarterly* 48 (1969): 117–139.

Vanderhill, Burke G., and Frank A. Unger. "Georgia–Florida Land Boundary, Product of Controversy and Compromise." *West Georgia College Studies in the Social Sciences* 18 (1979): 59–73.

Van Landingham, Kyle S., and Alma Hetherington. *History of Okeechobee County [Florida].* Fort Pierce, Fla.: Kyle S. Van Landingham, 1978.

Van Zandt, Franklin K. *Boundaries of the United States and the Several States.* Geological Survey Professional Paper 909. Washington, D.C.: Government Printing Office, 1976. The standard compilation for its subject.

Vignoles, Charles. *Observations upon the Floridas.* New York, 1823.

Warren, Harris G. "Textbook Writers and the Florida 'Purchase' Myth." *Florida Historical Quarterly* 41 (1963): 325–331.

Whitaker, Arthur Preston. *Spanish-American Frontier: 1783–1795.* Boston: Houghton Mifflin Co., 1927.

Williams, John Lee. *Territory of Florida: Or Sketches of the Topography, Civil and Natural History, of the Country, the Climate, and the Indian Tribes, from the First Discovery to the Present Time, with a Map, Views, Etc.* New York, 1837. Includes a very useful map of Florida.

Williams, John Lee. *View of West Florida, Embracing Its Geography, Topography, Etc. with an Appendix Treating of Its Antiquities, Land Titles, and Canals. And Containing a Map, Exhibiting a Chart of the Coast, a Plan of Pensacola, and the Entrance of the Harbour.* Philadelphia, 1827. Includes the detailed "Map of the Western Part of Florida."

Index of Places

This is an index of cities, towns, and other places that appear on the large-scale county maps in this volume. The index names the county where each place is located today. To find a place on a map, go to the section of individual county chronologies and maps and turn to the county named in the index; the 1990 map of the counties shows where the place is situated. Because of historical changes in county boundaries, the place may have been part of one or more different counties in the past. To find other counties in which the place may have been located in the past, trace that place back through the different configurations of its present county and other counties from which the current one was created or gained territory.

Place	Modern County	Place	Modern County
Acline	CHARLOTTE	Arredondo	ALACHUA
Adamsville	HILLSBOROUGH	Ashton	OSCEOLA
Agricola	POLK	Ashville	JEFFERSON
Alachua	ALACHUA	Astatula	LAKE
Alcoma	POLK	Astor	LAKE
Alford	JACKSON	Astor Park	LAKE
Allandale	VOLUSIA	Athena	TAYLOR
Allanton	BAY	Atlantic Beach	DUVAL
Allentown	SANTA ROSA	Auburn	OKALOOSA
Alliance	JACKSON	Auburndale	POLK
Altamonte Springs	SEMINOLE	Aucilla	JEFFERSON
Altha	CALHOUN	Avon Park	HIGHLANDS
Alton	LAFAYETTE		
Altoona	LAKE	Babson Park	POLK
Alturas	POLK	Bagdad	SANTA ROSA
Alva	LEE	Bahama Beach	BAY
Amelia City	NASSAU	Baker	OKALOOSA
American Beach	NASSAU	Baker Settlement	HOLMES
Anclote	PASCO and PINELLAS	Bakers Mill	HAMILTON
		Baldwin	DUVAL
Andalusia	FLAGLER	Balm	HILLSBOROUGH
Andytown	BROWARD	Bamboo	SUMTER
Angel City	BREVARD	Barberville	VOLUSIA
Ankona	ST. LUCIE	Barrineau Park	ESCAMBIA
Anna Maria	MANATEE	Barth	ESCAMBIA
Anona	PINELLAS	Bartow	POLK
Anthony	MARION	Bascom	JACKSON
Apalachicola	FRANKLIN	Basinger	OKEECHOBEE
Apopka	ORANGE	Bay Lake	LAKE
Arcadia	DE SOTO	Bay Ridge	ORANGE
Archer	ALACHUA	Bayard	DUVAL
Argyle	WALTON	Bayhead	BAY
Ariel	VOLUSIA	Bayou George	BAY
Aripeka	HERNANDO and PASCO	Bayport	HERNANDO
		Bayshore	LEE
Arlington	DUVAL	Bayshore Manor	LEE
Armstrong	ST. JOHNS	Beacon Hill	GULF
Arran	WAKULLA	Bean City	PALM BEACH

Place	Modern County	Place	Modern County
Bear Head	WALTON	Brooksville	HERNANDO
Beaver Creek	OKALOOSA	Browns Still	UNION
Becker	NASSAU	Bruce	WALTON
Bee Ridge	SARASOTA	Bryant	PALM BEACH
Bell	GILCHRIST	Bryceville	NASSAU
Belle Glade	PALM BEACH	Buckingham	LEE
Belleair Beach	PINELLAS	Bunnell	FLAGLER
Belleview	ESCAMBIA	Bushnell	SUMTER
Belleview	MARION		
Bellville	HAMILTON	Callahan	NASSAU
Bellwood	BREVARD	Callaway	BAY
Bereah	POLK	Campbell	OSCEOLA
Berkeley	HERNANDO	Campbellton	JACKSON
Berrydale	SANTA ROSA	Campton	OKALOOSA
Beverly Terrace	SARASOTA	Campville	ALACHUA
Big Pine	MONROE	Canal Point	PALM BEACH
Biltmore Beach	BAY	Candler	MARION
Bithlo	ORANGE	Cannon Town	OKALOOSA
Blackman	OKALOOSA	Canova Beach	BREVARD
Bland	ALACHUA	Cantonment	ESCAMBIA
Blitchville	GILCHRIST	Cape Canaveral	BREVARD
Bloomingdale	HILLSBOROUGH	Cape Coral	LEE
Blountstown	CALHOUN	Capitola	LEON
Bloxham	LEON	Capps	JEFFERSON
Blue Mountain Beach	WALTON	Captiva	LEE
Bluff Springs	ESCAMBIA	Carol City	DADE
Boardman	MARION	Carrabelle	FRANKLIN
Boca Grande	LEE	Caryville	WASHINGTON
Boca Raton	PALM BEACH	Cassadaga	VOLUSIA
Bogia	ESCAMBIA	Cassia	LAKE
Bokeelia	LEE	Cedar Hills	DUVAL
Bonifay	HOLMES	Cedar Key	LEVY
Bonita Springs	LEE	Center Hill	SUMTER
Bostwick	PUTNAM	Century	ESCAMBIA
Boulogne	NASSAU	Chaires	LEON
Bowling Green	HARDEE	Chancey	LAFAYETTE
Boyd	TAYLOR	Charlotte Beach	CHARLOTTE
Boyette	HILLSBOROUGH	Charlotte Harbor	CHARLOTTE
Boynton Beach	PALM BEACH	Chason	CALHOUN
Bradenton	MANATEE	Chassahowitzka	CITRUS
Bradenton Beach	MANATEE	Chattahoochee	GADSDEN
Bradfordville	LEON	Cherry Lake	MADISON
Bradley Junction	POLK	Chester	NASSAU
Branford	SUWANNEE	Chiefland	LEVY
Brannonville	BAY	Chipley	WASHINGTON
Bratt	ESCAMBIA	Choctaw	WALTON
Brent	ESCAMBIA	Chokoloskee	COLLIER
Brighton	HIGHLANDS	Chosen	PALM BEACH
Bristol	LIBERTY	Christmas	ORANGE
Broad Branch	CALHOUN	Chuluota	SEMINOLE
Bronson	LEVY	Chumuckla	SANTA ROSA
Brooker	BRADFORD	Citra	MARION

This is an index of cities, towns, and other places that appear on the large-scale county maps in this volume. The index names the county where each place is located today.

Place	Modern County	Place	Modern County
Citrus Park	HILLSBOROUGH	Day	LAFAYETTE
City Point	BREVARD	Daytona Beach	VOLUSIA
Clarcona	ORANGE	Daytona Beach Shores	VOLUSIA
Clark	ALACHUA	Deanville	FLAGLER
Clarksville	CALHOUN	DeBary	VOLUSIA
Clayno	BRADFORD	Deep Lake	COLLIER
Clear Springs	WALTON	Deer Park	OSCEOLA
Clearwater	PINELLAS	Deerfield Beach	BROWARD
Clermont	LAKE	Deerland	OKALOOSA
Cleveland	CHARLOTTE	De Funiak Springs	WALTON
Clewiston	HENDRY	Dekle Beach	TAYLOR
Cocoa	BREVARD	De Land	VOLUSIA
Cocoa Beach	BREVARD	DeLeon Springs	VOLUSIA
Coconut	LEE	Delespine	BREVARD
Coleman	SUMTER	Dellwood	JACKSON
College Park	ST. JOHNS	Delray Beach	PALM BEACH
Columbia	COLUMBIA	Denaud	HENDRY
Compass Lake	JACKSON	Denham	PASCO
Concord	GADSDEN	De Soto City	HIGHLANDS
Cooks Hammock	LAFAYETTE	Destin	OKALOOSA
Copeland	COLLIER	Dills	JEFFERSON
Coral Cove	SARASOTA	Dinner Island	FLAGLER
Coral Gables	DADE	Dinsmore	DUVAL
Corkscrew	COLLIER	Doctor Phillips	ORANGE
Cornwell	HIGHLANDS	Doctors Inlet	CLAY
Coronet	HILLSBOROUGH	Dorcas	OKALOOSA
Cortez	MANATEE	Dover	HILLSBOROUGH
Cottage Hill	ESCAMBIA	Dowling Park	SUWANNEE
Cotton Plant	MARION	Drexel	PASCO
Cottondale	JACKSON	Drifton	JEFFERSON
Courtenay	BREVARD	Duette	MANATEE
Crawfordville	WAKULLA	Dukes	UNION
Creels	FRANKLIN	Dundee	POLK
Crescent Beach	ST. JOHNS	Dunedin	PINELLAS
Crescent City	PUTNAM	Dunnellon	MARION
Crestview	OKALOOSA	Dupont	FLAGLER
Crewsville	HARDEE	Durant	HILLSBOROUGH
Cross City	DIXIE	Durbin	ST. JOHNS
Crows Bluff	LAKE		
Crystal Beach	PINELLAS	Eagle Lake	POLK
Crystal Lake	WASHINGTON	Earleton	ALACHUA
Crystal River	CITRUS	East Naples	COLLIER
Crystal Springs	PASCO	East Palatka	PUTNAM
Curlew	PINELLAS	East Williston	LEVY
Curtis	GILCHRIST	Eastlake Weir	MARION
Cutler Ridge	DADE	Eaton Park	POLK
Cypress	JACKSON	Eau Gallie	BREVARD
Cypress Quarters	OKEECHOBEE	Ebro	WASHINGTON
		Econfina	BAY
Dade City	PASCO	Edgar	PUTNAM
Dalkeith	GULF	Edgewater	VOLUSIA
Dallas	MARION	Edgewater Gulf Beach	BAY
Dania	BROWARD	Eldridge	VOLUSIA
Darby	PASCO	Eleven Mile	FRANKLIN
Darlington	WALTON	Elfers	PASCO
Davenport	POLK	El Jobean	CHARLOTTE
Davie	BROWARD	Ellaville	SUWANNEE

Place	Modern County	Place	Modern County
Ellzey	LEVY	Fort Meade	POLK
Elwood Park	MANATEE	Fort Myers	LEE
Emporia	VOLUSIA	Fort Myers Beach	LEE
Englewood	SARASOTA	Fort Myers Shores	LEE
Ensley	ESCAMBIA	Fort Myers Villas	LEE
Enterprise	VOLUSIA	Ft. Ogden	DE SOTO
Eridu	TAYLOR	Fort Pierce	ST. LUCIE
Espanola	FLAGLER	Fort Union	SUWANNEE
Estero	LEE	Fort Walton Beach	OKALOOSA
Esto	HOLMES	Fort White	COLUMBIA
Eucheeanna	WALTON	Fountain	BAY
Eureka	MARION	Fountain Heights	POLK
Eustis	LAKE	Foxtown	POLK
Eva	POLK	Francis	PUTNAM
Everglades	COLLIER	Freeport	WALTON
Evergreen	NASSAU	Frink	CALHOUN
Evinston	ALACHUA	Frontenac	BREVARD
		Frostproof	POLK
Fairbanks	ALACHUA	Fruit Cove	ST. JOHNS
Fairfield	MARION	Fruitland Park	LAKE
Falmouth	SUWANNEE	Fruitville	SARASOTA
Fannin	LEVY	Fullerville	LAKE
Farmton	VOLUSIA		
Favoretta	FLAGLER	Gainsville	ALACHUA
Felda	HENDRY	Galliver	OKALOOSA
Felicia	CITRUS	Galloway	POLK
Fellowship	MARION	Garden City	DUVAL
Fellsmere	INDIAN RIVER	Garden Grove	HERNANDO
Fenholloway	TAYLOR	Gardner	HARDEE
Fernandina Beach	NASSAU	Garnier	OKALOOSA
Ferndale	LAKE	Gaskin	WALTON
Ferry Pass	ESCAMBIA	Geneva	SEMINOLE
Fidelis	SANTA ROSA	Genoa	HAMILTON
Flagler Beach	FLAGLER	Georgetown	PUTNAM
Flamingo	MONROE	Gibsonia	POLK
Flemington	MARION	Gibsonton	HILLSBOROUGH
Florahome	PUTNAM	Gifford	INDIAN RIVER
Floral City	CITRUS	Glen St. Mary	BAKER
Florida City	DADE	Glendale	WALTON
Floridatown	SANTA ROSA	Glenwood	VOLUSIA
Florosa	OKALOOSA	Golden Beach	DADE
Flowersville	WALTON	Gomez	MARTIN
Foley	TAYLOR	Gonzalez	ESCAMBIA
Forest City	SEMINOLE	Good Hope	OKALOOSA
Forest Grove	ALACHUA	Goodland	COLLIER
Fort Basinger	HIGHLANDS	Goodno	GLADES
Fort Drum	OKEECHOBEE	Goulds	DADE
Fort George Island	DUVAL	Graceville	JACKSON
Ft. Green	HARDEE	Graham	BRADFORD
Fort Lauderdale	BROWARD	Grand Island	LAKE
Fort Lonesome	HILLSBOROUGH	Grand Ridge	JACKSON
Fort McCoy	MARION	Grandin	PUTNAM

This is an index of cities, towns, and other places that appear on the large-scale county maps in this volume. The index names the county where each place is located today.

Place	Modern County	Place	Modern County
Grant	BREVARD	Hollister	PUTNAM
Grayton Beach	WALTON	Holly Hill	VOLUSIA
Green Cove Springs	CLAY	Hollywood	BROWARD
Greenacres City	PALM BEACH	Holmes Beach	MANATEE
Greenhead	WASHINGTON	Holopaw	OSCEOLA
Greenland	DUVAL	Holt	OKALOOSA
Greensboro	GADSDEN	Homeland	POLK
Greenville	MADISON	Homestead	DADE
Greenwood	JACKSON	Homosassa	CITRUS
Gretna	GADSDEN	Homosassa Springs	CITRUS
Greyhound Key	MONROE	Honeyville	GULF
Grove Park	ALACHUA	Hopewell	MADISON
Groveland	LAKE	Horseshoe Beach	DIXIE
Gulf Beach	ESCAMBIA	Hosford	LIBERTY
Gulf Breeze	SANTA ROSA	Houston	SUWANNEE
Gulf Hammock	LEVY	Hudson	PASCO
Gulf Stream	PALM BEACH	Hugh	CLAY
Gulfport	PINELLAS	Hull	DE SOTO
		Hypoluxo	PALM BEACH
Hague	ALACHUA		
Haile	ALACHUA	Immokalee	COLLIER
Haines City	POLK	Indialantic	BREVARD
Hallandale	BROWARD	Indian River City	BREVARD
Hampton	BRADFORD	Indian Rocks Beach	PINELLAS
Hampton Springs	TAYLOR	Indian Town	MARTIN
Hanson	MADISON	Indrio	ST. LUCIE
Harbour Heights	CHARLOTTE	Inglis	LEVY
Hardaway	GADSDEN	Inlet Beach	BAY
Harold	SANTA ROSA	Intercession City	OSCEOLA
Hastings	ST. JOHNS	Interlachen	PUTNAM
Hatchbend	LAFAYETTE	Inverness	CITRUS
Havana	GADSDEN	Inwood	JACKSON
Haverhill	PALM BEACH	Irvine	MARION
Hawthorne	ALACHUA	Islamorada	MONROE
Hedges	NASSAU	Island Grove	ALACHUA
Hernando	CITRUS	Istachatta	HERNANDO
Hesperides	POLK	Italia	NASSAU
Hialeah	DADE	Izagora	HOLMES
Hialeah Gardens	DADE		
High Point	PINELLAS	Jacksonville	DUVAL
High Springs	ALACHUA	Jacksonville Beach	DUVAL
Highland	CLAY	Jacob	JACKSON
Highland Beach	PALM BEACH	Jamestown	SEMINOLE
Highland City	POLK	Jamieson	GADSDEN
Highland Park	POLK	Jasper	HAMILTON
Highland View	GULF	Jay	SANTA ROSA
Highlands Lakes	HIGHLANDS	Jena	DIXIE
Hiland Park	BAY	Jennings	HAMILTON
Hilden	ST. JOHNS	Jensen Beach	MARTIN
Hillcrest Heights	POLK	Jerome	COLLIER
Hilliard	NASSAU	Johnson	PUTNAM
Hillsboro Beach	BROWARD	Juno Beach	PALM BEACH
Hines	DIXIE	Jupiter	PALM BEACH
Hinson	GADSDEN	Jupiter Inlet Colony	PALM BEACH
Hobe Sound	MARTIN		
Holder	CITRUS	Kathleen	POLK
Holley	SANTA ROSA	Kelly Park	ORANGE

Place	Modern County	Place	Modern County
Kenansville	OSCEOLA	Lamont	JEFFERSON
Kendall	DADE	Lanark	FRANKLIN
Kendrick	MARION	Lantana	PALM BEACH
Kerr City	MARION	Largo	PINELLAS
Keuka	PUTNAM	Lauderdale-by-the-Sea	BROWARD
Key Biscayne	DADE	Laurel	SARASOTA
Key Colony Beach	MONROE	Laurel Hill	OKALOOSA
Key Largo	MONROE	Lawtey	BRADFORD
Key West	MONROE	Lealman	PINELLAS
Keystone Heights	CLAY	Lebanon	LEVY
Keysville	HILLSBOROUGH	Lecanto	CITRUS
Kinard	CALHOUN	Lee	MADISON
Kings Ferry	NASSAU	Leesburg	LAKE
Kingsley	CLAY	Lehigh Acres	LEE
Kissimmee	OSCEOLA	Leisure City	DADE
Kissimmee Park	OSCEOLA	Lemon Grove	HARDEE
Knights	HILLSBOROUGH	Leonia	HOLMES
Knox Hill	WALTON	Limestone	HARDEE
Korona	FLAGLER	Lithia	HILLSBOROUGH
Kynesville	JACKSON	Live Oak	SUWANNEE
		Lloyd	JEFFERSON
La Belle	HENDRY	Lochloosa	ALACHUA
Lacoochee	PASCO	Long Beach Resort	BAY
La Crosse	ALACHUA	Longbeach	MANATEE
Lady Lake	LAKE	Longwood	SEMINOLE
Lafayette	LEON	Loretto	DUVAL
La Grange	BREVARD	Lorida	HIGHLANDS
Laguna Beach	BAY	Lorraine	MANATEE
Lake Alfred	POLK	Lotus	BREVARD
Lake Bird	TAYLOR	Loughman	POLK
Lake Butler	UNION	Lovett	MADISON
Lake City	COLUMBIA	Lowell	MARION
Lake Clarke Shores	PALM BEACH	Ludlam	DADE
Lake Como	PUTNAM	Lulu	COLUMBIA
Lake Forest	DUVAL	Lumberton	PASCO
Lake Garfield	POLK	Lundy	PUTNAM
Lake Geneva	CLAY	Luraville	SUWANNEE
Lake Hamilton	POLK	Lutz	HILLSBOROUGH
Lake Harbor	PALM BEACH	Lynn Haven	BAY
Lake Helen	VOLUSIA	Lynne	MARION
Lake Kathryn Heights	LAKE		
Lake Lindsey	HERNANDO	McAlpin	SUWANNEE
Lake Mary	SEMINOLE	Macclenny	BAKER
Lake Monroe	SEMINOLE	McDavid	ESCAMBIA
Lake of the Hills	POLK	McIntosh	MARION
Lake Panasoffkee	SUMTER	McKinnon	ESCAMBIA
Lake Park	PALM BEACH	McNeal	CALHOUN
Lake Placid	HIGHLANDS	McNeils	GULF
Lake Wales	POLK	Madeira Beach	PINELLAS
Lake Worth	PALM BEACH	Madison	MADISON
Lakeland	POLK	Maitland	ORANGE
Lakewood	WALTON	Malabar	BREVARD

This is an index of cities, towns, and other places that appear on the large-scale county maps in this volume. The index names the county where each place is located today.

Place	Modern County	Place	Modern County
Malone	JACKSON	Mulberry	POLK
Manalapan	PALM BEACH	Munson	SANTA ROSA
Manatee	LEVY	Murdock	CHARLOTTE
Mandarin	DUVAL	Myakka City	MANATEE
Mango	HILLSBOROUGH	Myakka Head	MANATEE
Mangonia Park	PALM BEACH		
Marathon	MONROE	Naples	COLLIER
Marathon Shores	MONROE	Naples Park	COLLIER
Marco	COLLIER	Naranja	DADE
Margate	BROWARD	Narcoossee	OSCEOLA
Marianna	JACKSON	Nassauville	NASSAU
Marineland	FLAGLER	National Gardens	VOLUSIA
Martel	MARION	Navarre	SANTA ROSA
Martin	MARION	Neptune Beach	DUVAL
Mary Esther	OKALOOSA	New Berlin	DUVAL
Masaryktown	HERNANDO	New Hope	HOLMES
Mascotte	LAKE	New Hope	WASHINGTON
Matlacha	LEE	New Port Richey	PASCO
Maxville	DUVAL	New River	BRADFORD
Mayo	LAFAYETTE	New Smyrna Beach	VOLUSIA
Mayport	DUVAL	New York	SANTA ROSA
Maytown	VOLUSIA	Newberry	ALACHUA
Mecca	PINELLAS	Newburn	SUWANNEE
Medart	WAKULLA	Newport	WAKULLA
Medulla	POLK	Niceville	OKALOOSA
Melbourne	BREVARD	Nichols	POLK
Melbourne Beach	BREVARD	Nobleton	HERNANDO
Melbourne Village	BREVARD	Nocatee	DE SOTO
Melrose	ALACHUA	Nokomis	SARASOTA
Merritt Island	BREVARD	Noma	HOLMES
Mexico Beach	BAY	Norfleet	LEON
Miami	DADE	North Fort Myers	LEE
Miami Beach	DADE	North Miami	DADE
Miami Shores	DADE	North Miami Beach	DADE
Miami Springs	DADE	North Palm Beach	PALM BEACH
Micanopy	ALACHUA		
Micco	BREVARD	Oak Grove	ESCAMBIA
Miccosukee	LEON	Oak Grove	GULF
Middleburg	CLAY	Oak Hill	VOLUSIA
Midway	GADSDEN	Oakdale	JACKSON
Milligan	OKALOOSA	Oakland Park	BROWARD
Millview	ESCAMBIA	Oakwood Villa	DUVAL
Milton	SANTA ROSA	O'Brien	SUWANNEE
Mims	BREVARD	Ocala	MARION
Minneola	LAKE	Ocean City	OKALOOSA
Molino	ESCAMBIA	Ocean Ridge	PALM BEACH
Montbrook	LEVY	Oceanway	DUVAL
Monteocha	ALACHUA	Ochopee	COLLIER
Monticello	JEFFERSON	Ocoee	ORANGE
Montverde	LAKE	Odessa	PASCO
Moore Haven	GLADES	Ojus	DADE
Morriston	LEVY	Okahumpka	LAKE
Mossy Head	WALTON	Okeechobee	OKEECHOBEE
Mount Carmel	SANTA ROSA	Okeelanta	PALM BEACH
Mount Dora	LAKE	Oklawaha	MARION
Mount Pleasant	GADSDEN	Old Town	DIXIE
Mount Plymouth	LAKE	Oldsmar	PINELLAS

Place	Modern County	Place	Modern County
Olga	LEE	Penney Farms	CLAY
Olustee	BAKER	Pennsuco	DADE
Ona	HARDEE	Pensacola	ESCAMBIA
Oneco	MANATEE	Pensacola Beach	ESCAMBIA
Opa-Locka	DADE	Perrine	DADE
Orange	LIBERTY	Perry	TAYLOR
Orange City	VOLUSIA	Phifer	ALACHUA
Orange Heights	ALACHUA	Pickettville	DUVAL
Orange Lake	MARION	Picolata	ST. JOHNS
Orange Park	CLAY	Pierce	POLK
Orange Springs	MARION	Pierson	VOLUSIA
Oriole Beach	SANTA ROSA	Pine Barren	ESCAMBIA
Orlando	ORANGE	Pine Castle	ORANGE
Orlovista	ORANGE	Pine Log	BAY
Ormond Beach	VOLUSIA	Pinecrest	HILLSBOROUGH
Ormond-by-the-Sea	VOLUSIA	Pineda	BREVARD
Oslo	INDIAN RIVER	Pineland	LEE
Osprey	SARASOTA	Pinellas Park	PINELLAS
Osteen	VOLUSIA	Pineola	CITRUS
Otter Creek	LEVY	Pinetta	MADISON
Overstreet	GULF	Piney Point	MANATEE
Oviedo	SEMINOLE	Pinland	TAYLOR
Oxford	SUMTER	Pittman	HOLMES
Ozona	PINELLAS	Placida	CHARLOTTE
		Plains	HIGHLANDS
Pace	SANTA ROSA	Plant City	HILLSBOROUGH
Page Park	LEE	Plantation	BROWARD
Pahokee	PALM BEACH	Pleasant Grove	ESCAMBIA
Paisley	LAKE	Pleasant Grove	HILLSBOROUGH
Palatka	PUTNAM	Plymouth	ORANGE
Palm Bay	BREVARD	Point Washington	WALTON
Palm Beach	PALM BEACH	Polk City	POLK
Palm City	MARTIN	Pomona Park	PUTNAM
Palm Harbor	PINELLAS	Pompano Beach	BROWARD
Palm Valley	ST. JOHNS	Ponce de Leon	HOLMES
Palma Sola	MANATEE	Ponce Park	VOLUSIA
Palmdale	GLADES	Ponte Vedra Beach	ST. JOHNS
Palmetto	MANATEE	Port Charlotte	CHARLOTTE
Panacea	WAKULLA	Port Mayaca	MARTIN
Panama City	BAY	Port Orange	VOLUSIA
Panama City Beach	BAY	Port Richey	PASCO
Paola	SEMINOLE	Port St. Joe	GULF
Paradise	ALACHUA	Port Sewall	MARTIN
Paradise Beach	ESCAMBIA	Portland	WALTON
Parker	BAY	Princeton	DADE
Parmalee	MANATEE	Prosperity	HOLMES
Parrish	MANATEE	Providence	POLK
Pasco	PASCO	Punta Gorda	CHARLOTTE
Pass-a-Grille Beach	PINELLAS	Punta Gorda Beach	CHARLOTTE
Paxton	WALTON	Punta Rassa	LEE
Pembroke	POLK	Putnam Hall	PUTNAM
Pembroke Pines	BROWARD		

This is an index of cities, towns, and other places that appear on the large-scale county maps in this volume. The index names the county where each place is located today.

Place	Modern County	Place	Modern County
Summer Haven	ST. JOHNS	Venice	SARASOTA
Summerfield	MARION	Venus	HIGHLANDS
Summerland Key	MONROE	Vereen	WAKULLA
Sumterville	SUMTER	Vermont Heights	ST. JOHNS
Sun City	HILLSBOROUGH	Verna	MANATEE
Sun Garden	CLAY and PUTNAM	Vernon	WASHINGTON
Sunniland	COLLIER	Vero Beach	INDIAN RIVER
Sunnyland	SARASOTA	Vicksburg	BAY
Sunnyside Beach	BAY	Viking	ST. LUCIE
Sunset Harbor	MARION	Vilano Beach	ST. JOHNS
Surfside	DADE	Vilas	LIBERTY
Suwannee	DIXIE	Vineland	ORANGE
Suwannee	SUWANNEE		
Svea	OKALOOSA	Wabasso	INDIAN RIVER
Sweetwater	DADE	Wacissa	JEFFERSON
Switzerland	ST. JOHNS	Wakulla	WAKULLA
Sycamore	GADSDEN	Wakulla Beach	WAKULLA
Sydney	HILLSBOROUGH	Waldo	ALACHUA
		Walnut Hill	ESCAMBIA
Taft	ORANGE	Walton	ST. LUCIE
Tallahassee	LEON	Wannee	GILCHRIST
Tallevast	MANATEE	Warrington	ESCAMBIA
Tampa	HILLSBOROUGH	Watertown	COLUMBIA
Tangerine	ORANGE	Wauchula	HARDEE
Tarpon Springs	PINELLAS	Waukeenah	JEFFERSON
Tarrytown	SUMTER	Wausau	WASHINGTON
Tavares	LAKE	Waverly	POLK
Tavernier	MONROE	Webster	SUMTER
Taylor	BAKER	Weirsdale	MARION
Telogia	LIBERTY	Welaka	PUTNAM
Temple Terrace	HILLSBOROUGH	Wellborn	SUWANNEE
Terra Ceia	MANATEE	Wesconnett	DUVAL
Theressa	BRADFORD	West Frostproof	POLK
Thomas City	JEFFERSON	West Gate	PALM BEACH
Thonotosassa	HILLSBOROUGH	West Hollywood	BROWARD
Tice	LEE	West Lake Wales	POLK
Tisonia	DUVAL	West Miami	DADE
Titusville	BREVARD	West Palm Beach	PALM BEACH
Treasure Island	PINELLAS	West Pensacola	ESCAMBIA
Trenton	GILCHRIST	Westbay	BAY
Trilby	PASCO	Westville	HOLMES
Turnbull	BREVARD	Westwood Lakes	DADE
		Wewahitchka	GULF
Umatilla	LAKE	White City	GULF
Union Park	ORANGE	White City	ST. LUCIE
Usher	LEVY	White Springs	HAMILTON
Usinas Beach	ST. JOHNS	Whitehouse	DUVAL
		Whitfield Estates	MANATEE
Valkaria	BREVARD	Wilbur-by-the-Sea	VOLUSIA
Valparaiso	OKALOOSA	Wilcox	GILCHRIST
Valrico	HILLSBOROUGH	Wildwood	SUMTER
Vamo	SARASOTA	Williams Point	BREVARD

This is an index of cities, towns, and other places that appear on the large-scale county maps in this volume. The index names the county where each place is located today.

Place	Modern County	Place	Modern County
Williford	GILCHRIST	Woodville	LEON
Williston	LEVY	Wynnehaven Beach	OKALOOSA
Wilma	LIBERTY		
Wilton Manors	BROWARD	Yankeetown	LEVY
Wimauma	HILLSBOROUGH	Yeehaw Junction	OSCEOLA
Windermere	ORANGE	Yelvington	ST. JOHNS
Windsor	ALACHUA	Youngstown	BAY
Winfield	COLUMBIA	Yukon	DUVAL
Winter Beach	INDIAN RIVER	Yulee	NASSAU
Winter Garden	ORANGE		
Winter Haven	POLK	Zellwood	ORANGE
Winter Park	ORANGE	Zephyrhills	PASCO
Woods	LIBERTY	Zolfo Springs	HARDEE